Randall
Kiser

American
Law Firms
in Transition

Randall
Kiser

American
Law Firms
in Transition
Trends, Threats,
and Strategies

AMERICAN BAR ASSOCIATION
Defending Liberty
Pursuing Justice

Printed in the United States of America.

23 22 21 20 19 5 4 3 2 1

Library of Congress Cataloging-in-Publication Data

Names: Kiser, Randall, author.
Title: American law firms in transition : trends, threats, and strategies / Randall Kiser.
Description: Chicago : American Bar Association, [2019] | Includes index.
Identifiers: LCCN 2019003849 | ISBN 9781641053853 (hardcover)
Subjects: LCSH: Law firms—United States. | Practice of law—United States. |
    Law partnership—United States.
Classification: LCC KF300 .K57 2019 | DDC 338.4/73400973—dc23
LC record available at https://lccn.loc.gov/2019003849

ISBN: 978-1-64105-385-3

Contents

List of Figures and Tables

Acknowledgments

This book encompasses about 35 years of my professional life after law school graduation—20 years as a civil litigation attorney and law firm founder, partner, and principal and then 15 years as an author, researcher, consultant, and educator. Since this book attempts to integrate both practical and academic perspectives on American law firms, my dual-track experiences hopefully yield a more balanced view of law firms than currently exists in articles, law journals, and books. In this effort to blend the insights and wisdom of practitioners and academics, my views have been imprinted by literally hundreds of exceptional lawyers, law school professors, deans, journalists, analysts, and law firm leaders. I am indebted to each of them.

In writing this book, I have benefited from many of the best minds at law schools and in the legal services industry. William Henderson at the Indiana University Maurer School of Law has produced not only an enormous amount of data and research regarding law firms but also has led many innovations in law firms and corporate legal departments. My interactions with Professor Henderson have strongly influenced the themes and prescriptions in this book. Law firm consultants Peter Zeughauser and Kent Zimmerman at The Zeughauser Group also have shared, over many years of friendship, their keen insights into law firm leadership and operations.

My understanding of law firms' challenges has been greatly enhanced by multiple meetings with law firm managing partners, chief operating officers, and chief marketing officers at leadership roundtables and conferences during the last 10 years. I also am indebted to many law firm leaders and executive committee members who, expecting confidentiality, have described their concerns, challenges, and goals in connection with my presentations, programs, and consulting assignments.

The final versions of this book were prepared while I was a Scholar-in-Residence at the Indiana University Maurer School of Law. I am grateful for the law school's commitment to innovation and its ongoing efforts to transform legal education to benefit society and promote ethical leadership.

I also thank Samantha Cassetta, who has served as an editor of my four books, for her expert assistance in reviewing the draft chapters and initially suggesting that the book's content would be a good match with the American Bar Association's publications.

John Palmer, the Acquisitions Editor at the American Bar Association, merits special attention because he recognized the book's value at an early stage and adroitly guided me through the association's review, approval, publication, and marketing processes. His ideas consistently reflected the association's mission to promote professional growth and legal professionalism.

The last acknowledgment, for my wife, Denise, is the most important. Her deep sense of humanity and belief in the power of education, literature, and grace always enlighten and inspire me.

1
Introduction

Law firms fulfill privileged, yet vital, roles in American society. They simultaneously protect the resources, reputations, and prerogatives of the nation's leading corporations, businesses, and families; supply many of the political leaders serving in state and national governments; manage about 500,000 partners and associate attorneys; and effectuate a massive transfer of assets from clients to law firms in payment of legal fees.[1] Although law firms serve as protectors of established wealth, status, and power, they also dedicate millions of attorney hours every year to pro bono representation of indigent and historically underserved populations. Many law firm attorneys, moreover, act as another conscience for their clients, and their ethical duty to exercise independent judgment generally has heightened the quality of clients' decision making and the integrity of commercial conduct. The pivotal role of law firms, however, is now challenged by a series of economic dislocations and strategic errors that have disturbed, destabilized, and weakened law firms. Those dislocations and errors—and methods of recovering from them—are the subject of this book.

Law firms are remarkably profitable but surprisingly fragile. Their profit margins vastly exceed those of Fortune 100 corporations,

---

[1] The estimate of 500,000 attorneys in law firms is based on the American Bar Association National Lawyer Population Survey, Historical Trend in Total National Lawyer Population, 1878–2018, and the American Bar Association Lawyer Demographics Year 2016 data regarding practice setting and private practitioners.

and Citi Private Bank depicts them as "one of the most profitable personal services businesses in the world."[2] Despite their profitability, law firms become insolvent and collapse at exceptionally high rates. Nearly one-half of the firms listed in the Am Law 100 in 1987, the first year in which *The American Lawyer* publicly ranked law firms by gross revenue and profits per partner, have now dissolved, merged with stronger firms, or failed to maintain sufficient revenue or profitability to remain in the Am Law 100.[3] Although law firms attempt to project an aura of stability consistent with the staid image of the legal profession, many law firms are, in reality, only a few months away from a devastating defection of partners, a disappointing revenue report, or a rushed merger with a stronger firm.

The Great Recession inflicted a severe economic blow from which most law firms did not recover.[4] The period from 1990 to 2008 is now called the "Golden Era" of law firms. The period after that has been marked by fewer billable hours per attorney, declining revenue per lawyer, intense competition from corporate law departments and alternative legal service providers, fewer employment opportunities for law school graduates, and a wave of law firm

---

2   Citi Private Bank and Hildebrandt Consulting LLC. (2017). *2018 client advisory* (p. 15). Parnell, David. (2015). *The failing law firm: Symptoms and remedies* (p. 12). Chicago: American Bar Association. Parnell, David. (2017, April 26). Profits per equity partner. *The American Lawyer.* (In 2016, the average profit margin of the 100 firms ranked highest in profits per equity partner was 37.8%.) Christensen, Clayton M., & Anthony, Scott D. (2003, January 21). *Transforming legal services* (p. 2). Innosight LLC. ("Law firms are among the most profitable and least risky businesses in the world. The profit margins of the top 100 U.S. law firms are at least twice those of America's largest publicly traded corporations.")

3   Henderson, William D. (2012, June). Rise and fall. *The American Lawyer.* (2016, April 25). Firms ranked by profits per partner. *The American Lawyer.* (2016, April 25). Firms ranked by revenue per lawyer. *The American Lawyer.* Um, Jae. (2018, June 20). Outwit, outplay, outlast: A post-recession view of the survivors. *The American Lawyer.*

4   See Georgetown Law Center for the Study of the Legal Profession & Thomson Reuters Legal Executive Institute. (2018). *2018 report on the state of the legal market.* Simons, Hugh. (2018, June 12). Law and lemmings: Associate salary increases are a mass act of self-harm. *The American Lawyer.* Shunk, Marcie Borgal. (2018, May 22). The second hundred are stuck in the middle. *The American Lawyer.*

consolidations and mergers.[5] As the U.S. economy recovered after the Great Recession, it left most law firms behind, competing for a stagnant number of billable hours and scrambling to maintain their partners' income levels.

The apex of client demand for law firms' services occurred in 2008, and overall demand has been static or declining since then.[6] To the extent that lawyers' income increased after 2008, this increase is attributable to hourly billing rate increases, not increased billable hours. The collapse of demand for law firms' legal services has been well hidden by incremental increases in their billing rates and, hence, their gross revenue—giving the impression that firms are thriving financially when in fact they have simply changed the prices on their billable hours. As the annual *Report on the State of the Legal Market* succinctly states, "the financial performance of law firms over the past 10 years has essentially been driven by only one factor: rate increases."[7] This palliative treatment, masking with annual hourly rate increases the industry's underlying infirmity of declining demand, will be withdrawn in the next economic downturn as law firms exhaust their clients' tolerance for higher rates.

The rate of law firm implosions has doubled since the beginning of the Great Recession.[8] Dewey & LeBoeuf's dissolution in 2012 was the largest law firm bankruptcy in history, expelling 1,100 attorneys and revealing liabilities exceeding $300 million. The demise of Dewey & LeBoeuf was preceded by the disintegration of well-regarded firms such as Howrey, Brobeck, Heller Ehrman, Coudert

---

[5]   Zeughauser, Peter. (2017, October 16). New post-recession metrics for BigLaw partner success. *Law 360*. Georgetown Law Center for the Study of the Legal Profession & Thomson Reuters Legal Executive Institute (2018), *supra* note 4.

[6]   Press, Aric. (2014, October 29). Special report: Big Law's reality check. *The American Lawyer*. Georgetown Law Center for the Study of the Legal Profession & Thomson Reuters Legal Executive Institute. (2017). *2017 report on the state of the legal market*. Clay, Thomas S., & Seeger, Eric A. *2018 law firms in transition* (p. 3). Willow Grove, PA: Altman Weil ("Only 40% of law firms reported growth in demand in each of the last three years.")

[7]   Georgetown Law Center for the Study of the Legal Profession & Thomson Reuters Legal Executive Institute (2017), *supra* note 6 at 9.

[8]   Citi Private Bank. (2013). *2013 Client Advisory*, p. 5. See Scheiber, Noam. (2013, July 21). The last days of Big Law: You can't imagine the terror when the money dries up. *New Republic*.

Brothers, Shea & Gould, WolfBlock, and Thelen.[9] The frequency and magnitude of law firm implosions seem to have inured both attorneys and clients to the transient nature of law firm alliances. As a partner who left Dewey & LeBoeuf and joined Winston & Strawn in 2012 notes, "All we really did for clients was change the firm name and the address where they sent their bills."[10]

No one has determined whether attorneys and law firms have developed a preoccupation with short-term revenue as a result of law firms' instability or whether law firms' instability is caused by attorneys' preoccupation with short-term revenue. In any event, this instability has engendered among many attorneys a transitory, opportunistic attitude that derides loyalty as naïveté and perseverance as quixotic. Law firms now serve as upscale docks for transient, highly talented attorneys whose allegiance to the firm may be as variable as *The American Lawyer*'s annual ranking of its profits per partner. Rather than await the outcome of financial setbacks, attorneys flee their law firms when managing partners, recruiters, or journalists alert them to sudden changes in their firms' financial condition or other unanticipated risks. Consequently, the viability of many law firms is precarious, their very existence threatened by the next recession, loss of a key client, or defection of a few rainmaker partners. Today's venerated law firm is quickly transformed into tomorrow's legend as soon as its most profitable partners lose confidence in its financial prospects or leadership.

Causes of Law Firm Instability

Dewey & LeBoeuf, a law firm with 26 offices and annual revenue of $782 million, filed its bankruptcy petition on May 28, 2012. During the preceding five years, its debt had increased from $140 million to

---

[9]   Ax, Joseph, & Prasad, Sakthi. (2012, May 29). Dewey files for Chapter 11 in record law firm collapse. *Reuters.*

[10] Flaherty, Scott. (2017, May 4). Dewey survivors share lessons from their old firm's demise. *The American Lawyer.* Retrieved from https://www.law.com/americanlawyer/sites/americanlawyer/2017/05/04/dewey-survivors-share-lessons-from-their-old-firms-demise/.

$315 million.[11] Within hours after this bankruptcy filing, attorneys throughout the United States began asking themselves, "Is there anything that we need to do differently to avoid making Dewey's mistakes?"[12] They quickly assured themselves that the problems besetting Dewey & LeBoeuf—excessive debt, compensation guarantees to partners, and an overly aggressive growth strategy—either did not exist at their firms or existed in a small, benign form. They convinced themselves that the conditions leading to Dewey & LeBoeuf's demise were unique, episodic, and purgative.

In regarding Dewey & LeBoeuf's collapse as an isolated event, attorneys missed an opportunity to objectively evaluate their own law firms' weaknesses and to correct attitudes and practices that could lead to a debacle every bit as momentous and unexpected as Dewey & LeBoeuf's downfall. The fact that an existing law firm does not exhibit the same maladies as a defunct law firm does not make it any less vulnerable to collapse. Vulnerability is now embedded in most law firms due to weak demand for their services and the absence of methods, systems, and incentives essential to detecting and responding to major changes in clients' expectations of professional service providers. What distinguishes Dewey & LeBoeuf's collapse from that of a contemporary law firm are the manifestations and depth of the problems, not their nature and breadth.

The critical question for law firm leaders is not whether their firms have problems identical to those that afflicted Dewey & LeBoeuf and other failed firms but rather whether their firms have any vulnerabilities that could lead to their demise. A comprehensive assessment of law firm vulnerabilities is required because "law firms, like human beings, usually do not die from a single cause but from a combination of systemic failures."[13] In their comparative study of

---

[11] Frank, Allan Dodds. (2012, May 29). The end of an era: Why Dewey & LeBoeuf went under. *Fortune*. Lat, David. (2012, May 11). Dewey violate Rule 10b-5? A detailed look at the firm's 2010 offering memorandum. *Above the law.com*. Lattman, Peter. (2012, April 4). *American Lawyer* to revise Dewey's financials. *The New York Times*. Lattman, Peter. (2012, May 28). Dewey & LeBoeuf files for bankruptcy. *The New York Times*.

[12] Zimmerman, Kent. (2012, June 8). Four steps every firm should consider in the wake of Dewey & LeBoeuf. *Chicago Daily Law Bulletin*.

[13] Raasch, Janet Ellen. (2007, September 30). Why do some law firms fail while others succeed?

failed and successful law firms, consultants Burkey Belser and Mark Greene found that "many of the failed firms had some or nearly all of the characteristics of the firms that succeeded. It would be simpler if we could point to a single fatal flaw."[14]

Among the 60 variables that Belser and Greene determined were associated with success and failure, "none was predictive in and of itself."[15] They concluded that law firms' failures were not caused by a single factor or incident but instead resulted from multiple characteristics and a sequence of events. This conclusion is consistent with general catastrophic failure theories, which find that "disasters do not simply occur; they evolve. In complex systems, a single failure rarely leads to harm."[16] Because law firm failures are multifaceted and unfold in a series of deleterious processes and events, Belser and Greene observe, "there is no such thing as a precipitous firm collapse. It only appears that way."[17]

Over the next decade, many law firms will vanish in a Dewey & LeBoeuf–like implosion or will merge with other firms in rescue operations marketed as bold, strategic actions. They will fail for the same reasons that other companies dissolve, governments fail, leaders are ousted, and industries become obsolete: failure to anticipate, failure to learn, and failure to adapt.[18] Law firm critics like Paul Lippe, the founder of the technology firm Legal OnRamp,

---

14   Belser, Burkey, & Greene, Mark T. (2004, May 10). What makes firms fail?: A new study compares the characteristics of firms that prosper with those that don't. *The National Law Journal*. See also Belser, Burkey. (2012, June 28). Why firms fail: A diagnosis of the death of Dewey LeBoeuf. Retrieved from http://greenfieldbelser.com/big-ideas/why-firms-fail-a-diagnosis-of-the-death-of-dewey-leboeuf

15   Raasch, *supra* note 13. In a similar vein, Dan DiPietro, former chairman of the Law Firm Group at Citi Private Bank, identifies multiple causes for law firm failures: poorly conceived growth strategies; "disconnects" in partner compensation ranges between lower and higher echelon partners; excessive concentration in practice areas; and "poorly conceived and implemented" lateral hiring strategies. Di Pietro views high debt "as a complicating factor and not necessarily a precipitating factor." Wilkins, David B. (2017, March). Bank on more failures. *The Practice*, 3(3).

16   Gawande, Atul. (2002). *Complications* (p. 63). New York: Picador.

17   Belser & Greene, *supra* note 14.

18   Cohen, Eliot, & Gooch, John. (1990). *Military misfortunes* (p. 26). New York: Free Press.

believe that the problems afflicting law firms are largely irreversible: "Large firms are entering a Bermuda Triangle of management challenges: slower growth, greater pressure for change, and a governance model designed to be anti-nimble. The problem for firms is that they are designed to *not* be especially good at change, so it's crazy to imagine that they will be able to transcend that architecture."[19] The approach taken in this book, however, is less pessimistic than Lippe's prognosis. This book's thesis is that the problems facing law firms are severe, chronic, endemic—and solvable.

Themes and Premises of This Book

Law firms' problems are rooted deeply in attorney personality characteristics; law firms' recruitment processes, professional development programs, and partnership admission criteria; practice group and law firm leader selection; and attorneys' short-term perspectives exacerbated by law firms' cash basis method of accounting. Law firms' adaptability is further hindered by the impractical nature of legal education and a general misconception that law firms are unique and have little or nothing to learn from other businesses and organizations. This admixture of errors, oversights, arrogance, and isolation buttresses a collective intransigence that now threatens the continued existence of many law firms. To better understand law firms' vulnerabilities and to show how they can be reduced, mitigated, or surmounted, this book analyzes their practices, leadership, cultures, systems, strategies, challenges, and deficiencies. This book posits that effective law firms must be proficient, professional, positive, prescient, and profitable, and it demonstrates how those qualities can be realized.

This book's analysis of law firms employs an analogy developed by James Collins, a noted business consultant and author of the best sellers *Good to Great, How the Mighty Fall,* and *Great by Choice.* Collins asserts that business successes are attributable to three basic achievements: getting the right people on the bus, placing

---

[19] Parnell, David. (2014, April 21). Paul Lippe of Legal OnRamp: Every legal department will seek to Cisco-ify themselves. *Forbes.* Retrieved from: http://www.forbes.com/sites/davidparnell/2014/04/21/paul-lippe-of-legal-onramp-on-the-legal-market-david-parnell.

the right people in the right seats, and sending the bus in the right direction. Business failures, conversely, are attributable to poor recruiting, hiring, and promotion decisions; mismatches between people and their positions; and mistaken strategies. The leader's primary responsibility in every organization, Collins explains, centers on people, assignments, and strategies:

You are a bus driver. The bus, your company, is at a standstill, and it's your job to get it going. You have to decide where you're going, how you're going to get there, and who's going with you.

Most people assume that great bus drivers (read: business leaders) immediately start the journey by announcing to the people on the bus where they're going—by setting a new direction or by articulating a fresh corporate vision.

In fact, leaders of companies that go from good to great start not with "where" but with "who." They start by getting the right people on the bus, the wrong people off the bus, and the right people in the right seats. And they stick with that discipline—first the people, then the direction—no matter how dire the circumstances.[20]

When Collins' model is applied to law firms, it is evident that law firms get far too many of the wrong people on the bus; they place many of the right people in the wrong seats; and, collectively, the wrong people, the misseated right people, and the leaders are steering the bus in the wrong direction. Although it is impracticable for law firms to change the people, their seats, or the direction of the bus immediately, they can initiate four critical changes by:

- realistically assessing and eventually changing the types of attorneys they hire.
- modifying their recruiting, hiring, and professional development practices to more closely align attorneys' skills and propensities with clients' needs and expectations.

---

[20]   Collins, James. (2001, October). Good to great. *Fast Company*.

- selecting leaders based on their leadership capabilities instead of their legal expertise and rainmaking success.
- developing and executing more incisive, intelligent, and durable strategies than the current "expansion fever" in law firm mergers and lateral hiring, the overemphasis on premium pricing, and the obsession with "chasing stars" in compensation decisions and lateral partner acquisitions.

The solutions proposed in this book will require a frank acknowledgment of misconceptions that currently impair attorney performance and mislead law firm management; a willingness to abandon behavior that was debatably successful in the past but is now dangerously maladaptive; a receptiveness to personal change and the adoption of higher standards of professional conduct and client service; and the implementation of contemporary management and leadership practices that have been tested and validated in other disciplines and industries. These solutions also require a degree of humility and openness in a profession whose most prominent members are popularly portrayed as argumentative, aggressive, confident, and not particularly reflective.

Organization of This Book

This book provides an overview of economic and demographic trends in the legal services industry and explains how law firms' current practices and strategies are misaligned with clients' needs and unsupported by empirical research. After providing this overview of current conditions, the book shows how improvements in culture, character, practices, systems, and leaders can enable law firms to survive and thrive in the next decade.

A brief summary of the book's chapters appears below to orient readers to the book's organization, content, and progression:

- *Chapter 2—Trends.* This chapter presents a snapshot of the legal services industry and of law firms' declining role in that industry. It summarizes key indicators and trends that signal high risks for law firms: law firm revenue, employees, billable hours, hourly rates, collections, profitability, volatility, corporate legal departments, alternative legal service providers, and surplus partners. This chapter also illuminates two major demographic changes that will reconstitute law firms: the impending retirement of nearly one-half of all current partners and the surge of Millennial generation attorneys joining firms and becoming partners.

- *Chapter 3—Mismatches.* This chapter describes and challenges traditional attorney hiring criteria and the attendant overemphasis on grade point averages and law school ranking. It explains how law firms' hiring strategies, incentives, biases, and compensation systems result in a low level of diversity and a high level of attrition among female and racial and ethnic minority attorneys. This chapter also documents the extraordinary costs of attorney attrition and describes the financial benefits that firms can realize with a diverse workforce.

- *Chapter 4—Missteps.* Law firms generally adopt eight strategies to increase market share and profitability: head count growth, mergers, lateral partner hiring, star partner recruiting, client origination incentives, rate increases, premium pricing, and leverage. This chapter examines the empirical evidence regarding these strategies and finds that they promote short-term perspectives and generally fail to achieve the intended results.

- *Chapter 5—Culture.* The role of culture in law firms has been neglected. This chapter describes the meaning and importance of firm culture. It discusses and shows how effective law firms develop the key features of culture: shared objectives, commitment to clients, trust and collegiality, continuous learning and improvement, social purpose, and accountability.

- *Chapter 6—Character.* This chapter identifies the personal traits that law firms must seek when recruiting attorneys and should enhance in their talent development programs: likeability, humility, engagement, realism, openness, and resilience. Law firms have overlooked these traits, and as a result, many clients have been subjected to suboptimal legal service. This chapter also examines what psychologists call the "dark traits" that law firms should detect and avoid in attorney candidates.

- *Chapter 7—Practices.* The practices that distinguish effective law firms, derived from studies of high-performance organizations, are identified and discussed in this chapter. Those practices include collaboration, decision making, civility, readiness, and diversity and inclusion. The chapter explains the benefits of those practices, along with specific methods of improving them.
- *Chapter 8—Systems.* Successful law firms operate with systems that facilitate client service and attorney professionalism. When systems are working well, they are taken for granted and hence may receive less attention than they merit. This chapter highlights and explains the importance of these key law firm systems: quality control, feedback, and evaluation; compensation; technology and information management; lateral attorney integration; succession planning; attorney wellness; and pro bono services.
- *Chapter 9—Leaders.* Law firm leaders occupy ill-defined roles that are often circumscribed by a predecessor's model or directed by their own interests. As a result, law firm leadership is often more idiosyncratic than perdurable. This chapter delineates the six major responsibilities that law firm leaders must understand and undertake: awareness; vision and strategy; innovation and change management; crisis management; talent development; and execution.

Purposes of This Book

As indicated by these brief chapter summaries, this book's purpose is to animate attorneys' deep intelligence and strong analytical skills to enable them to (1) become more effective attorneys and law firm leaders; and (2) recognize and possibly reverse the downward trends that currently threaten their client relationships and destabilize their law firms. Those trends, unless halted, will lead to the termination of thousands of attorneys and the demise of multiple law firms. Although clients ultimately may benefit from that disruptive process as competitors seize new opportunities from law firms, it is not clear that these competitors will provide the breadth of expertise or the independent judgment traditionally offered by law firms.

Nor is it clear that these competitors will fulfill the community service roles and undertake the pro bono responsibilities traditionally assumed by law firms. Law firms have a singular role and purpose in American society that may not be fully understood or appreciated until many of them vanish.

The transformation of the legal services industry has been largely ignored by attorneys and their law firms. This transformation is driven as much by law firms' passivity as it is by competitors' advantages, as much by law firms' acquiescence as it is by competitors' ambitions. It is critical for law firms to explicitly decide whether they will continue to succumb to competitive forces that promise clients less expensive, more efficient legal services or whether they will reassert themselves by adopting new attitudes and modern practices. Although client attrition from law firms is not inexorable, it will become irreversible if it is continually minimized or disregarded.

Clients' expectations and their alternatives have expanded markedly since most attorneys graduated from law school, and the gap between clients' demands and law firms' performance widens every year. This gap is both tangible and perceptual. Clients are convinced that their law firms are not serious about changing their legal services delivery model and providing greater value to clients, but their law firms report significant progress in increasing their efficiency.[21] This book can help law firm attorneys bridge this gap or narrow it sufficiently to preserve their firms' distinct contributions to American society and its legal system.

---

[21] See Altman Weil. (2016). *2016 Chief Legal Officer survey* (p. 23). Newtown Square, PA: Altman Weil. Clay & Seeger, *supra* note 6 at 53.

2
Trends

Preoccupied with their law practices, many attorneys are unaware of the strong forces and dramatic changes that have overtaken the legal profession. While attorneys were diligently working on client matters and enjoying the financial rewards of their expertise and success during the last 10 years, the rest of the world decided to curtail its use of lawyers and their law firms. Corporate law departments sharply reduced their spending on outside law firms, alternative legal service providers (ALSPs) exploited market niches like electronic discovery and contract management, and accounting firms captured large segments of the legal services market. New competitors, technological advances, and innovative business models now threaten to disrupt, if not upend, conventional law firms.[1]

This chapter presents an overview of the financial trends, competitors, and demographic changes that are destabilizing and displacing law firms. It first examines law firms' financial conditions and trends, focusing on gross revenue, the number of employees and average hours worked, billable hours, surplus partners, realization rates, and collection rates. The chapter then describes the growth of corporate legal departments, clients' increasing use of

---

[1] See Press, Aric. (2014, October 29). Special report: Big Law's reality check. *The American Lawyer.* Georgetown Law Center for the Study of the Legal Profession & Thomson Reuters Legal Executive Institute. (2018). *2018 report on the state of the legal market.* Georgetown Law Center for the Study of the Legal Profession & Thomson Reuters Legal Executive Institute. (2017). *2017 report on the state of the legal market.*

ALSPs, competition from the Big Four accounting firms, and law firms' responses to major changes in the legal services industry. The balance of the chapter discusses law school graduate employment opportunities and highlights two demographic trends affecting law firms: an increase in Millennial generation attorneys and a decrease in Silent Generation and Baby Boomer attorneys due to their retirements.

Financial Condition and Trends

Gross Revenue

Law firm revenue is no longer growing and in fact entered a long period of decline beginning in 2008. As shown in Figure 2.1, total annual revenue in the legal services industry peaked in 2008. Adjusted for inflation, average annual revenue after 2008 is roughly 10 percent less than average annual revenue in the 1997–2008 period.[2] Figure 2.1 also indicates that the decline in legal services industry revenue is not attributable to general economic conditions since annual revenue for "other professional and business services" steadily increased after 2009.

Revenue per lawyer in Am Law 100 firms, considered to be the most reliable measure of law firms' financial health, is below its 2007 level, after adjusting for inflation.[3] Hugh Simons, formerly the chief operating officer at Ropes & Gray, succinctly describes this revenue drop-off: "the law firm revenue engine shut down in 2007. It hasn't restarted; it won't restart."[4] The demand for *business legal services*—the mainstay of large law firms—has decreased significantly. Business clients reduced their spending on law firms, in inflation-adjusted dollars, by 25.8 percent between 2004 and 2014.[5] Two-thirds of chief legal officers anticipate that their future spending on outside law firms will be reduced or maintained at current

---

2   Bureau of Economic Analysis. (2016, November 23). Real value added by industry, 1997–2015 [Millions of chained (2009) dollars].

3   Simons, Hugh. (2018, June 12). Law and lemmings: Associate salary increases are a mass act of self-harm. *The American Lawyer*. Cipriani, Gina Passarella. (2018, April 24). The 2018 Am Law 100 ranked by: Revenue per lawyer. *The American Lawyer*.

4   Simons, *supra* note 3.

5   Sobowale, Julie. (2016, April). Beyond imagination. *ABA Journal*, p. 50.

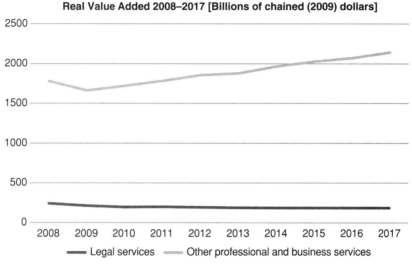

Figure 2.1   Real Value Added by Legal Services Industry
Source: Bureau of Economic Analysis.

levels; and 43 percent of chief legal officers are planning to terminate their company's relationship with an outside firm.[6]

Law firm partners often point to increases in profits per equity partner as evidence of financial growth. Their reliance on profits per equity partner, however, is misplaced and misleading. To the extent that profits per partner have increased, that increase generally is due to higher hourly billing rates, a reduction in the number of equity partners, and adroit expense management. Seventy-four percent of the Am Law 100 firms that reported increases in profits in 2017, for example, "worked their way to higher PPP [profits per partner] by combining equity partner reductions, higher leverage, and lowered cost-per-lawyer."[7] Any nominal increases in annual revenue have been confined to a small cohort—roughly 20 percent of Am Law 100 firms.[8]

---

6   Association of Corporate Counsel. (2018). *Chief Legal Officers 2018 survey* (p. 6). Spiezio, Caroline. (2018, February 8). A third of CLOs fired outside counsel in 2017, and that number's set to rise. *The American Lawyer.*

7   Simons, Hugh A., & Bruch, Nicholas. (2018, April 24). Success in the Am Law 100 is being driven by management. *The American Lawyer.*

8   MacEwen, Bruce. (2017, September 27). But what do the Am Law numbers really show? Thomson Reuters.

The levers used to increase profits per partner, despite flat or declining client demand, are of limited utility and duration. These levers may not survive the next recession, as legal technologists Richard Lau and Thomas Suh explain:

The tactics used by law firms to survive the Great Recession will not be effective during the next recession. These tactics, broadly, include raising prices; cutting expenses, primarily via layoffs; and slowing or shrinking equity partner ranks. Going forward, however, raising prices will be less effective. ... Higher rates will simply drive business toward cheaper firms and ALSPs, accelerating the continued erosion of the law firm franchise. Layoffs and de-equitizing partners present a different problem. Those solutions are exhaustible, and the expenses and lawyer/partner head counts haven't come close to their peaks in 2007. Law firms can't rely on cuts in those areas to maintain profitability again because there is simply less available to cut.[9]

Increasing prices to offset slackening demand may sustain law firms in a growing economy, but that strategy will collapse in a weakening economy with an abundant supply of attorneys and ALSPs.

The absence of organic revenue growth in the legal services industry is compounded by volatility. Very few firms demonstrate a consistent competitive advantage, and their financial results reflect the instability inherent in a constantly changing client base. "None of us are getting a huge percentage of our revenue from repeat institutional clients the way we all did 20 years ago or even 10 years ago," an Am Law 50 managing partner states. "That is a form of volatility in itself because you have to replace work every year, every six months, every two years."[10] In 2005–2007, 64 percent of law firms experienced two years of consecutive revenue

---

[9] Lau, Richard, & Suh, Thomas. (2018, November 6). What law firms need to know to prepare for the next recession. *The American Lawyer*.

[10] Cipriani, Gina Passarella. (2018, April 24). Volatility is now a fact of life for America's biggest firms. *The American Lawyer*.

increases, but 10 years later only 29 percent of firms reported consecutive annual revenue increases.[11]

Revenue volatility is reflected in erratic revenue per lawyer (RPL), profits per lawyer (PPL), and profits per partner (PPP). In 2015, for example, only 38 percent of Am Law 100 firms reported consecutive years of growth and decline in profits per lawyer, but in 2017, 60 percent of law firms experienced consecutive years of growth and decline in profits per lawyer.[12] Analyzing data from Am Law 100 firms in 2017, ALM Legal Intelligence analyst Nicholas Bruch concludes that "volatility is on the rise in almost every key metric. The percentage of firms that have reported reversals in RPL, PPL, or PPP growth has increased in each of the past three years."[13]

Number of Employees, Average Weekly Hours, and Billable Hours

Although law firm revenue, adjusted for inflation, peaked in 2008, the total number of employees in the legal services industry crested one year earlier in 2007. As shown in Figure 2.2, the legal services industry now employs about 50,000 fewer people than it did in 2007.[14] Other professional and business services, in contrast, increased employee headcount after 2009 by 27 percent, as shown by Figure 2.3.

Law firm employees who kept their jobs after 2007 did not pick up the slack following other employees' departures because there

---

[11] Citi Private Bank & Hildebrandt Consulting. (2018). *2018 client advisory.*
[12] Bruch, Nicholas. (2017, May 2, updated 2017, December 19). The Am Law 100: Dark clouds on the horizon. *The American Lawyer.*
[13] Ibid.
[14] Some commentators attribute part of the decline in the number of employees to the fact that law firm partners are classified as business owners, not employees. As William Henderson notes, "it is quite possible that the diminution in legal services employment is occurring because law firms contain more partners who are, on balance, older and less leveraged in terms of associates, paralegal and staff." Henderson, William. (2018, July). *Legal market landscape report,* p. 2. But the percentage of law firm partners has not increased during the last 10 years and, in fact, appears to have decreased. Aric Press, the former editor-in-chief of *The American Lawyer*, finds that the percentage of partners "dropped by a full three percentage points. In 2013, the percentage of equity partners in the firms had dropped to 25.4 percent of total head count. To put that in perspective, in 2004, equity partners represented 28.7 percent of the total firm." Press, Aric. (2014, October 29). Special report: Big Law's reality check. *The American Lawyer.*

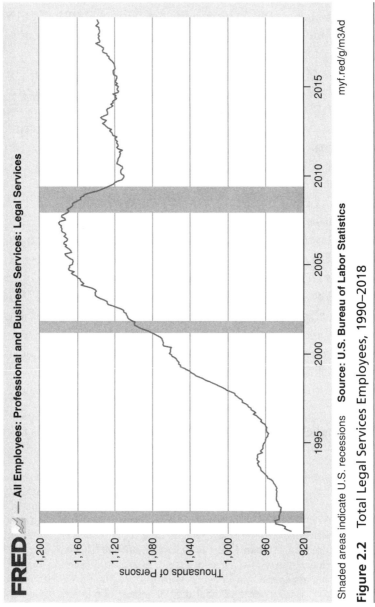

Shaded areas indicate U.S. recessions   **Source: U.S. Bureau of Labor Statistics**

myf.red/g/m3Ad

Figure 2.2   Total Legal Services Employees, 1990–2018

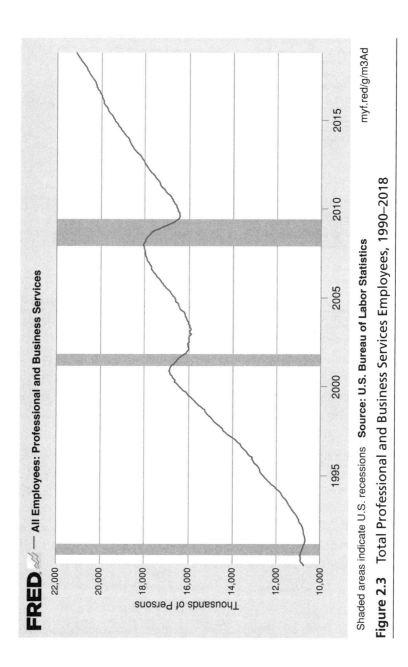

Shaded areas indicate U.S. recessions **Source: U.S. Bureau of Labor Statistics**   myf.red/g/m3Ad

Figure 2.3 Total Professional and Business Services Employees, 1990–2018

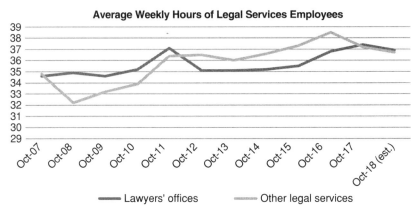

Figure 2.4   Average Weekly Hours of Employees in Lawyers' Offices and Other Legal Services
Source: Bureau of Labor Statistics.

was no slack to pick up. Average weekly hours worked in law firms varied only slightly in 2007, 2008, and 2009, indicating that employee workloads remained steady despite employee layoffs and attrition.[15] During the last five years, as shown by Figure 2.4, average weekly hours in *lawyers' offices* have increased slightly. But the average weekly hours of those employees in the legal services industry who are employed *outside of lawyers' offices* increased at a faster rate during that period.

Although total law firm employee hours have increased slightly, attorneys' billable hours have dropped appreciably. During the last 10 years, attorneys' average billable hours declined by about 10 percent, and during the last five years, average billable hours decreased every year.[16] The *2018 Report on the State of the Legal Market* describes the decline in billable hours and the practical consequences for law firm revenue:

---

[15]   See Table B-16. Average hours and earnings of production and nonsupervisory employees on private nonfarm payrolls by detailed industry [for years 2007–2009]. U.S. Department of Labor, Bureau of Labor Statistics.

[16]   Georgetown Law Center for the Study of the Legal Profession & Thomson Reuters Legal Executive Institute (2017), *supra* note 1 at 4.

Since 2011, there has been an overall downward trend in the productivity of all categories of timekeepers except associates, and the downward trend has been particularly serious in the of-counsel ranks. For all lawyers, the current level of billable worked hours per month is some 13 total hours below the level at the beginning of 2007 (just before the onset of the Great Recession). That represents a total of 156 billable worked hours per year which, if multiplied by the average hourly worked rate for all lawyers in 2017 ($475), indicates that the decline in productivity over the past decade is costing firms about $74,100 per lawyer per year.[17]

For many law firms, the decline in billable hours has been sudden and substantial. The *2016 Real Rate Report*, for instance, shows that "total hours billed per law firm—often referred to as demand—fell 8 percent from 2013 to 2015" and that "hours billed in specific client-firm relationships fell 8 percent in 2015 after growing 6 percent in 2014 and 22 percent in 2011."[18]

Law firm partners' billable hours have declined at a more rapid rate than associate attorneys' billable hours. During the last 10 years, associate attorney billable hours declined by three percent, and hours billed by equity and nonequity partners declined by 11 percent and 16 percent, respectively.[19] Dan DiPietro, the former chair of Citi Private Bank's Law Firm Group, noted that "average annual partner hours billed at the country's 15 most profitable firms had declined by about 10 percent since 2009."[20] The average equity partner now bills about 30 hours per week, and many equity partners are billing about 21 hours per week.[21] DiPietro's conservative

---

[17] Georgetown Law Center for the Study of the Legal Profession & Thomson Reuters Legal Executive Institute (2018), *supra* note 1 at 6.

[18] Strom, Roy. (2017, March 27). With hourly rates rising, report shows spotty record for GC's cost-constraint tactics. *The American Lawyer.*

[19] Ibid.

[20] Triedman, Julie. (2013, June 24). Weil slashes 60 associates, 110 staffers. *The Am Law Daily.*

[21] Randazzo, Sara. (2016, October 10). Law firms demote partners as pressure mounts over profits. *The Wall Street Journal.*

estimate is that law firms "have 6.5 percent excess lawyer capacity, with those 'higher up in the food chain' closer to 8 percent or 8.5 percent."[22] His grim views are echoed by Jeff Grossman, senior director of banking for Wells Fargo Private Bank's Legal Specialty Group. Grossman concludes that chronically underperforming partners are "a very difficult issue to deal with. To me this is the biggest challenge the industry faces."[23]

The scope of this "chronically underperforming partner" problem is revealed in a recent survey of large law firm partners. They report that 51 percent of equity partners and 59 percent of nonequity partners are "not sufficiently busy."[24] This problem is especially acute in the largest law firms. In firms with 250 or more attorneys, 62 percent of equity partners are not sufficiently busy, and 72 percent of nonequity partners are not sufficiently busy.[25] "There are more partners than there's work to go around," observes Grossman.[26]

The number of surplus partners in Am Law 200 firms varies markedly with their ranking in profits per partner. Firms in the 1–50 and 101–150 quartiles, based on profits per partner, have no surplus partners.[27] But firms ranked in the 51–100 and 151–200 quartiles have 3,400 and 1,200 surplus partners, respectively.[28] The high number of surplus partners in firms ranked 51–100 is surprising and risky, states former Ropes & Gray COO Hugh Simons:

That's a whopping surplus for a mere 50 firms (an average of 68 surplus partners per firm). It's particularly so in the eighth year of an economic expansion with a downturn overdue by historical norms.

---

22 Ibid.
23 Randazzo, Sara. (2013, August 9). Bank says firms on track for anemic growth in 2013. *The Am Law Daily*.
24 Clay, Thomas S., & Seeger, Eric A. (2018). *2018 Law firms in transition* (p. 25). Willow Grove, PA: Altman Weil.
25 Ibid. at 26.
26 Gluckman, Nell. (2017, January 23). Richest firms pulled ahead in 2016 as some regions struggled. *The Am Law Daily*.
27 Simons, Hugh. (2017, August 30). How many excess partners does your firm have? *The Am Law Daily*.
28 Ibid.

The leaders of these second 50 firms are playing a dangerous game. When the downturn hits they'll be caught needing to out-place partners in such numbers that they simply won't be able to do it. Some unproductive partners will remain in place, dragging down the comp of the most commercially productive partners and forcing them to migrate to stronger platforms, such as those offered by the top 50 firms. The departure of strong partners will beget the departure of even stronger partners and, in a run-on-the-bank dynamic, the firm will be forced into closure, bankruptcy or uncomfortable merger.[29]

Realization and Collection Rates

Concurrent with decreases in their attorneys' billable hours, law firms are experiencing declines in their realization and collection rates. Their partners bill fewer hours, and those hours are less valuable than they were five years ago for two reasons: clients are less willing to pay standard hourly rates ("rack rates"), demanding and routinely receiving discounted rates; and an increasing number of clients simply do not pay their legal bills.

Although standard hourly rates have increased by 30 percent during the last 10 years, many clients refuse to pay the higher rates.[30] Noting strong client "pushback" to hourly rate increases, the *2017 Report on the State of the Legal Market* confirms that law firms are consistently discounting their hourly rates: "Since 2007, collection realization as measured against standard rates, has declined 11 percent for Am Law 100 firms, 7.6 percent for Am Law Second 100 firms, and 7.3 percent for midsize firms. During 2016, the average realization rate for all firms has been consistently below 83 percent, the lowest level ever recorded."[31] After reaching their lowest point in 2016, Am Law 100 firms' realization rates continued to decline, while Am Law 101-200 firm's realization rates stabilized

---

[29] Ibid.
[30] Georgetown Law Center for the Study of the Legal Profession & Thomson Reuters Legal Executive Institute (2017), *supra* note 1 at 5.
[31] Ibid.

at the record low.[32] (The average realization rate for solo, small, and medium-sized law firms is 81 percent, and some practice areas within those firms, e.g., insurance, employment, immigration, criminal, and bankruptcy, exhibit even lower realization rates.)[33]

Whether their bills are based on standard or discounted rates, law firms frequently face a fresh round of cost cutting after the bills are sent. In 2007, clients paid about 94 percent of the amounts billed by their law firms, but by 2017 that collection rate had declined to 89 percent.[34] For many clients, the bill is simply an invitation to start negotiations. "Clients are becoming more sophisticated and systematic about invoice review and invoice rejections," states Mark Medice, a former Senior Director at Thomson Reuters Peer Monitor.[35]

Law Firm Competitors

Hidden in the bleak data about law firms' financial performance is a critical fact: the legal services industry is growing rapidly in dimensions that have been minimized by law firms and inadequately documented by law professors and economists. Law firms may be inert or failing, but corporate legal departments and ALSPs like contract management, document review, and coding companies are expanding. The total U.S. legal market, according to Thomson Reuters' Legal Executive Institute, is estimated to be $437 billion.[36] Law firms capture about 63 percent of that market; the balance of the market is allocated between corporate legal departments (about 37 percent) and ALSPs (>1 percent).[37] "Large law firms are not the

---

[32]   Georgetown Law Center for the Study of the Legal Profession (2018), *supra* note 1.

[33]   (2016). *Legal Trends Report* (pp. 5, 31). Burnaby, British Columbia: Themis Solutions, Inc.

[34]   Georgetown Law Center for the Study of the Legal Profession & Thomson Reuters Legal Executive Institute (2018), *supra* note 1. Solo, small and medium-sized law firms have an average collection rate of 86 percent. See *Legal Trends Report, supra* note 33 at 5.

[35]   Smith, Jennifer. (2013, December 22). Law firms press to get bills paid by year-end. *The Wall Street Journal*.

[36]   Thomson Reuters Legal Executive Institute. (2016, January 11). The size of the US legal market: Shrinking piece of a bigger pie—an LEI Graphic.

[37]   Ibid.

THE NUMBER OF IN-HOUSE LAWYERS HAS TRIPLED.

% Change in Number of Employed Lawyers by Practice Setting, 1997 to 2016.

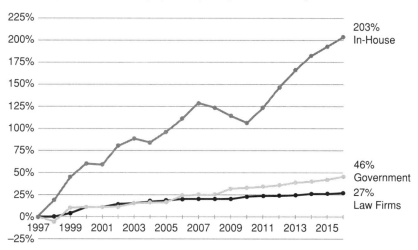

Figure 2.5   Corporate Legal Department Employee Growth

Reprinted with permission of Legal Evolution LLC.
Source: Bureau of Labor Statistics.

only option for corporate legal work," concludes the Legal Executive Institute. "In fact, they are no longer the primary option."[38]

Corporate Legal Departments

Corporate legal departments have increased attorney headcount and their annual budgets at a remarkably rapid rate. Between 1997 and 2016, the number of attorneys employed by corporate legal departments increased by 203 percent, as shown in Figure 2.5. During that period, the number of attorneys employed by law firms increased by only 27 percent. The overall budget for most corporate legal departments has increased during the last eight years, and the increases in the "inside" budget for corporate law departments' internal operations are greater than the increases in their "outside" budgets for external law firms.[39] In 2018, for instance,

---

[38]   Ibid.

[39]   Association of Corporate Counsel. (2018). *ACC Chief Legal Officers 2018 Survey.* Association of Corporate Counsel. (2017). *ACC Chief Legal Officers 2017 Survey.* Altman Weil. (2016). *Altman Weil 2016 Chief Legal Officer Survey* (p. iii). Newtown Square, PA: Altman Weil.

average budgeted expenditures for outside counsel declined from 40 percent of the total budget to 36 percent; and average budgeted expenditures on inside expenses increased from 53 percent to 56 percent.[40] Thirty-seven percent of corporate counsel report that they increased the number of attorneys in their law departments during the preceding 12 months, and 28 percent expect to add attorneys to their department within the next 12 months.[41] Only 8.5 percent of chief legal officers plan to decrease the number of attorneys in their departments.[42]

The increased spending on corporate legal departments comes at the expense of outside law firms. Forty percent of corporate counsel report that they "shifted law firm work to in-house lawyer staff" during the preceding 12 months, and 26 percent intend to decrease their use of outside firms in the future.[43] Of the firms intending to decrease their spending on outside counsel, 81 percent report that the work will be redirected to in-house lawyer staff.[44] Only one in three chief legal officers intends to increase the amount of work assigned to outside law firms.[45] Evaluating more than 10 different steps they have taken to control costs, corporate counsel find that the most effective step is shifting work from outside counsel to in-house legal departments.[46]

Alternative Legal Service Providers (ALSPs)

ALSPs are increasing their share of clients' legal expenditures. They currently generate about $8.4 billion in worldwide revenue, of which $6.2 billion is spent on e-discovery and document review service providers.[47] In a survey of 800 law firms and corporations,

---

40   Association of Corporate Counsel. (2018), *supra* note 39.

41   Association of Corporate Counsel. (2018), *supra* note 39. Association of Corporate Counsel. (2017), *supra* note 39.

42   Altman Weil. (2016), *supra* note 39 at 2.

43   Altman Weil. (2014). *2014 Chief Legal Officer Survey* (pp. 4, 9). Newtown Square, PA: Altman Weil.

44   Altman Weil. (2016), *supra* note 39 at 3.

45   Association of Corporate Counsel. (2018), *supra* note 39.

46   Altman Weil. (2014), *supra* note 43 at 10.

47   Thomson Reuters Legal Executive Institute, Georgetown University Law Center for the Study of the Legal Profession, & University of Oxford Saïd Business School. (2017). *Alternative Legal Service Providers* (p. 4).

51 percent of law firms and 60 percent of corporations report that they currently use ALSPs.[48] An additional 21 percent of law firms and 14 percent of corporate law departments report that they intend to start using ALSPs within 12 months.[49] Corporate law departments estimate that, during the preceding 12 months, the average dollar value of work "shifted from law firms to non-legal vendors" was $754,644.[50] Overall, two percent of corporate legal departments expenditures are allocated to ALSPs.[51] General counsel expect that allocation to increase significantly, and D. Casey Flaherty, former corporate counsel at Kia Motors America, Inc., estimates it will be 10 percent within five to ten years.[52]

Law firms most commonly use ALSPs for electronic discovery services, document review and coding services, and litigation and investigation support. But ALSPs are rapidly expanding the range of services they provide to include legal research, intellectual property management, contract management, regulatory compliance, and project management services.[53] Kent Zimmerman, a law firm consultant with The Zeughauser Group, notes that "they used to do just the diligence and e-discovery, but now they are going upstream." As "the U.S. law firms are getting smaller," he adds, their competitors "are getting bigger."[54]

Corporations generally use ALSPs for regulatory risk and compliance services, specialized legal services, and legal research services.[55] They intend to expand their use of ALSPs for electronic discovery services, nonlegal/factual research, intellectual property

---

[48] Ibid. at 2.
[49] Li, Victor. (2017, January 31). Study finds law firms and corporations increasingly turning to alternative legal service providers. *ABA Journal*.
[50] Altman Weil. (2016), *supra* note 39 at 4.
[51] Williams-Alvarez, Jennifer. (2017, June 26). Legal departments keep huge percentage of work in-house. Here's why. *The American Lawyer*.
[52] Ibid.
[53] Thomson Reuters Legal Executive Institute, Georgetown University Law Center for the Study of the Legal Profession, & University of Oxford Saïd Business School, *supra* note 47 at 7.
[54] Brown, Liam. (2013, February 18). Are LPOs really "stealing dealwork from law firms"?!
[55] Thomson Reuters Legal Executive Institute, Georgetown University Law Center for the Study of the Legal Profession, & University of Oxford Saïd Business School, *supra* note 47 at 7.

management, and contract management.[56] About one-third of corporate legal departments report that they used non-law firm vendors for litigation discovery and document review within the preceding 12 months, and payments to non-law firm vendors increased by 59 percent between 2012 and 2016.[57] Both corporate legal departments and law firms are likely to expand their use of ALSPs, according to a report prepared jointly by the Georgetown University Law Center for the Study of the Legal Profession, the University of Oxford Saïd Business School, and Thomson Reuters Legal Executive Institute: "ALSPs represent one of the most dynamic segments of the legal services industry, and they are likely to continue to play a role as competitors and disruptors for years to come."[58]

The Big Four Accounting Firms

In attempting to identify competitors, law firms have underestimated the market share and growth rates of the Big Four accounting firms (Deloitte, PwC, EY, and KPMG). Their impact has been obscured because they evade consistent labeling in surveys and studies; some articles classify them as ALSPs, while others simply ignore them because they appear to provide accounting services exclusively. In reality, the Big Four accounting firms are adept, powerful competitors that pose a growing challenge to law firms. As Citi Private Bank's *2018 Client Advisory* explains,

---

The sheer depth and reach of the Big Four potentially makes them formidable competitors. The three largest of them combined have global revenues that exceed the aggregate revenues of the Global 100 [law firms]. They spend more on technology

---

[56] Ibid. at 10.

[57] Altman Weil. (2016), *supra* note 39 at 4, 17.

[58] Thomson Reuters Legal Executive Institute, Georgetown University Law Center for the Study of the Legal Profession, & University of Oxford Saïd Business School, *supra* note 47 at 4. See Blasé, Friedrich. (2016, March 15). Sooner than you think! When do law firms need to take alternative legal providers seriously? Thomson Reuters Legal Executive Institute. Dzienkowski, John S. (2014). The future of big law: Alternative legal service providers to corporate clients. *Fordham Law Review, 82,* 2995.

and training each year than the revenue of any law firm. They are very experienced at developing multi-point client relationships and "solutions" to clients' business issues.

While this is not the first time that the Big Four have built legal services businesses, this time they are building them as part of an integrated service offering rather than a stand-alone product. Regulation in some markets (especially the US) may impede their progress as there are too many restrictions on what ancillary work they can do for audit clients. Still, their renewed interest and recent progress in offering legal services make them a market force to watch.[59]

The Big Four accounting firms already outrank most of their Am Law 100 competitors in size and revenue growth rates. If the Big Four's legal services units were regarded as law firms, they would tower over most of the Am Law 100 firms. PwC Legal, for instance, has 2,500 lawyers and ranks as the world's sixth largest legal services provider based on attorney headcount.[60] Each of the Big Four accounting firms' legal services units currently generates estimated annual revenue of $900 million and plans to increase that revenue to $1 billion by 2021.[61] That goal should be easy to achieve since annual revenue from the legal services units has increased by more than 10 percent in recent years.[62] Most Am Law 200 firms, in contrast, experienced negative revenue growth in 2017.[63] Small wonder,

---

[59] Citi Private Bank & Hildebrandt Consulting LLC. (2018). *2018 Client Advisory* (p. 6). See Thomson Reuters Legal Executive Institute, Georgetown University Law Center for the Study of the Legal Profession, & University of Oxford Saïd Business School, *supra* note 47 at 4. To avoid prohibitions against the unauthorized practice of law (Rule 5.5) and nonlawyer ownership of law firms (Rule 5.4), "the Big Four accounting firms now routinely supplies legal services to major corporations, albeit under the supervision of the companies' legal departments." Henderson, William. (2018, July). Legal market landscape report, p. 29.

[60] Ibid. Bruch, Nicholas, & Mayer, James. (2017, September 17). *Elephants in the room* (p. 9). New York: ALM Intelligence.

[61] Ibid.

[62] Johnson, Chris. (2017, September 14). Do the Big Four accounting firms pose a big threat to big law? *The American Lawyer.*

[63] Shunk, Marcie Borgal. (2018, May 22). The second hundred are stuck in the middle. *The American Lawyer.*

then, that management consultant Michael Roch describes the Big Four accounting firms as "the biggest underestimated threat to the legal profession today."[64]

Law Firms' Reactions to Competitors

Lawyers appear to be aware that the legal work they used to perform has been siphoned off to their corporate clients' legal departments and nontraditional legal services vendors. Despite this loss of business, most lawyers do not recognize the need to change or understand how they could change. Sixty-eight percent of law firms report that they are losing business to corporate law departments; and 19 percent acknowledge losing business to non-law firm providers of legal services.[65] Sixty-five percent of law firm leaders believe that "corporate clients doing more work in-house will be a permanent trend going forward"; and 66 percent believe that "the erosion of demand for work done by law firms" is a permanent trend.[66] Yet when asked "Why isn't your firm doing more to change the way it delivers legal services?" 59 percent of law firm leaders state that "clients aren't asking for it;" and 60 percent concede that "we are not feeling enough economic pain to motivate more significant change."[67] Attorneys' lack of motivation to change is aggravated by their lack of self-awareness: 56 percent of law firm leaders believe that "most partners are unaware of what they might do differently."[68]

Lawyers' recognition that clients are abandoning their law firms has not resulted in serious, continuous changes in individual attorney behavior or law firm management. In the few firms that acknowledge the necessity for change, the lawyers generally lack the managerial discipline to require new behavior from their colleagues and to enforce new behavior standards with financial penalties. When asked, "How has your firm addressed underperforming

---

[64]   (2015, March 9). Attack of the bean-counters. *The Economist*.

[65]   Clay, Thomas S., & Seeger, Eric A. (2017). *2017 Law firms in transition* (p. 4). Newton Square, PA: Altman Weil.

[66]   Ibid. at 1.

[67]   Ibid. at 14.

[68]   Ibid.

partners?," 59 percent of managing partners responded, "we want to do something about it, but have yet to act."[69] When asked, "To what extent has your firm's strategy changed in light of disruptive changes going on within the legal profession?," 66 percent of managing partners responded, "not at all."[70]

Attorneys' reluctance to change their behavior is not limited to large law firms and therefore reflects more of an individual bias against change than an institutional intransigence. In a Thomson Reuters survey of small law firms, for instance, 60 percent of partners identified "lack of internal efficiency" as a moderate or significant challenge, yet 74 percent of firms facing that challenge acknowledge that they are not addressing it.[71] "Cost control" and "rate pressures from clients" were cited as moderate or significant challenges by about 60 percent of partners in small law firms, yet about four out of every five law firms confronted by those challenges had not addressed them.[72] As Thomson Reuters reports, "firms may be aware of what sorts of obstacles lie in their way, but are unsure of how to confront them, challenged to find the time necessary to do so, or find it difficult to spur change within their firm."[73]

Attorneys' reactions to changes and challenges are a perplexing admixture of resistance, intransigence, and indifference. Although 94 percent of law firm leaders are convinced that "focus on improved practice efficiency will be a permanent trend going forward," only 39 percent believe that their firm "has significantly changed its strategic approach to efficiency of legal service delivery."[74] Sixty-five percent of law firm leaders state that law firms do not change because "partners resist most change efforts"; and less than one-half of law firms provide incentives for change by "rewarding efficiency and profitability" in partner compensation decisions.[75] Efficiency and profitability, in fact, do not appear to

---

[69] The Remsen Group & Jaffe. *Re-envisioning the law firm: How to lead change and thrive in the future* (p. 88).

[70] Ibid. at 92.

[71] Thomson Reuters. (2017). *2017 State of U.S. small law firms* (p. 6).

[72] Ibid.

[73] Ibid.

[74] Clay & Seeger (2017), *supra* note 65 at 1, 60.

[75] Ibid. at 14, 56.

be factors in most law firms' evaluations of their attorneys; only 20 percent of law firms measure attorney productivity by any metric other than billable hours.[76]

Lawyers' reluctance to acknowledge clients' dissatisfaction with their law firms and the resultant need for attorneys to change how they provide legal services may be caused, in large part, by law firms' failure to elicit clients' opinions. Only 60 percent of law firms with 250 or fewer attorneys report that they regularly seek "client input of what they want and value."[77] Consistent with this lack of interest in client input, less than one-third of law firm leaders consider "client performance management and client satisfaction measurement" to be among their top three priorities.[78]

Entry-Level Attorney Employment

Law firms' financial problems have resulted in diminished employment opportunities for new law school graduates. In 2007, 82.3 percent of new law school graduates were employed in full-time positions requiring bar passage.[79] By 2016, only 75.6 percent of the recent graduates were working in full-time positions requiring bar passage.[80] Reflecting the increased financial uncertainty of the legal services industry, legal employers delayed their hiring decisions as long as possible. Although 66 percent of law school graduates in 2007 had secured a job before graduation, only 54 percent of the law school class in 2015 knew where they would be employed when they graduated.[81] Summarizing legal employment trends between 2007 and 2017, Professor William Henderson

---

[76] Exterro, Inc. (2017). *2017 Law firm benchmarking report*, p. 25.

[77] Ibid. at 21.

[78] ALM Legal Intelligence. (2012, October). *Thinking like your client: Law firm strategic planning* (p. 19).

[79] National Association for Law Placement. (2008, June). *Class of 2007 National Summary Report.*

[80] National Association for Law Placement. (2017, August). *Class of 2016 National Summary Report.*

[81] National Association for Law Placement (2008), *supra* note 79. National Association for Law Placement (2017), *supra* note 80.

notes that "the number of private practice jobs is lower now than at any time since the beginning of the recession."[82]

Large law firms have wielded a disproportionately negative impact on the market for new attorneys:

[W]hile most sectors of the entry-level legal employment market have changed only modestly during the Great Recession, one sector—the larger private law firms colloquially known as "BigLaw"—has contracted proportionally six times as much as all the others. Though this sector has historically hired only 10% to 20% of each graduating class, it is responsible for over half the entry-level Law Jobs lost since 2008. And because BigLaw historically has hired a disproportionate number of the candidates most attractive to most employers, this contraction has sent a new cohort of highly accomplished and credentialed law graduates previously absorbed by BigLaw into the competition for non-BigLaw jobs, disrupting common understandings regarding where new graduates with particular ranges of credentials could expect to find work.[83]

Consistent with this cutback in entry-level positions, large law firms also have decreased the size of their summer associate classes and the number of summer associate offers made to second-year law students.[84]

Although the impending retirement of Boomer generation attorneys will create new job openings for younger attorneys, the total number of new job openings to be filled between 2014 and 2024

---

[82] Henderson, William. (2018, August 5). Four charts to better understand the class of 2017. Legal evolution. Available at: https://www.legalevolution. org/2018/08/four-charts-better-understand-class-2017-060.

[83] Burk, Bernard A. (2014). What's new about the new normal: The evolving market for new lawyers in the 21st century. *Florida State University Law Review, 41,* 544–545.

[84] Sloan, Karen. (2018, January 25). Summer associate hiring slowed at largest firms. *The American Lawyer.*

is estimated to be 157,700.[85] Considering that about 410,000 law students will graduate during that period, 252,300 law school graduates may not find law-related employment—a number sufficient to populate an entire city the size of Laredo, Texas, or Madison, Wisconsin, with unemployed attorneys.[86]

Demographic Changes

Entry-level attorneys encounter extreme competition for their initial law firm jobs, but in the long term they will be riding a demographic wave that will rapidly place them in law firm leadership positions. They will benefit from both the sheer number of peers in the Millennial generation and the impending retirements of attorneys in the Silent and Boomer generations. Millennial generation attorneys already comprise a majority of all practicing lawyers.[87] Although they presently are clustered in the associate attorney ranks, they are projected to constitute a majority of equity and non-equity partners within 10 years.[88] Assuming that partner promotion rates remain steady over the next 10 years, Millennial generation attorneys will experience the greatest leadership opportunities since the Silent generation first entered the workforce in the 1950s and 1960s.

Concurrent with the rising number of Millennial generation attorneys in law firms is the anticipated retirement of aging partners. The average age of Am Law 20 partners is 51, and about one in every three partners at large law firms is at or approaching retirement age.[89] Thirty-nine percent of partners whose tenure exceeds 20 years are planning to retire within five years, and an additional 41 percent of those 20+ year partners expect to retire within 6 to

---

[85] Weiss, Debra Cassens. (2016, January 28). Revised outlook for growth in lawyer jobs is glum. *ABA Journal Daily News.*

[86] See Sloan, Karen. (2016, December 15). Number of students enrolling in law school basically flat. *The National Law Journal.*

[87] Citi Private Bank & Hildebrandt Consulting, *supra* note 59 at 14.

[88] See McLellan, Lizzy. (2017, November 6). Where the Millennials are: Tracking the generations in Big Law. *The American Lawyer.*

[89] McQueen, M. P. (2016, February 29). How old is your firm? *The American Lawyer.* Citi Private Bank & Hildebrandt Consulting, *supra* note 59 at 12.

10 years.[90] Overall, retirements will cause law firms to lose about 16 percent of their partners by 2021 and 38 percent of their partners by 2026.[91]

Although these demographic changes should open up leadership positions for Millennial generation attorneys, it is not clear that older partners will yield their positions or that law firms can survive the conflicts resulting from older partners' resistance. Many senior partners refuse to transition their clients to other partners, and when asked to retire, they choose to join another law firm with an intact book of business.[92] New partners cite law firms' lack of succession planning as a principal source of anxiety, expressing a concern that "some senior partners won't let go."[93] At firms where rainmaking and client origination credits play an outsize role in attorney compensation, younger attorneys describe senior attorneys as enacting "sort of a Charlton Heston at the NRA [National Rifle Association] moment: You'll take these clients out of my hands when you pry my cold dead fingers off their files."[94]

When senior partners refuse to transition clients and vacate leadership positions, talented senior associates and junior partners move on to other firms that afford superior opportunities. Millennial generation attorneys are especially likely to join another firm when senior partners thwart their advancement; Millennials generally are more mobile, risk tolerant, and entrepreneurial than attorneys in previous generations.[95] As Heather Morse, marketing director at Greenberg Glusker, observes, "the rising generation—people who are less afraid of risk because they grew up more independent—are more likely to jump to other firms instead of

90   Lowe, Jeffrey A. (2016). *2016 Partner compensation survey* (p. 84). Washington, DC: Major, Lindsey, & Africa.
91   Triedman, Julie. (2016, August 29). Retiring boomers pose big challenges for firms. *The American Lawyer*.
92   Rozen, Miriam. (2018, April 5). Carrot & stick used to motivate retirement-age partners to hand off clients. *The American Lawyer*.
93   Press, Aric. (2011, November 22). The talent. *The Am Law Daily*.
94   Ibid.
95   McQueen, M. P. (2016, February 29). Here come the Big Law millennials. *The American Lawyer*.

waiting their turn for promotion to head practice groups and later to become part of firm management."[96]

Chapter Capsule

This chapter has presented an overview of the legal services industry and law firms' declining role in that industry. It has summarized key features and trends—law firm revenue, employees, average weekly hours, billable hours, realization and collection rates, corporate legal departments, ALSPs, and Big Four legal services units—that signal hazardous working conditions and compel fundamental changes. Across nearly all key performance metrics, law firms, on average, have experienced decreased demand for their services, lower realization rates, and thinning margins. Even successful law firms cannot assume that their past success presages future success, as volatility has increased throughout the Am Law 200.

Although many firms are reporting increased revenue and profitability in 2018, those financial achievements are built upon the same business model that sustained law firms after the Great Recession—weak client demand for legal services offset by hourly rate increases, expense vigilance, and fewer equity partners. In the second quarter of 2018, for example, the overall economy grew at a 4.1 percent annualized rate, but the demand for legal services rose only 1.4 percent.[97] Worked billing rates, though, rose by 3.4 percent in the second quarter.[98] Attorney productivity increased by 0.9 percent in the second quarter, but that productivity increase "was mostly due to shrinking or stagnant head count at firms."[99] Financial results in the third quarter of 2018 also appeared to signal a financial turnaround for law firms. Closer scrutiny of those results, however, indicates that price increases vastly exceeded demand increase. Although law firms raised their average rates by 3.1 percent in the third quarter, total demand rose only 0.9 percent for the first nine months of

---

[96]   Olson, Elizabeth. (2015, November 4). Graying firms wrestle with making room for younger lawyers. *The New York Times.*

[97]   Strom, Roy. (2018, August 14). Report says law firm demand hit new heights in second quarter. *The American Lawyer.*

[98]   Ibid.

[99]   Ibid.

2018—"which may sound miniscule but represents the strongest performance since 2014."[100]

Attorneys and their law firms appear to be resigned to the diversion of their work to corporate legal departments, ALSPs, and the Big Four accounting firms. They have adroitly squeezed a stagnant revenue pool into higher profits per partner through short-term strategies. This gives equity partners the impression that the revenue pool is rising when, in fact, it is level or lower after adjustments for inflation.

Associate attorneys and non-equity partners, who do not benefit from the machinations necessary to boost profits per partner, are not visibly agitated by their declining prospects. When asked to rate attorneys' "awareness of the challenges of the new legal market" on a scale of 1 (low)—10 (high), the median response from law firm leaders is "6."[101] That median response has not changed during the last five years. Consistent with that low level of awareness, 59 percent of law firm leaders report that law firms are not changing how they deliver legal services because "we are not feeling enough cco nomic pain to motivate more significant change."[102]

Instead of adapting to clients' evolving demands and expectations, many law firms embrace five quick fixes that temporarily boost income and divert their attention from the underlying problems. Law firm consultant Stephen Mabey describes these palliative measures:[103]

- Let's "eat our young" by laying off associates.
- Let's "eat our old" by forcing older partners into retirement.
- Let's offer larger client discount rates.

---

[100] Strom, Roy. (2018, November 12). Demand for Big Law hits post-recession high: Report. *The American Lawyer*. See Legal Executive Institute. (2018, November 12). PMI Rises for second consecutive quarter. Thomson Reuters Peer Monitor Index. ("This marks the fifth consecutive quarter with average rate growth of three percent or higher.")

[101] Clay & Seeger. (2018), *supra* note 24 at 22.

[102] Ibid. at 15.

[103] Mabey, Stephen. Law firms in transition. Don't shoot the messengers—change them! Ross Intelligence blog. Retrieved from https://rossintelligence.com/law-firms-in-transition.

- Let's agree to alternative fee arrangements, although we don't understand their financial effect.
- Let's "cut our way to profitability" by reducing expenses without considering their actual long-term impact on profitability.

These remedies will not be sufficient to forestall the fundamental changes that clients expect, technology facilitates, and competitors deliver.

3
Mismatches

If law firms were attempting to assemble a "dream team" for client service or law firm leadership, they might select attorneys who are quite different from their current partners and associate attorneys. The recruiting, hiring, professional development, evaluation, and compensation practices that produced the present generation of law firm attorneys and leaders were not based on empirical methods and tended to promote personal similarities and existing hierarchies within the legal profession. These practices did not consistently identify and promote attorneys who possess the skills and qualities most important to clients, and they did not reliably assist law firms in recognizing and developing many attorneys who could have become outstanding partners and leaders.

Law firms' employment practices continue to disaffect and exclude many superb attorneys, perpetuate biases against female attorneys and racial and ethnic minority attorneys, and lead to the hiring of many attorneys unsuitable for client service and uncomfortable with collaborative professional relationships. From an empirical perspective, law firms' practices are failing to meet the expectations of both their external market (clients) and their internal market (law firm employees and partners). These practices are suboptimal in at least six respects:

- They give undue weight to Law School Admission Test (LSAT) scores and grade point averages (GPAs), despite research indicating that these two factors are not predictive of attorney performance and may, in fact, signal performance problems.

- They result in a low level of diversity and a high level of attrition among female and racial and ethnic minority attorneys.
- They promote gender biases in law school admissions and discriminate against female attorneys in hiring decisions.
- They deprive clients and law firms of the superior service and outcomes provided by a diverse workforce.
- They fail to objectively assess and properly weight personal qualities and "soft skills" predictive of attorney performance.
- They cause astronomical attrition costs that ultimately are borne by clients.

Each of these problems is analyzed and discussed below.

LSAT Scores and Grade Point Averages

Undergraduate GPAs and LSAT scores are the primary determinants of law school admissions decisions and, most importantly, whether an applicant is accepted by an elite law school.[1] Enrollment at an elite law school thus serves as a symbol of and proxy for high undergraduate GPAs and LSAT scores. Although these two factors are positively correlated with law school grades, they bear little or no relation to attorney success after graduation from law school.[2] Law school grades, moreover, are not predictive of attorney

---

[1] Henderson, William D., & Zahorsky, Rachel M. (2012, July 1). The pedigree problem: Are law school ties choking the profession? *ABA Journal.* Marks, Alexia Brunet, & Moss, Scott A. (2016, June). What predicts law student success? A longitudinal study correlating law student applicant data and law school outcomes. *Journal of Empirical Legal Studies, 13*(2), 205–265.

[2] Gerkman, Alli, & Cornett, Logan. (2016, July). *Foundations for practice: The whole lawyer and the character quotient.* Denver, Colorado: Institute for the Advancement of the American Legal System. Gerkman, Alli, & Harman, Elena. (2015, January). *Ahead of the curve: Turning law students into lawyers* (p. 21). Denver, Colorado: Institute for the Advancement of the American Legal System. Gibson, Steve, Henderson, William, Stacy, Caren Ulrich, & Zorn, Chris. (2011, October 10). Moneyball for law firms. *The Am Law Daily.* Marks & Moss, *supra* note 1 at 205, 217. Lempert, R. O., Chambers, D. L., & Adams, T. K. (2000). Michigan's minority graduates in practice: The river runs through law school. *Law & Social Inquiry, 25,* 395–505. Shultz, Marjorie, & Zedeck, Sheldon. (2009,

performance after graduation; and other academic achievements like undergraduate honors and law review "have been strong negative predictors of essential associate competencies or success traits."[3] Since the determinants of admission to an elite law school and a student's grades at the law school are practically irrelevant in assessing future performance as an attorney, law firms' practice of hiring attorneys based on academic credentials appears to be as sensible as selecting Olympic sprinters based on shoe size.

Summarizing the results of a study that identified 26 factors essential to an attorney's success after graduation, law professor William Henderson notes, "Remarkably, LSAT scores, undergraduate GPA, and first year law school grades were correlated at statistically significant levels with between zero and six of the 26 success factors."[4] Thus, the conventional attorney hiring factors (LSAT scores and GPAs) are related to 23 percent or less of the factors that determine an attorney's success. Academic credentials, Henderson adds, "were negatively associated with other success factors, such as networking, building relationships, practical judgment, ability to see the world through the eyes of others, and/or commitment to community service."[5] In other words, high academic performance actually signaled possible shortcomings in critical success factors such as judgment, relationship skills, and perspective taking.

Other analyses have found a negative correlation between attorneys' undergraduate GPAs and integrity, suggesting that conventional measures of academic success could portend unconventional

January 30). *Final report—Identification, development and validation of predictors for successful lawyering.* Retrieved from http://ssrn.com/abstract=1353554. Stilwell, Lisa Anthony, Dalessandro, Susan P., & Reese, Lynda M. (2011, October). *Predictive validity of the LSAT: A national summary of the 2009 and 2010 LSAT correlation studies.* Newton, PA: Law School Admission Council. Shultz, Marjorie M., & Zedeck, Sheldon. Predicting professional effectiveness: Broadening the basis for law school admission decisions. *Law & Social Inquiry, 36,* 620. Weiss, Debra Cassens. (2008, October 16). School rank and GPA aren't the best predictors of BigLaw success. *ABA Journal Law News Now.*

3   Gibson, Henderson, Stacy, & Zorn, *supra* note 2.
4   Henderson, William. (2009, June). The bursting of the pedigree bubble. *NALP Bulletin.*
5   Ibid.

judgment and behavior.[6] Illustrative of potential problems is the fact that 60 percent of attorneys in their first 10 years of practice at firms with 250–500 attorneys report that having "a commitment to justice and the rule of law" is either "not relevant" or "advantageous but not necessary" for an attorney's success.[7] Large law firms can boast that they hire the most academically accomplished law school graduates, but like the physician who reports that the operation was successful although the patient died, law firms cannot be certain that their clients will survive their hiring successes.

Despite the absence of a statistically reliable relationship between attorneys' career performance and their LSAT scores and undergraduate and law school GPAs, major law firms continue to base their hiring decisions on law school rankings, law review participation, grades, class standing, and cursory interviews. This system has existed for decades and, Henderson notes, "would be as familiar to today's partner as it was to the partner who first interviewed him or her 25 years ago. Anchored by the one-on-one interview and an unwavering bias towards a cookie cutter educational pedigree, law firms make million dollar hiring decisions using little or no analytics."[8] Henderson's conclusions are mirrored in the study, "Assessing Lawyer Traits & Finding a Fit for Success." Its authors, Mark Levin and Bruce MacEwen, find that law firms "employ the same metrics (GPA, school attended, law review or moot court participation and a brief impression of the person from a series of short, unstructured interviews) that they have always used, even though these metrics have no true correlation to success within a firm setting."[9]

---

6 Henderson, William. (2014). Successful lawyer skills and behaviors. In Haskins, Paul (Ed.). *Essential qualities of the professional lawyer* (p. 63). Chicago: American Bar Association.

7 This data is derived from the interactive feature, "Explore all foundations for practice," developed by the Institute for the Advancement of the American Legal System. It is available at: http://iaals.du.edu/foundations/explore/all. See Gerkman & Cornett, *supra* note 2.

8 Henderson, Bill, Stacy, Caren Ulrich, & Gibson, Steve. (2011, October 10). Everything you think you know about lawyer recruiting is wrong: The new science of evidence-based hiring practices. *Bloomberg Law*.

9 Levin, Mark, & MacEwen, Bruce. (2014). Assessing lawyer traits & finding a fit for success: Introducing the Sheffield Legal Assessment (p. 7).

Emblematic of law firms' emphasis on conventional hiring criteria is this interview of an Am Law 50 hiring partner, conducted by *The American Lawyer* columnist Vivia Chen:

Sidley's D.C. practice sounds very high-powered. Is it more elitist about hiring than the other offices in your firm? I can't say that. We all look for the top students at the top schools.

What qualities do you look for in your new hires? We pride ourselves on our collegial and collaborative environment. We look for lawyers who are not sharp-elbow types, who show maturity and good judgment. We give them a lot of responsibility early on.

And how do you figure all that out in a 20-minute interview? We engage in substantive conversations. We ask them about their law review notes or their judicial clerkships. You can gauge a lot from how someone explains what they've worked on.[10]

Although this partner emphasizes "top" students and law schools, law review notes, and judicial clerkships, many attorneys now recognize that other criteria and experiences may be more predictive of an attorney's success. In a recent survey, for instance, about 24,000 attorneys reported that "legal employment," "recommendations from practitioners or judges," "legal externship," "other experiential education," and "life experience between college and law school" were the five most helpful hiring criteria for new attorneys.[11] Among 17 hiring criteria listed in the survey, conventional hiring criteria such as "law review experience" and "journal experience" were ranked second to last and last, respectively.[12] "Class

---

[10] Chen, Vivia. (2010, August 20). Sidley Austin: Bring on the work/life balance seekers! *Law.com.*

[11] Gerkman, Alli, & Cornett, Logan. (2017). *Foundations for practice: Hiring the whole lawyer* (p. 5). Denver, CO: Institute for the Advancement of the American Legal System.

[12] Ibid.

rank" and "law school attended" were ranked eleventh and twelfth, respectively.[13]

So why would law firms base their hiring decisions on criteria that seem relatively insignificant and arguably irrelevant? The primary reason appears to be inertia, but another reason may be more compelling. When asked why he relies on conventional hiring factors like law school ranking, a managing partner responded, "If I hired a lawyer from Harvard and he doesn't work out, it's his fault. But when a candidate from a regional school washes out, it's my fault."[14] Just as "no one ever got fired for buying IBM" in an earlier age, no one evidently gets blamed for hiring from the elite law schools.

In their recruiting efforts, law firms cast a wide net over a very small number of law schools. Most entry-level associates in the nation's 250 largest law firms are selected from the top 14 law schools, as ranked by *U.S. News and World Report*.[15] These 14 law schools comprise only seven percent of the 205 law schools approved by the American Bar Association. And those 14 law schools inhabit a stagnant pool; no school among the 14 has fallen out of that elite group, although their rankings periodically change within the group.[16]

Despite this fixation on the top 14 law schools, large law firms cannot demonstrate that the attorneys hired from those law schools are more likely to meet their partnership criteria. In fact, attorneys who graduate from lower-ranked law schools are more likely to make partner in those firms. The employment data regarding the 250 largest law firms shows that 53.7 percent of their entry-level associate attorneys graduated from a top 14 law school, but only 29.4 percent of the lawyers promoted to partner at those firms attended those schools.[17] As Henderson explains,

---

[13]   Ibid.
[14]   Henderson (2009), *supra* note 4.
[15]   Henderson (2014), *supra* note 6 at 64–65.
[16]   Ibid. at 65.
[17]   Ibid.

for every 5.4 graduates from elite law schools, one elite graduate is promoted to partner. For all other law schools, that cor-
responding statistic is 1.95. Further, even when the analysis
is limited to the top 50 [law firms] based on profitability, there
remains a large, persistent disparity that favors regional law
graduates. Among the 50 most profitable firms, there are 4.9 top
14 associates hired for every top 14 lawyer promoted to partner,
compared to regional law schools, where the ratio of associates
hired to partners promoted is only 1.9.[18]

Surveying the results of law firms' hiring practices, Henderson
finds that "the heavy emphasis placed on academic credentials by
elite legal employers, such as large law firms, is misplaced."[19] These
practices, he states, "are largely the relics of a bygone era that persist
long after their original business purpose has evaporated. For new
and aspiring attorneys who may lack the cognitive markers to make
the cut for these seemingly elite institutions, the encouraging word
is that the markers themselves have precious little ability to predict
future performance as a lawyer."[20]

Graduates of elite national law schools are not only less likely to
make partner at large law firms; they also exhibit different attrition
patterns, career satisfaction levels, client generation capabilities,
and evaluation biases. Studies indicate that attorneys who graduate from elite law schools are more likely to voluntarily leave their
employer law firm;[21] are more likely to be laid off by their employer
law firm;[22] are less satisfied working in large law firms;[23] are less

---

[18] Ibid.
[19] Ibid. at 54.
[20] Ibid.
[21] Dinovitzer, Ronit, & Garth, Bryant G. (2007, March). Lawyer satisfaction in the
process of structuring legal careers. *Law & Society Review, 41*(1), 1–50.
[22] Oyer, Paul, & Schaefer, Scott. (2010, March 2.). What drives turnover and
layoffs at large law firms. Available at: https://www.law.georgetown.edu/
academics/centers-institutes/legal-profession/documents/upload/Confer-
ence-Papers-March-23-oyerlayoffs.pdf.
[23] Dinovitzer & Garth, *supra* note 21.

likely to be successful rainmakers;[24] and tend to receive higher performance ratings when evaluated by partners who also graduated from elite law schools.[25] The disparity between the attributes required to excel in top-ranked law schools and those required to advance in law firms becomes acute when partnership admission decisions are made, as Noam Scheiber explains in "The Last Days of Big Law":

Even lawyers with a dedicated mentor have trouble making equity partner unless they meet a second criterion: demonstrating a potential for attracting clients. There is an irony that flows from this. Lawyers at an elite firm like Mayer Brown [an Am Law 50 firm] have typically spent their lives amassing intellectual credentials. They are high-school valedictorians and graduates of elite universities, with mantles full of Latin honors. They have made law review at top law schools and clerked for federal judges. When, somewhere between the second and fifth year of their legal careers, they discover that brainpower is only incidental to their professional advancement—that the real key is an aptitude for schmoozing—it can be a rude awakening.[26]

Client origination and retention may be particularly challenging for attorneys whose lives have been distinguished by extraordinary academic achievement. That achievement, writes Ann Hulbert in her study of child prodigies, "takes a toll. It demands an intensity that rarely makes kids conventionally popular or socially comfortable."[27]

---

24 Gillette, Patricia K. (2015, August 15). Rainmakers: Born or bred? *Law Practice Today.* Drake, Monique, & Parker-Stephen, Evan. (2013). *The rainmaking study: How lawyer's personality traits and behaviors drive successful client development* (p. 6). Lawyer Metrics.
25 Gibson, Henderson, Stacy, & Zorn, *supra* note 2.
26 Scheiber, Noam. (2013, July 21). The last days of Big Law: You can't imagine the terror when the money dries up. *New Republic.*
27 Hulbert, Ann. (2018). *Off the charts* (p. xvii). New York: Alfred A. Knopf.

Although many graduates of elite law schools are superb attorneys and their law firms benefit immensely from their intelligence, skills, and commitment, law firms cannot justify allocating a disproportionate number of associate attorney positions to them. Instead of fixating on elite law schools, law firms should undertake the more productive task of identifying and recruiting outstanding graduates of all law schools. This effort would require law firms to develop selection criteria that are more closely related to actual client needs and attorney performance predictors. If the academic credentials required for admission to elite law schools are not predictive of professional success, as demonstrated in numerous studies, when will large law firms stop converging on a small fraction of elite law schools whose students, on average, may perform worse than many graduates of lower-ranked law schools?

Law firms' reluctance to expand the list of "accepted" recruitment schools, according to professional development experts Jeanne Picht and Caren Stacey, is "based largely on anecdotal information or internal politics."[28] This obstinacy fosters attorney hiring decisions and an entire hierarchy of lawyers and law schools based more on status than merit, more on motivated reasoning than actual data. Every year it stymies the careers of thousands of dedicated and capable graduates of lower-ranked law schools while appearing to be both merit-based and time-honored. As the French philosopher Pierre Bourdieu observed, "Every established order tends to make its own entirely arbitrary system seem entirely natural."[29]

Female and Minority Attorneys

Apart from the hiring biases reflected in law firms' emphasis on academic credentials and elite law schools, many law firms exhibit

---

[28] Picht, Jeanne M., & Stacy, Caren Ulrich. (2013, May/June). Solving the multimillion-dollar C player problem. *Law Practice, 39*, 3. See Sander, Richard, & Bambauer, Jane. (2012, December). The secret of my success: How status, eliteness and school performance shape legal careers. *Journal of Empirical Legal Studies, 9*(4), 893–930 (finding "there is little empirical basis for the overwhelming importance students assign to 'eliteness' in choosing a law school").

[29] Bourdieu, Pierre. (1977). *Outline of a theory of practice* (p. 164). Cambridge, UK: Cambridge University Press.

a distinct pattern of bias against female attorneys and racial and ethnic minority attorneys. This pattern of bias begins with law school admissions, continues through associate attorney hiring and partnership admission decisions, and remains robust in partner compensation determinations. It corrupts the hiring, talent development, and evaluation process and ultimately forces thousands of outstanding attorneys out of the nation's law firms. Eighty-five percent of minority female attorneys, for example, leave large firms within seven years after they are hired.[30] As attorney/writer Liane Jackson explains in her *ABA Journal* article, "Invisible Then Gone," "it's not because they want to leave, or because they 'can't cut it.' It's because they feel they have no choice."[31] Black women, for instance, leave their law firms at especially high rates (about 17 percent per year) because "the firm culture is not conducive to success for people of color or people of color who are women"—they "simply see no place for themselves in Big Law."[32]

Law firms tend to be models of homogeneity and exclusion, more reflective of the college-educated workforce in the 1960s than today's workforce.[33] While racial and ethnic minorities will soon constitute more than 50 percent of the U.S. population, racial and ethnic minority attorneys comprise only 15 percent of all attorneys employed by law firms in the United States; about 20 percent are associate attorneys and nearly 9 percent are partners.[34] Only 2 percent of law firm partners are Black, and the representation of Blacks among partners "barely budged" during the last 10 years.[35]

---

[30] Jackson, Liane. (2016, March). Invisible then gone: Minority women are disappearing from Big Law—and here's why. *ABA Journal.*

[31] Ibid.

[32] Russell-Kraft, Stephanie. (2017, January 6). Law firms struggle to hire and keep black women. *Bloomberg Law.*

[33] See Goldin, Claudia, Katz, Lawrence F., & Kuziemko, Ilyana. (2006, Fall). The homecoming of American college women: The reversal of the college gender gap. *Journal of Economic Perspectives, 20*(4), 133. McKay, Ruth B. (2007). A black community with advanced labor force characteristics in 1960. *Monthly Labor Review.*

[34] Bell, Jacqueline. (2017, August 20). The best firms for minority attorneys. *Law 360.* See Silkenat, James R. (2014, March). Major push for diversity. *ABA Journal,* p. 8.

[35] Olson, Elizabeth. (2016, March 3). Law firm's first Latina partner, with boost from N.Y.U. program. *The New York Times.* National Association for Law

Women of color, moreover, represent only 2 percent of all equity partners; Black women constitute a mere 0.64 percent of all partners.[36] Although Asian Americans comprise 10.3 percent of top-30 law schools graduates, they "have the highest attrition rates and the lowest ratio of partners to associates among all groups."[37]

The biases and lack of diversity in the legal profession extend to nearly every facet of the legal services industry, law schools, and the judicial system, including mediators,[38] judges,[39] corporate counsel,[40] court appearances,[41] first-chair positions on litigation teams,[42] oral arguments,[43] law school deans,[44] federal judicial law clerks,[45] law clerk positions at the Supreme Court of the United States[46] and Supreme Court appointments to argue as an amicus.[47] "One irony of this nation's struggle for diversity and gender equity," asserts law

Placement. (2017). *2016 report on diversity in U.S. law firms* (p. 6). Washington, DC: National Association for Law Placement.

[36] Chen, Vivia. Female equity partner rate is at all-time high (But it's not that great). (2017, September 20). *The Am Law Daily*. Russell-Kraft, *supra* note 32.

[37] Chung, Eric, Dong, Samuel, Hu, Xiaonan, Kwon, Christine, & Liu, Goodwin. (2017, October 5). A portrait of Asian Americans in the law. Available at: https://papers.ssrn.com/sol3/papers.cfm?abstract_id=3045905.

[38] Hanft, Noah. (2017, March 20). Making diversity happen: No more lip service. *The New York Law Journal.*

[39] Negowetti, Nicole E. (2015, Spring). Implicit bias and the legal profession's "diversity crisis:" A call for self-reflection. *Nevada Law Journal, 15*, 934. ABA Commission on the Future of Legal Services. (2016, August). Report on the future of legal services in the United States (p. 38). Chicago: American Bar Association.

[40] McQueen, M. P. (2016, August 1). Minority women: Still out. *The American Lawyer*. Silkenat, *supra* note 34.

[41] Braff, Danielle. (2018, February). Trial by data: Legal analytics are being used to determine gender diversity of firms. *ABA Journal.*

[42] Ward, Stephanie Francis. (2017, March). Female first chairs. *ABA Journal.*

[43] Jackson, Liane. (2018, January). Judges push for diverse voices in court. *ABA Journal.*

[44] Huang, Andrew. (2015, July 8). Year of the female dean. *National Jurist.*

[45] Chung, Dong, Hu, Kwon, & Liu, *supra* note 37.

[46] Weiss, Debra Cassens. (2017, December 12). Supreme Court law clerks are still mostly white men; Which justices had the most diverse clerks? *ABA Journal.* Mauro, Tony. (2017, December 11). Shut out: SCOTUS law clerks still mostly white and male. *The American Lawyer.*

[47] Weiss, Debra Cassens. (2016, May 17). Supreme Court favors white males in amicus appointments, study says. *ABA Journal.*

professor Deborah Rhode, "is that the profession leading the struggle has failed to set an example in its own workplaces."[48]

Female law students have comprised nearly 50 percent of law school enrollees during the last two decades, yet only 18 percent of law firm equity partners and 4 percent of managing partners are female.[49] "Although collegiality may be a dominant motif in law firms," law professor John Flood notes, "gender equality is not. Law firms are primarily male institutions even though greater proportions of women are entering the legal profession."[50] Despite having reached parity in law school admissions, women continue to be disfavored in partnership promotion decisions. In 2016, for instance, five Am Law 100 firms failed to elevate a single female to partner status, and only "36.7 percent of all partner promotions in the Am Law 100 went to women."[51] In its survey of the nation's 200 largest law firms, the National Association of Women Lawyers found that "100 percent of firms reported that its highest U.S. paid partner is male."[52] These biases are driven, in part, by male clients' tendency to select male lead partners. Male clients choose a female lead attorney in only 17 percent of cases.[53]

Although the percentage of female attorneys in partner and managing partner positions is strikingly low, the actual distribution of female attorneys among legal practice areas reveals a deeper level of bias. Female attorneys are concentrated in immigration, family law, health care, and labor and employment practices.[54] These practice

---

48   Rhode, Deborah L. (2011). From platitudes to priorities: Diversity and gender equity in law firms. *Georgetown Journal of Legal Ethics, 24*, 1041.

49   American Bar Association. First year and total J.D. enrollment by gender, 1947–2011. Casazza, Lauren O., & Morris, Madelyn A. (2016, November 11). Counsel's table should mirror real-life diversity. *New York Law Journal*.

50   Flood, John. (2007). Law firms. In Clark, D. (Ed.). *Encyclopedia of law and society: American and global perspectives*. Thousand Oaks, CA: Sage Publications.

51   Russell-Kraft, Stephanie. (2017, January 11). These law firms made the most women partners in 2016. *Bloomberg Law*.

52   Rikleen, Lauren Stiller. (2015). Women lawyers continue to lag behind male colleagues (p. 4). National Association of Women Lawyers.

53   Chen, Vivia. (2018, January 17). Male clients disfavor women partners. *The American Lawyer*.

54   Isaacson, Daniella. (2017, April). *Where do we go from here?: Big Law's struggle with recruiting and retaining female talent* (p. 5). ALM Intelligence.

areas are among the lowest when ranked by prestige and income.[55] When rated by "prestige of practice scores," female attorneys, on average, have been placed substantially below other practicing lawyers.[56] (Black lawyers, too, were ranked below other practicing lawyers in prestige of practice scores, but unlike the prestige and income disparities affecting female attorneys, the difference "is not statistically significant.")[57]

The most lucrative practice areas in large law firms are dominated by male attorneys, while the less lucrative practice areas show higher concentrations of female attorneys:

In looking at female lawyers at Am Law 200 firms, the ALI study ["Where Do We Go from Here?: Big Law's Struggle with Recruiting Female Talent"] found substantial gender diversity variances across all practice areas. Women in Big Law made up 60 percent of immigration practices, followed by 48 percent of family law groups and 45 percent of those lawyers specializing in health care work. But the study found that they were the anomalies. The majority of Am Law 200 practices have an average female head count ratio of 30 percent. Practice areas with the highest compensation and focus within Big Law, such as banking, intellectual property, and litigation, had the lowest percentages of women. Women made up only 35 percent of Am Law 200 litigation departments, 31 percent of banking and taxation practices and accounted for 27 and 23 percent of IP and M&A teams, respectively.[58]

These disparities in practice areas result in large income disparities between female and male partners. Average partner income in labor and employment practices (44% female attorneys) is

---

55 Heinz, John P., Nelson, Robert L., Sandefur, Rebecca L., & Laumann, Edward O. (2005). *Urban lawyers* (pp. 87–88). Chicago: University of Chicago Press.
56 Ibid. at 96.
57 Ibid. at 95.
58 Tribe, Meghan. (2017, April 17). Study shows gender diversity varies widely across practice areas. *The Am Law Daily.*

$597,000, a relatively low amount when compared with the average partner income in intellectual property practices (27% female attorneys) and litigation practices (35% female attorneys) of $880,000 and $873,000, respectively.[59] Across all practice areas, female partners' total annual compensation is about 69 percent of male partners' total annual compensation ($659,000 vs. $949,000).[60]

Although substantial disparities exist between female and male partner compensation in large law firms, surveys indicate that racial and ethnic minority partners, on average, earn compensation roughly similar to that of White partners in those firms.[61] Black partners (comprising only two percent of surveyed partners) earn average compensation of $797,000, compared with White partners' average compensation of $876,000.[62] Hispanic partners (two percent of surveyed partners) and Asian Pacific partners (three percent of surveyed partners), earn an average annual compensation of $956,000 and $875,000, respectively.[63]

Despite compensation parity, minority partners display markedly higher rates of dissatisfaction with their compensation than their White counterparts. Only 19 percent of White partners report that they are "not very satisfied" or "not at all satisfied" with their compensation, while 43 percent of Black partners state that they are "not very" or "not at all" satisfied.[64] Thus, the percentage of Black partners dissatisfied with their compensation is more than twice that of White partners. Thirty-two percent of Hispanic and Asian Pacific partners state that they are "not very" or "not at all" satisfied, evidencing again a significantly higher level of dissatisfaction than shown by White partners (19 percent). The most frequently cited

---

[59]   Isaacson, *supra* note 54 at 5. Lowe, Jeffrey. (2016). *2016 Partner compensation survey* (p. 50). Washington, DC: Major, Lindsey, & Africa.

[60]   Lowe, *supra* note 59 at 50. See Olson, Elizabeth. (2016, October 12). A 44% pay divide for female and male law partners, survey shows. *The New York Times.*

[61]   The female/male apportionment among minority law firm equity partners is estimated to be: Hispanic (24 percent female/76 percent male); Black (33 percent female/66 percent male) and Asian (29 percent female/71 percent male). Rikleen, *supra* note 52 at 7.

[62]   Lowe, *supra* note 59 at 50.

[63]   Ibid.

[64]   Ibid at 33–34.

reason for dissatisfaction with compensation is "cronyism" within the firm.[65]

To understand partners' attitudes about their careers, independent of compensation, the attorney placement company Major, Lindsey, & Africa asked partners, "Overall, how satisfied are you with your life as an attorney when you DO NOT factor your compensation into the equation? Sixty-one percent of White partners stated that they were "very satisfied" or "moderately satisfied."[66] But only 54 percent of Black attorneys reported being "very" or "moderately" satisfied.[67] The satisfaction levels of Hispanic and Asian Pacific attorneys were even lower. Only 50 percent of Hispanic partners and 47 percent of Asian Pacific partners stated that they were "very" or "moderately" satisfied with their life as an attorney, independent of compensation.[68]

Consistent with their relatively lower levels of satisfaction, Black and Hispanic attorneys are more likely to be planning their exits from their law firms. In firms of 100+ attorneys, 30 percent of Black attorneys and 25 percent of Hispanic attorneys are considering leaving their positions, but only 20 percent of White and Asian Pacific attorneys are considering departures.[69] In law firms with 21–100 attorneys, one-half of all Black attorneys are considering a job change.[70] Asian Pacific attorneys' lower level of "mobility intentions" does not reflect job satisfaction: "Asian respondents reported below-average levels of satisfaction across all factors, except for the power track [compensation, evaluation, recognition], and they were least satisfied with the social index [pro bono opportunities, workplace diversity]."[71]

[65] Ibid at 35. Rivera, Lauren A., & Tilcsik. (2016). Class advantage, commitment penalty: The gendered effect of social class signals in an elite labor market. *American Sociological Review, 81*(6), 1097, 1111.

[66] Lowe, *supra* note 59 at 68.

[67] Ibid.

[68] Ibid.

[69] Dinovitzer, Ronit, et al. (2014). *After the JD III: Third results from a national study of legal careers* (p. 78). American Bar Foundation & NALP Foundation for Law Career Research and Education.

[70] Ibid.

[71] Ibid. at 77.

Minority partners' dissatisfaction often centers on their firms' lack of diversity and the perception that evaluations and compensation are not performance based. These sources of dissatisfaction not only fuel a minority partner's determination to leave a firm but also discourage the partner from recruiting or mentoring other minority attorneys. As a minority partner relates,

I almost don't want to recruit students of color here [into the firm] any more. I bring these talented young people here, and I know that, behind the scenes, people are setting the stage for them to fail. No matter how qualified, no matter how much star quality these recruits have, they are going to be seen as people who will most likely not cut it. So, they are under the microscope from the first moment they walk in. And, every flaw is exaggerated. Every mistake is announced. And, it's like, aha. As soon as a minority makes a mistake, they immediately say that that's what they were expecting all along.[72]

Significantly, when a law firm instituted "blind" evaluations of minority summer associates' work product ("the partners evaluating the work did not know which associate had completed the work"), the blind evaluations "were generally more positive for minorities and women and less positive for majority men."[73] Before the blind evaluations were implemented, the firm's minority summer associates "were consistently being evaluated more negatively than their majority counterparts."[74]

Barriers to Female Attorney Employment

The foundation for disparities in employment opportunities and compensation for female attorneys is laid a few years before they begin their first law firm job. Recent analyses of law school

---

[72] Negowetti, *supra* note 39 at 930, 949.
[73] Ibid. at 957.
[74] Ibid.

admissions practices show that female applicants are less likely to be admitted to an elite law school and more likely to be admitted to a law school with a low job placement rate. Law schools in general admit 79.5 percent of male applicants but only 75.8 percent of female applicants.[75] This discrepancy has existed since 2000, the first year reliable data was available, and it has ranged as high as 5.9 percentage points.[76] Although women constituted 49.4 percent of all law students in 2015, they accounted for 46 percent of the students at the top 50 law schools and 53 percent of the students at the bottom quarter of law schools, as ranked by *U.S. News and World Report.*[77]

Female applicants' lower admission rates appear to be attributable to their lower LSAT scores. Although female applicants tend to score higher than male applicants on undergraduate grade point averages (UGPAs), male applicants, on average, have higher LSAT scores.[78] Law schools are far more likely to admit high-LSAT/low-UGPA candidates than low-LSAT/high-UGPA candidates.[79] But an exhaustive statistical analysis of applicant data and law school performance demonstrates that high-LSAT/low-GPA applicants actually "perform subpar, controlling for all other variables," in law school grades.[80] The analysis shows that low-LSAT/high-UGPA candidates "are no less promising than those with a more balanced profile or a high LSAT, so schools need not fear admitting low-LSAT candidates with high UGPAs, or other pluses."[81] The law school admission process that favors male applicants in its overemphasis on LSAT scores thus appears to lack an objective basis.

Female law students also are more likely to be enrolled in a law school with lower job placement rates. Law schools with 70–84 percent placement rates show an average female student enrollment of 45.7 percent, but law schools that place fewer than 40 percent

---

[75] Merritt, Deborah Jones, & McEntee, Kyle. (2016, November). The leaky pipeline for women entering the legal profession.

[76] Ibid.

[77] Ibid.

[78] Ibid.

[79] Marks & Moss, *supra* note 1 at 247.

[80] Ibid. at 248.

[81] Ibid.

of their graduates show an average female student enrollment of 55.9 percent. As Deborah Merritt, a law school professor at the Moritz College of Law, and Kyle McEntee, Executive Director of Law School Transparency, explain, "The negative correlation between the percentage of women and percentage of jobs requiring bar passage constitutes a major leak in the pipeline carrying women into the legal profession. Women occupy almost half of all law school seats, but they are significantly less likely than men to attend the schools that send a high percentage of graduates into the profession."[82]

In their job search after law graduation, female attorneys encounter multiple barriers to employment. Even when their credentials are equivalent to those of male law school graduates, female law school graduates are less likely to be interviewed and hired by large law firms.[83] To determine whether female law school graduates are subjected to bias by large law firms, management professors Lauren Rivera and András Tilcsik sent fictitious resumes to 316 law firm offices in 14 cities. The applicants' credentials were identical (top one percent of class, law review, dean's merit scholarship, Phi Beta Kappa), but the first names were changed to signal gender (James or Julia), and some resume features were changed to signal social class. Higher-class candidates' resumes, for example, showed extracurricular activities and personal interests like "sailing team, polo, classical music," while lower-class candidates' resumes included involvement in "track and field team, pick-up soccer, country music." Four candidate profiles, therefore, appeared on the fictitious resumes (higher-class male, higher-class female, lower-class male, and lower-class female), yet "all educational academic, and work-related achievements were identical."[84]

The law firms' responses to the resumes revealed a strong preference for the male candidate with the higher-class background:

---

[82] Merritt & McEntee, *supra* note 75.
[83] See Rikleen, *supra* note 52.
[84] Rivera, Lauren, & Tilcsik, Andras. (2016, December 21). Research: How subtle class cues can backfire on your resume. *Harvard Business Review*.

Even though all educational and work-related histories were the same, employers overwhelmingly favored the higher-class man. He had a callback rate more than four times of other applicants and received more invitations to interview than all other applicants in our study combined. But most strikingly, he did significantly better than the higher-class woman, whose resume was identical to his, other than the first name.[85]

The higher-class male received considerably more interview requests than the lower-class male (13 vs. 1), but the higher-class signals in the females' resumes did not benefit them. In fact, the higher-class female candidates received slightly fewer interview requests than the lower-class female candidates (3 vs. 5).[86]

To explore the reasons for the law firms' disparate responses to the resumes, Rivera and Tilcsik sent the resumes to 210 practicing lawyers and asked them to rate the applicants. Like the law firms, the practicing lawyers rated the higher-class male as a superior interview candidate and "significantly more committed than the higher-class woman to working and building a career at a law firm."[87] The higher-class male also was perceived to be "more compatible with the culture and clients of a large law firm."[88] The attorneys' explanations for their inferior ratings of the higher-class female candidates are illuminating:[89]

- "An upper-class man is always going to be working. He's always gonna stay in the workforce, and chances are he's well connected, and that might be a good person to have at your firm. But an extremely upper-class woman, she might have all of the sort of like entitled asshole issues the guy does, plus you

---

[85] Ibid. ("The differences in callback rates for higher-class women, lower-class men, and lower-class women were not statistically significant. But higher-class men received significantly more callbacks than all other categories.")

[86] Ibid.

[87] Rivera & Tilcsik (2016), *supra* note 65 at 1113.

[88] Ibid. at 1116.

[89] Ibid. at 1120–1121.

add in the fact that she might not take the job that seriously. ... There's not the same societal pressure on women to work and to have some sort of high-earning job."

- "This is the question we always ask ourselves, really. Why would you do this job if you didn't have to, right? Like if you had another option, if you could do anything, if you could live the lifestyle that this job provides but you didn't actually have to put in the work involved, I'm not sure that I would do it. And so I think people look at women from affluent backgrounds or classes—if they come from money or if they're marrying into money—because they already live in that strata [sic] and ask that question."

- "[With] a female associate from a privileged background, there is an unspoken concern—which is not good—that they may go off track. And leave the firm. Or pursue other interests. Or perhaps a family focus or what have you. ... With unhealthy 100-hour weeks, you can see why that concern is prevalent. Those types of expectations, people assume that women will bow out of them. ... If you come from a more privileged background, that optionality is of a greater concern."

A female attorney who served as a member of her law firm's hiring committee recalls, "There's ... a sense that these women don't really need this job. 'Cause they have enough money or they are married to somebody rich and they should be, you know, they're going to end up being a helicopter mom." Higher-class female attorneys, she asserts, are perceived to be flight risks: "They're eventually going to leave law."[90]

The lower-class female candidates were subjected to different preconceptions and biases. A female practicing attorney expected the lower-class female candidate to be "immature on the phone" and lacking in confidence, incapable of conveying to clients that "these are my ideas and they're worth listening to."[91] But other attorneys thought her commitment might be strong and that she

---

[90]   Ibid. at 1121.
[91]   Ibid. at 1120.

would "work hard for the money" because she was "hungry," had "law school debt to pay," and would have "mouths to feed."[92] (The resumes did not mention student debt or parental status.) Whether female or male, the lower-class candidates generally "were seen as misfits and rejected."[93]

Diversity Benefits

Although the most damaging results of bias appear to be inflicted upon the attorneys personally subjected to the bias, the harm actually extends far beyond them to the firms themselves and the clients who otherwise would have obtained a superior level of service. That the firms and their clients also are harmed when women and racial and ethnic minority attorneys are underrepresented is established by studies showing that:

- Diverse teams "provide a superior performance to their clients across all key performance areas. The most significant difference is in relation to the value delivered. Statistical evidence also confirms enhanced performance across other key attributes including responsiveness, strength of relationship, commerciality and efficiency. Overall satisfaction is also significantly improved when clients are working with very diverse teams."[94]
- "Mixed gender teams significantly outperform single gender teams. Analysis of 12 KPIs [Key Performance Indicators] has revealed an uplift in performance across the full suite of industry-recognized metrics according to 996 clients interviewed by Acritas, with the biggest gain in performance for strength of relationships."[95]

---

[92] Ibid.
[93] Rivera & Tilcsik, *supra* note 84.
[94] (2016). Acritas diversity report: Uncovering the positive impacts of a fully diverse legal team. New York: Acritas Research Ltd.
[95] Acritas. (2015, December 15). Gender diverse legal teams outperform single gender teams.

- Diverse legal teams earn "higher performance ratings and they're more likely to be recommended to clients' peers than nondiverse teams."[96]
- Diverse legal teams "get 25 percent more of clients' total legal spending than teams that are not at all diverse."[97]
- Defense litigation teams led by a female and male partner are less likely to be overconfident in their case assessments. Mixed-gender defense teams are correlated with a 31 percent reduction in settlement decision errors (rejecting pretrial settlement offers that turn out to be financially superior to the results later obtained at trial) when compared with litigation teams consisting of two male partners.[98]

These findings are consistent with other research demonstrating that diverse teams are better at analytical thinking, complex problem solving, and divergent thinking, and their companies achieve better financial results and higher levels of employee engagement and client retention.[99] Diversity thus has shifted from

---

[96] McQueen, M. P. (2016, May 12). GCs spend more on diverse legal teams, survey finds. *The American Lawyer*.

[97] Ibid.

[98] Kiser, Randall. (2010). *Beyond right and wrong: The power of effective decision making for attorneys and clients* (p. 81). Berlin, Heidelberg: Springer.

[99] Adamy, Janet. (2016, February 8). Companies where more women lead are more profitable, a new report says. *The Wall Street Journal*. Barta, Thomas, Kleiner, Markus, & Neumann, Tito. (2012). Is there a pay-off from top-team diversity? *McKinsey Quarterly*. Cecchi-Dimeglio, Paola. (2017, February 1). What it costs when talent walks out the door. *The American Lawyer*. Fuhrmans, Vanessa. (2018, January 18). Companies with diverse executive teams posted bigger profit margins, study shows. *The Wall Street Journal*. Hunt, Vivian, Layton, Dennis, & Prince, Sara. (2015, February 2). Diversity matters. McKinsey & Company. Levine, Sheen S., et al. (2014, December). Ethnic diversity deflates price bubbles. *PNAS*, *111*(52), 18524–18529. Levine, Sheen S., & Stark, David. (2015, December 9). Diversity makes you brighter. *The New York Times*. Negowetti, *supra* note 39 at 930, 950. Page, Scott. (2008). *The difference.* Princeton, NJ: Princeton University Press. Perlberg, Heather. (2012, July 31.) Stocks perform better if women are on company boards. *Bloomberg*. Semuels, Alana. (2016, December 27). When women run companies. *The Atlantic*. Simons, John. (2017, February). In Trump age, taking a different tack on workplace diversity. *The Wall Street Journal*. Cf. Bar, Michaela, Niessen, Alexandra, & Ruenzi, Stefan. (2007, September). The impact of work group diversity on performance: Large sample evidence from the mutual fund industry [finding "significantly negative

being seen by many companies as a legal mandate and a moral benefaction to being regarded as a financial imperative. This realization, however, has not spread to many law firms. As Lisa Hart Shepherd, chief executive officer of Acritas Research Ltd., notes, "From my experience with working with a lot of these firms, [diversity] is important but they see it as a socially responsible thing to do, rather than as a driver of higher financial performance. Now that it seems that it is a driver of financial performance, it requires more serious action."[100]

In light of the extensive evidence demonstrating the benefits of diversity, one would expect law firms to vigorously recruit, carefully develop, and assiduously retain female attorneys and other attorneys who comprise a diverse professional workforce based on their race, ethnicity, nationality, and LGBT identification.[101] Instead of being in the vanguard of diversity and inclusion, however, many law firms are in the rear guard, minimizing diversity and inclusion strategies, bemoaning the lack of "qualified" minority candidates, and defending their hiring and partner admission decisions in terms of "standards" and "quality."[102] When asked what their law firms do to recognize and reward those working on diversity and inclusion strategies, for instance, 30 percent of attorneys responded, "does not do anything."[103]

Law firms tend to excuse their lack of diversity by citing the paucity of qualified minority candidates. This justification is suggestive of prejudice and encourages confirmation bias. As Raymond Ocampo, former general counsel of Oracle Corporation, notes, "What is most dangerous about this argument ["our law firm has been unable to hire a qualified woman/minority"] is that it tends to be a self-fulfilling prophecy because the person holding the assumption

---

impact of gender diversity on performance while age diversity has no significant impact on performance"].

[100] McQueen, *supra* note 96.

[101] Ibid.

[102] See Ocampo, Raymond. (1994, Summer). Hiring women and minority attorneys—One General Counsel's perspective. *ACC Docket*.

[103] Bloomberg Law. (2016). *Big Law business diversity & inclusion annual report* (p. 6).

is the same person doing the judging."[104] The excuse also is impudent since the existing standards and quality of practice, deemed to be sacrosanct, are not optimal. Client satisfaction surveys show that only one-third of chief legal officers would recommend their law firm to a peer, and trial court judges rate attorney performance in intellectual property and commercial litigation cases (both high-status practice areas dominated by elite law firms) as 4.1 on a scale where 4 is "good" and 5 is "excellent."[105] The most elite and presumably selective firms, moreover, rank lower on client service metrics (responsiveness, legal expertise, solutions focus, likelihood to recommend, outcome, and cost/efficiency) when surveyed corporate counsel compare Am Law 20 firms with Am Law 21-200 firms.[106] What law firms, especially the more elite law firms, are preserving under the banner of high standards is not exactly clear.

Personality Assessments

Attorneys' personal qualities—their traits, habits, ethics, judgment, grit, and maturity—are strong predictors of professional performance. Eight of the ten most important factors in attorney success, as ranked by *attorneys*, are personal qualities largely attributable to individual values, beliefs, and experiences rather than technical legal competence.[107] Nine of the ten most important factors, as ranked by *clients*, are personal qualities.[108] These qualities and their rankings are shown in Table 3.1. Considering the critical importance of these personal qualities, law firms would be irresponsible, if not negligent, in failing to conduct behavioral assessments before hiring attorneys. Nevertheless, only a small fraction of law firms currently undertakes these assessments for any positions,

---

[104] Ibid.

[105] BTI Consulting Group. (2017, May 10). CLOs to law firms: Fix your client service or we're leaving. Posner, Richard A., & Yoon, Albert H. (2011). What judges think of the quality of legal representation. *Stanford Law Review, 63*, 317, 331.

[106] Dattu, Firoz, & Kotok, Aaron. (2018, June 12). Large, pedigreed firms underperform on service quality compared to other firms. *The American Lawyer*.

[107] Kiser, Randall. (2017). *Soft skills for the effective lawyer* (p. 34). New York: Cambridge University Press.

[108] Ibid.

Table 3.1 Comparison of Attorneys' and Clients' Competency Rankings

Attorneys' Rankings of Competencies	Clients' Ranking of Competencies
Top 10 competencies	
Legal expertise/competence; knowledge of applicable law	Ongoing communication with clients; keeping clients informed and updated on case status, progress, and new developments that could affect clients; promptly responding to client emails and telephone calls; asking questions and seeking information from clients
Honoring client confidentiality; keeping information confidential	Attentive listening skills
Punctuality/arriving on time for meetings, appointments, and hearings	Responsiveness to clients and their needs, interests, and goals; anticipation of client needs
Ability to determine appropriate risk mitigation strategies	Explanation of fee arrangements; accurate estimates of fees and costs and range of variance from estimates
Honoring commitments	Strategic problem solving, legal advice, and case/project management
Delegation to and management of support staff	Understanding of client needs, expectations, and priorities, including need for closure
Integrity and trustworthiness	Empathy and compassion
Ability to objectively assess the soundness of a deal or proposed solution in terms of risks and rewards	Respectfulness
Treating others with courtesy and respect	Legal expertise/thorough knowledge of law
Ability to prepare a case for trial	Trust

Source: Kiser, *Soft Skills for the Effective Lawyer*, 2017, Cambridge University Press.

and a smaller number use them in entry-level associate hiring decisions.[109] The vast majority of law firms prefer to rely on academic factors proven to be of nominal value and unstructured interviews demonstrated to be unreliable.[110]

Law firms' reluctance to administer personality assessments results in acute problems for the firms and their clients. Many attorneys present a unique blend of personal characteristics that are antithetical to client service, constructive problem solving, and teamwork. Studies of attorney personalities, as indicated in the following summaries, reveal a host of traits not usually associated with effective communication, analysis, conflict resolution, professional development, decision making, collaboration, and leadership:

- "[L]awyers share the same six traits that set them dramatically apart from the general population. Lawyers tend to be skeptical and 'urgent,' or results-oriented. They need autonomy and are abstract reasoners, but they aren't very sociable or resilient. . . . The lowest lawyers' scores came in sociability and resiliency. . . . They may find it uncomfortable to develop intimate relationships. Low scorers in resiliency tend to be defensive, resistant to feedback and hypersensitive to criticism."[111]
- "Law schools, and hence the legal profession itself, have recruited individuals whose modal Myers Briggs Type indicator preference is either I(E)STJ or I(E)NTJ—decision makers and problem solvers who 'do not see the wider ramifications of current, expedient decisions,' 'quibble over abstract issues and terms that have little meaning or relevance to others,' and 'rush into premature judgments and actions without considering

---

[109] See Levin & MacEwen, *supra* note 9. ("Less than 5% of the Am Law 250 currently uses assessments during the hiring process, and none uses instruments purpose-built for the legal profession.") The Remsen Group. (2016). *Re-envisioning the law firm: How to lead change and thrive in the future* (p. 74). (Three percent of surveyed law firms report that they use psychological assessment tools as part of their attorney hiring and recruiting practices.) Simons, Hugh A., & Ellenhorn, Michael A. (2018, January 28). Recent survey shows firms aren't doing right due diligence on laterals. *The American Lawyer.*

[110] Picht & Stacy, *supra* note 28. Henderson, Stacy, & Gibson (2011), *supra* note 8.

[111] Tribe, Meghan. (2017, February 2). Putting law firm hires to the test. *The American Lawyer.*

new information.' Although they are serial decision makers, they may 'take in only that information that fits their insights,' 'overlook details or facts that do not fit into their Intuitive patterns,' and 'decide too quickly before taking in enough information' or 'considering alternatives or exploring possibilities.'"[112]

- "Attorneys are more likely to avoid situations where they may be rejected or criticized. This trait is often tied to difficulties in business development. . . . There is also a clear profile of trait markers for those attorneys that choose to leave the practice of law altogether after working in their first law firm role; higher levels of resilience, empathy, initiative and sociability are among the traits where these attorneys differ from those lawyers who continue to stay in the practice of law."[113]

- "Another trait that distinguishes lawyers from the general public is their higher Urgency scores. A high score on Urgency is characterized by impatience, a need to get things done, a sense of immediacy. . . . They may finish others' sentences, jump to conclusions, be impulsive. . . . They seek efficiency and economy in everything from conversations to case management to relationships. While clients certainly reward many lawyers for moving their matters along, Urgency can have a negative side as well. Urgent people are sometimes brusque, poor listeners, and can be annoying to many people. This can add a level of tension to meetings, a level of frustration to mentor/mentee relationships, and a sense of oppression to lawyer/secretary interactions."[114]

- "HDS [Hogan Development Survey] results reveal a general tendency among many lawyers to shy away from others when under pressure. This stands in direct contrast to many

---

[112] Kiser (2010), *supra* note 98 at 150.
[113] Levin & MacEwen, *supra* note 9.
[114] Richard, Larry. (2008, Winter). Herding cats: The lawyer personality revealed. *LAWPRO*, 7(1), 3, 4. Another version of this article appears in Richard, Larry. (2002, August). Herding cats: The lawyer personality revealed. *Report to Legal Management.* The Managing Partner Forum also has published a version of this article.

managers and highly educated professionals in other fields who are more likely to engage in confrontation."[115]

- "[M]ost Am Law 250 firms, and particularly those in the 150–500 attorney range show attorney trait patterns that look particularly prone to siloed practices and siloed business development. Attorney assessments from firms this size showed the strongest preferences for working alone on issues and individual problem solving even where issues might be outside the attorney's practice area. Coupled with higher introversion and higher self-sufficiency than other firms, these traits will strengthen silos and limit collaboration. . . . [T]he vast majority of attorneys at these firms and the pervasive firm culture in this segment would prefer to work alone and build business alone."[116]

A former law firm managing partner observes, "Most partners were recognized and rewarded for being the smartest person in the class or the most accomplished. They have rarely experienced or understood the power of succeeding as part of a larger group or team."[117] His experience indicates that partners tend to have a short-term focus that is "selfish and self-serving, even narcissistic." This selfishness, he believes, "leads to a shortsighted approach to decision making that inhibits long-range success because investments of time or money that don't yield immediate results are rarely made."[118]

Perhaps the most glaring mismatch between typical attorney personalities and large law firms' needs occurs when firms try to transform their bright, introverted partners into rainmaker partners. Stated bluntly, most large law firm attorneys "are basically wired to fail at this activity."[119] Essential personality traits for successful rainmaker partners include resilience and empathy, both of which are in limited supply among typical attorneys.[120] In addition, successful rainmaker

---

[115] Foster, Jeff, Richard, Larry, Rohrer, Lisa, & Sirkin, Mark. (2010). *Understanding lawyers: Why we do the things we do.* Hildebrandt Baker Robbins.

[116] Levin & MacEwen, *supra* note 9.

[117] Maister, David. (2006, April). Are law firms manageable? *The American Lawyer.* See Hulbert, *supra* note 27.

[118] Maister, *supra* note 117.

[119] Levin & MacEwen, *supra* note 9.

[120] Richard, *supra* note 114.

partners, when compared with a firm's service partners, are "more assertive, sociable, risk-taking and confident, and significantly less cautious (less perfectionistic) and less skeptical (more trusting)."[121]

Rainmaker partners also differ from ordinary partners in their ability to see the "big picture," willingness to work on teams, capacity to motivate other team members, receptiveness to creative and flexible problem solving, and genuine interest in their clients' lives.[122] Statistical analyses of rainmaker partners' personal backgrounds yield additional insights into what makes them distinct. As Patricia Gillette, a former partner with Orrick, Herrington & Sutcliff LLP, notes, "The results raise questions about many traditional notions of what makes a lawyer successful. For example, going to one of the top law schools is not necessarily predictive of success as a rainmaker; people from blue-collar families tend to be better rainmakers than those from privileged backgrounds."[123]

Attrition Rates and Costs

Law firms' current hiring, evaluation, and compensation practices exact an enormous toll on their attorneys, clients, and firm profitability. Annual associate attorney attrition rates are about 20 percent, and, cumulatively, 71 percent of associates leave their firms within five or fewer years.[124] Fourteen percent of entry-level male associates and 12 percent of entry-level female associates leave their firms within two years of being hired.[125] For lateral associates, the attrition rates are bleaker; "31% of males and 25% of females left within two years of being hired," reports the National Association for Law Placement.[126] Minority female and male lateral associates both exhibit higher attrition rates at 38 percent and 28 percent, respectively.[127]

---

[121] Ibid.

[122] Gillette, *supra* note 24. Drake & Parker-Stephen, *supra* note 24.

[123] Gillette, *supra* note 24.

[124] Patterson, Tammy A. (2016, May). Highlights from the NALP Foundation's annual study of law firm associate hiring and attrition. *NALP Bulletin.*

[125] Ibid.

[126] Ibid.

[127] Ibid. See NALP Foundation. (2011, June 2). The future of law according to the data: Research findings from the NALP Foundation and NALP.

Most associate attorney departures are attributed to "an improper fit between the attorney and the firm, job role and/or practice area."[128]

When an associate attorney leaves a firm, the total costs resulting from that departure range from $350,000 to $800,000.[129] (This cost estimate is remarkably similar to the estimated cost of $400,000–$600,000 when a hospital medical group loses a physician.)[130] These costs include recruiting, search, interviewing, training, summer program, human resource, and administrative expenses; placement company fees; lost billings during the attorney replacement period; write-offs of recorded time for both the departing and the replacement attorney; and unbilled time for supervising attorneys to oversee assignments to the replacement attorneys. Intangible costs attributable to attorney attrition—client dissatisfaction with attorney turnover, reputational damage, and delays in completing projects—are excluded from the $350,000–$800,000 estimate. For a firm of 400 attorneys, the estimated annual cost of associate attorney attrition exceeds $25 million; and the total attrition costs for the 400 largest firms in the United States are nearly $10 billion.[131] These costs, of course, must be borne by the firms' clients.

---

[128] Levin & MacEwen, *supra* note 9 at 5. "Interestingly, there has been little change in the reasons cited for associate departures in surveys and exit interviews over the last 20 years." Prescott, Blane R. (2018, September 27, 2018). Are firms fighting the associate salary war with the wrong weapon? *The American Lawyer.*

[129] Ibid. Cohen, Tim, & Henderson, Jennifer. (2017, July 3). Why associates leave and how you can get them to stay. *The American Lawyer.* Harper, Steven J. (2012, February 24). The non-equity partner bubble. *The Am Law Daily.* Reeser, Edwin B., & McKenna, Patrick J. (2012, February 1). Crazy like a fox; Why the increase in nonequity partners (and decrease in associate ranks) makes business sense. *The American Lawyer.* Reeser, Edwin B. (2015, February 4). 9 ways to change the carnivorous partnership model and save Big Law firms. *ABA Journal.*

[130] Vuong, Khuong. (2017, February 1). Turnover rate for hospitalist groups trending downward. *The Hospitalist.* Vuong cites Frenz, David A. (2016, August). The staggering cost of physician turnover. *Today's Hospitalist.* For a model that includes the revenue losses as a new physician "increases initial productivity to reach the practice norm," see Atkinson, William, Misra-Hebert, Anita, & Stoller, James. (2006). The impact on revenue of physician turnover: An assessment model and experience in a large healthcare center. *Journal of Medical Practice Management, 21*(6), 351–355.

[131] Levin & MacEwen, *supra* note 9.

Table 3.2   Associate Attorney Attrition Costs

	Firm #1	Firm #2	Firm #3
	250 associates @ $375 real rate	500 associates @ $400 real rate	750 associates @ $425 real rate
Annual associate attorney billings (1,800 hours)	$168,750,000	$360,000,000	$573,750,000
Annual collections @ 93% collection rate	$156,937,500	$334,800,000	$533,587,500
Number of associate attorneys leaving at 17% annual attrition rate	43	85	128
Attrition costs at $400,000 per associate attorney	$17,200,000	$34,000,000	$51,200,000
Attrition costs as % of total associate billings	10%	9%	9%
Attrition costs as % of total associate collections	11%	10%	10%

If clients' invoices for legal services were itemized by component costs like salaries, rent, and partners' compensation, clients would be startled to find that about 10 percent of each charge for associate attorney time represents the firm's attrition costs—essentially a surcharge to clients for the firm's hiring errors and inability to retain highly talented associate attorneys. As shown in Table 3.2, the attrition costs at three illustrative firms with 250, 500, and 750 associate attorneys represent 9–10 percent of total associate billings and 10–11 percent of total collected associate billings (assuming attrition costs in the lower range of $400,000 per attorney). Although even the best managed companies will experience some level of annual attrition, attrition rates ranging from 12 to 25 percent in large law firms are alarming, destructive of attorney morale, and financially damaging to clients. As the general counsel for a major corporation exclaims, "No other company would treat its most important commodity poorly enough to cause a turnover rate of 85% for first year lawyers who are gone by the sixth year. Why are you doing it? How can you get away with that?"[132]

The Right People in the Right Seats

Even when law firms hire and retain effective attorneys, **they frequently place them in the wrong positions.** This usually occurs when partners seek or are asked to perform leadership roles separate from their conventional legal services to clients. It may take months to recognize that a partner has been installed in an unsuitable position and many more months to nudge, prod, and eventually extract that partner. During that period, law firm morale, operations, planning, and profitability deteriorate and are sometimes set back irreversibly. The fact that the partner was placed in an unsuitable position may not have been evident to many of the other partners because they share similar deficiencies. Since they would have employed the same ideas, practices, and standards as the misplaced partner, the other partners are more likely to have served as facilitators than monitors.

As discussed in Chapter 1, business consultant and author Jim Collins describes this dilemma as getting "the right people in the right seats."[133] This dilemma is particularly challenging in law firms because smart people like attorneys tend to think they are proficient in multiple dimensions and often overestimate the range of responsibilities they can perform competently. This overestimation is called the "general-ability fallacy"—the belief that "if you are smart in one thing, you are smart in everything."[134] People who have performed well on tests and in school, psychologist Robert Sternberg explains, "often think that their high levels of performance in these domains mean they will be expert in any domain."[135] Usually, Sternberg points out, "they are wrong."[136]

---

[132] Harper, Steven J. (2013). *The lawyer bubble* (p. 174). New York: Basic Books.

[133] Collins, James. (2001, October). Good to great. *Fast Company.*

[134] Sternberg, Robert. (2003). *Wisdom, intelligence, and creativity synthesized* (p. 46). New York: Cambridge University Press.

[135] Ibid.

[136] Ibid.

Attorneys frequently occupy the wrong seats because they lack leadership skills and training;[137] do not know how to improve group performance;[138] tend to be conflict avoidant, risk averse, and change resistant;[139] mistake intelligence for judgment;[140] assign a low priority to management training;[141] assume that attorneys who have successful relationships with clients will have successful relationships with their colleagues;[142] and occasionally regard leadership positions as rewards rather than responsibilities.[143] Nearly all of these obstacles can be overcome with self-awareness, knowledge, and training. But the development process is often thwarted because attorneys do not recognize or accurately assess their shortcomings. If they commit themselves to self-reflection, feedback, and practice, however, they can become credible

---

[137] See Cullen, Robert W. (2010). *The leading lawyer.* Eagen, Minnesota: West. Normand-Hochman, Rebecca (Ed.). (2015). *Leadership for lawyers.* Surrey, UK: Globe Law and Business Ltd. Rhode, Deborah. (2013). *Lawyers as leaders.* New York: Oxford University Press.

[138] See Catmull, Ed. (2014). *Creativity, Inc.* (p. 84). New York: Random House. Goleman, Daniel. (1998). *Working with emotional intelligence* (p. 204). New York: Bantam Dell. Goleman, Daniel. (2004, January). What makes a leader. *Harvard Business Review.* Maister, *supra* note 117.

[139] See Carr, Jeffrey, Lamb, Patrick, McKenna, Patrick L., & Reeser, Edwin R. (2009, October 20). Value-focused fees, now is the time. *San Francisco Daily Journal.* Moliterno, James E. (2013). *The American legal profession in crisis: Resistance and responses to change.* New York: Oxford University Press. Poor, Stephen J. (2012, May 7). Re-engineering the business of law. *The New York Times.* Maister, *supra* note 117.

[140] See Argyris, Chris. (1991). Teaching smart people how to learn. *Harvard Business Review, 69*(3), 99, 103. Ericsson, K. Anders, Prietula, Michael J., & Cokely, Edward T. (2007, July–August). The making of an expert. *Harvard Business Review,* pp. 114–121. Hogarth, Robin M. (2001). *Educating intuition* (p. 164). Chicago: University of Chicago Press. Wenke, Dorit, & Frensch, Peter A. (2003). Is success or failure at solving complex problems related to intellectual ability? In Davidson, Janet E., & Sternberg, Robert J. (Eds.). *The psychology of problem solving* (p. 94). Cambridge: Cambridge University Press.

[141] Shanker, Deena. (2013, January 11). Why are lawyers such terrible managers? *Fortune.*

[142] See Gardner, Heidi. (2015). Leading the campaign for greater collaboration within law firms. In Normand-Hochman, *supra* note 137 at 18. Westfahl, Scott. (2015). Learning to lead: Perspective on bridging the lawyer leadership gap. In Normand-Hochman, *supra* note 137 at 79.

[143] See Reeser, Edwin. (2013, September 12). Big Law is looking for change in all the wrong places, Part II. *ABA Journal.*

leaders.[144] "A mindful lawyer who is willing to mentally rehearse new thoughts and behavioral repertoires," states psychologist Larry Richard, "can dramatically improve their leadership effectiveness."[145] Richard's experience in working with attorneys for 30 years has convinced him that lawyers who want to become leaders must acknowledge their "outlier" personality traits and then adopt a more patient, collaborative, and respectful attitude toward people and a more innovative, risk-taking, and inspiring approach to their law firms.

At the very least, attorneys misplaced in leadership positions should acknowledge that their education, training, and experience usually have been narrow and could not have prepared them adequately for leadership positions. As Paul Lippe, an attorney and founder of OnRamp Systems, explains,

If you think about it, there's no particular reason to imagine that the people running large firms are well prepared to manage change. As lawyers, we're oriented to a particular style of thinking—detail oriented, somewhat abstract, risk-averse, not especially emotionally intelligent, very short-term focused in terms of business activities, and with a somewhat odd presumption both that we're more virtuous than other people and that more selfishness is usually a good thing.

If you have those attributes, spend 20–30 years working hard and loyally as a lawyer, find yourself in a position of middle or upper middle management, and then are selected to run the firm, what would have prepared you to lead a few thousand people in many offices with hundreds of millions or even a billion dollars of revenue?[146]

---

[144] Mack, Olga V., & Bloom, Katia. (2017, June 12). Lawyers as leaders: Is your personality too legal? *Above the Law*.

[145] Ibid.

[146] Lippe, Paul. (2012, March 27). Dewey or don't we: Abnormal or new normal? *ABA Journal*.

As Lippe's comments reveal, attorneys generally do not acquire rudimentary leadership skills before they assume complex leadership duties. Their deficiencies in leadership skills should compel them to immediately and conscientiously develop those skills when they are thrust into leadership positions. Better yet, law firms should initiate leadership training years before their attorneys become responsible for leading their colleagues. The quest to develop leadership skills will require an openness to eliciting advice and feedback from colleagues and leadership experts, immersion in executive leadership courses, familiarity with leadership research and texts, and systematic, objective performance evaluation. If attorneys are unwilling to accept that responsibility and insist on remaining in the wrong seat—occupying the position of a leader while refusing to fulfill that role—they place their law firms at a high risk of failure.[147]

Chapter Capsule

Law schools admit students based on criteria largely irrelevant to client needs and factors immaterial to attorneys' career success. Many law firms, in turn, select students who excel in law school on tasks unrelated to client satisfaction and professional achievement. Like adolescents picking their first car, law schools and law firms frequently employ a superficial selection process separated from value, safety, and reliability. They focus on a few salient features expected to heighten their popularity and status and overlook the features essential to long-term service.

Neither law schools nor law firms attempted to empirically determine the most important attorney performance factors before they established their selection criteria, and the criteria have changed very little over the last 50 years. Since the selection criteria have not materially changed, many biases in attorney hiring and promotion practices have been allowed to evolve from nascent prejudices to

---

[147] See Reeser, *supra* note 143. ("Partners in leadership positions are increasingly not leaders, but those with enough power to demand positions and allocate to themselves, and to their friends, increasing shares of money and other rewards. The confusion of the position of leader, with the fulfillment of the role of a leader, has never been more apparent.")

accepted conventions. As a result, law firms display statistically high levels of bias in attorney hiring, evaluation, compensation, and promotion. They also induce markedly low levels of satisfaction among female and ethnic minority attorneys, leading to high attrition rates.

Attorney personality characteristics pose special challenges to law firms. Many attorneys are exceptionally intelligent but immature. Studies indicate that attorneys, when compared with the general population, tend to be skeptical, impatient, conflict avoidant, impulsive, insensitive, and unsociable. These characteristics are antithetical to client service, sound decision making, collaborative problem solving, and client development. The problems caused by these characteristics are minimized because they are widespread. As law firm consultant David Maister observes, "If everyone else does things equally poorly, and clients and recruits find little variation between firms, even the most egregious behavior will not lead to a competitive disadvantage."[148]

Although law firms' practices may not put them at a competitive disadvantage relative to other firms, they would benefit from conducting preemployment personality assessments and behavioral interviews, adopting more ambitious diversity goals, and implementing programs designed to eliminate or reduce explicit and implicit bias. Law firms' inability to accurately identify and retain attorneys who will thrive in their law practices results in extraordinary attrition rates and outsized costs, which are ultimately borne by clients. Clients' legal costs could be reduced substantially—and law firms' profits could be increased significantly—if law firms reevaluated and improved their employment practices.

---

[148] Maister, David. (2006, April). Are law firms manageable? *The American Lawyer.*

4

Missteps

Once the right people are on the bus and seated in the right seats, Jim Collins advises, leaders must steer the bus in the right direction. For law firms, the right direction usually means the direction in which other law firms are going. Educated and trained in the doctrine of *stare decisis*, law firm members and leaders are most comfortable looking at their peers' strategies to ascertain their own. While this approach offers a degree of predictability and reliability, it constrains creativity and forestalls innovation.

Law firms have a unique method of vetting new ideas and strategies. Law firm consultant David Maister finds that law firms, unlike other business organizations, do not seek a competitive advantage by adopting ideas and strategies undiscovered by their competitors. Instead, when presented with a new business idea, "the first thing they ask is, 'Which other law firms are doing this?' Unless it can be shown that the idea has been implemented by other law firms, lawyers are skeptical about whether the idea applies to their world."[1]

The corollary to this rule of replication is that, once other law firms have implemented an idea, its soundness and value are not questioned for long periods. Precedent and widespread adoption become proxies for merit. Ongoing testing and evaluation of ideas and strategies, routinely performed by healthy business organizations, are considered unnecessary and arguably wasteful in many law firms. The result is that law firms sometimes mimic other firms'

---

[1]   Maister, David. (2006, April). Are law firms manageable? *The American Lawyer*.

ideas and strategies that either lacked empirical validity from the outset or were later proven to be of limited utility.

Because law firms tend to imitate other law firms, they risk adopting a strategic platform and financial structure that are unimaginative, unproductive, and, ultimately, unsustainable. The major components of that platform and structure currently include growth, mergers, lateral partners, star partner recruiting and compensation, client origination incentives, rate increases, premium pricing, client relegation, leverage, and short-term planning and profitability. This chapter examines these elements to determine whether they warrant emulation and will continue to support the roughly 250,000 attorneys working in midsize and large law firms.[2]

Growth

"Expansion fever" has gripped many Am Law 200 firms during the last 20 years.[3] It intensified after the Great Recession in 2007–2009 as law firm leaders became convinced that larger law firms were more likely to be insulated from the financial upheavals that afflicted their smaller brethren.[4] Some leaders embraced the "too big to fail" concept that appeared to save the largest financial institutions from ruin in the Great Recession, while other leaders thought that larger firms would at least be "too big to fail quickly."[5] The larger the law firm, the theory holds, the greater the revenue cushion against client or partner defections. And some law firm leaders simply thought that clients would equate size with quality and prestige. As Steven Kumble,

---

[2] See American Bar Association. ABA national lawyer population survey: Historical trend in total national lawyer population 1878–2017. American Bar Association, Lawyer Demographics Year 2015.

[3] Finkelstein, Sydney. (2003). *Why smart executives fail* (p. 155). New York: Penguin Group. ("Call it 'expansion fever.' It's what a company is suffering from when it pursues rapid expansion at the expense of profitability and without controlling liabilities.") See Harper, Steven J. (2014, October 9). A myth that motivates mergers. *The American Lawyer.* Strom, Roy. (2017, June 19). 'For growth's sake,' enough already. *The American Lawyer.*

[4] Gordon, Leslie A. (2017, June). Make me a match. *ABA Journal.*

[5] Henderson, William D. (2013). From Big Law to lean law. *International Review of Law and Economics, 3.* Indiana Legal Studies Research Paper No. 271. Available at SSRN: https://ssrn.com/abstract=2356330.

an early advocate of law firm growth at Finley Kumble, asserted, "When you're the biggest, everyone will think we're the best."[6]

The empirical research on firm size and growth indicates that expansion strategies are unlikely to promote profitability. Illustrative studies find that law firm size is not positively correlated with profitability or other measures of success:

- "Bigger is not better, at least for profitability. . . . Lawyers and firm managers often associate size with safety, and thus pursue head count and top-line revenue increases as key strategic goals. Indeed, the departure of 30 lawyers is a much bigger blow to a 300-lawyer firm than a 900-lawyer firm. Yet our findings strongly indicate that this too-big-to-fail mentality exacts a toll on profitability. Firms with higher attorney head counts are less profitable, all else being equal. A bigger firm is harder to manage and more prone to factions, and generally dilutive of the cultural aspects that inspire trust and risk-sharing. So in the longer term, the return on growth for growth's sake appears to be mediocrity."[7] (William Henderson, Indiana University Maurer School of Law, and Evan Parker, Lawyer Metrics.)

- "If you start by saying that we want to grow our market share, or we want to be a particular size, as a strategic goal that is a terrible choice for a number of reasons. First, and most important, is that market share is not that correlated with profitability. The second is that the most natural way to gain market share is by charging lower fees, which is what we see throughout the industry in this misguided effort to gain size and market share."[8] (Felix Oberholzer-Gee, Harvard Business School.)

---

6   Harper, Steven J. (2013, October 11). Assessing the latest possible large law firm combo. *The Am Law Daily.*

7   Henderson, William D., & Parker, Evan. (2017, January 3). The five strategies of highly successful firms. *The American Lawyer.*

8   McQueen, M. P. (2015, November 23). Growth won't solve your firm's problems: Harvard business prof. *The Am Law Daily.* See Halaburda, Hanna, & Oberholzer-Gee, Felix. (2014, April). The limits of scale: Companies that get big fast are often left behind. Here's why. *Harvard Business Review* 92(4), 95–99.

- "More than half of the mergers we have seen and researched in the legal sector have, after three to five years, either produced neutral results or have failed to unlock the promised rewards of enhanced market position, improved competitive positioning and profit performance. It seems that firms which merge are relatively weak and do not realize the full growth and profitability potential of an enhanced platform."[9] (Gerard Tanja, Venturis Consulting Group.)

- "The imperative for law firms to grow is groundless. Smaller firms that don't expand internationally are not losing [market] share; they've gained share through the Great Recession. The data could not be clearer. . . . Running a U.S.-centered, organically growing law firm is a strategy with enormous validity and tremendous potential for strong profit growth."[10] (Hugh Simons, Simons Advisors, and Nicholas Bruch, ALM Legal Intelligence.)

- "For over 30 years, the Altman Weil Survey of Law Firm Economics has shown, generally, that there are no economies of scale in private law practice. Larger firms almost always spend more per lawyer on staffing, occupancy, equipment, promotion, malpractice and other nonpersonnel insurance coverages, office supplies and other expenses than do smaller firms. This is counterintuitive, in the sense that larger firms should be able to spread fixed costs across a larger number of lawyers, reducing per lawyer costs, overall. However, that principal does not take into account the excess plant and equipment capacity necessary to support growth, or the increases in staff and communications costs as firms become larger."[11] (Ward Bower, Altman Weil.)

[9]   Tanja, Gerard J. (2015). Leading post-merger integration processes. In Normand-Hochman, Rebecca (Ed.). *Leadership for lawyers* (p. 137). Surrey, UK: Globe Law and Business Ltd.

[10] Simons, Hugh A., & Bruch, Nicholas. (2018, May 22). Debunking the consolidation myth. *The American Lawyer*.

[11] Bower, Ward. (2003). *Mining the surveys: Diseconomies of scale?* Newtown Square, PA: Altman Weil.

Despite the evidence that firm size is not correlated with efficiency, profitability, or durability, law firms continue to be driven by the intuitive conviction that bigger is better. Dewey & LeBoeuf's former chairman, Steve Davis, expressed this belief in 2009: "Size, in and of itself, gives you greater flexibility in key markets. You're taken more seriously when you have 500, 600 attorneys in New York."[12] (Dewey & LeBoeuf filed its bankruptcy petition three years later in 2012.) In sharp contrast with the pervasive emphasis on firm size and growth is Wachtell, Lipton, Rosen & Katz, the firm "you go to when you are not willing to take any risk at all."[13] Wachtell is a relatively small firm of 260 lawyers with average profits per partner in 2017 of $5.7 million.[14] The other Am Law 100 firms reported an average profit per partner of $1.76 million in that year.[15]

Mergers

The number of law firm mergers and acquisitions set a record in 2017. In that year, 102 mergers or acquisitions occurred. The previous record of 91 was set in 2015.[16] In 2018, the number of law firm mergers increased to 103, establishing a new record. "The law firm merger market is white hot," states Thomas Clay, a principal at the law firm consulting firm Altman Weil. "Not only is there a broad-based, ongoing interest in acquiring small, high-quality firms to buy market share, but there is also a newly intensifying appetite for larger combinations as more law firms feel the pinch of flattening demand and look for new ways to differentiate themselves from competitors."[17]

---

12 Lewis, Al. (2012, May 5). A living lawyer joke. *The Wall Street Journal*.
13 Roumeliotis, Greg A. (2017, June 8). Small is lucrative for Wachtell, corporate America's legal defense force. *Reuters*.
14 Cipriani, Gina Passarella. (2018, April 24). The 2018 Am Law 100 ranked by: Profits per equity partner. *The American Lawyer*.
15 Strom, Roy. (2018, April 24). Despite anxiety-inducing trends, Am Law 100 rose to the challenge in 2017. *The American Lawyer*.
16 Olson, Elizabeth. (2018, January 3). 2017 record year for law firm mergers. *Bloomberg Law*. For 2018 data, see Packel, Dan. (2019, January 2). Law firm mergers were red hot in 2018 with no slowdown in sight. *The American Lawyer*.
17 Ibid.

Are these mergers, in fact, increasing market share, raising demand, and enabling firms to differentiate themselves? Again, the empirical evidence does not support conventional strategies, and it shows specifically that mergers are not usually successful in increasing revenue or decreasing costs:

[M]ost major law firm combinations since 2000 have not resulted in significant growth. . . . [F]ive years after a merger most firms had underperformed their peers in revenue growth and saw their costs increase. Those outcomes, according to the report, are often glossed over by managing partners who fail to account for the complexity involved in cross-selling, expanding into new cities and installing technologies to tie their firms together. Five years after a merger, 30 percent of firms saw their gross revenue fall and 73 percent reported revenue gains less than their group of peer firms in revenue per lawyer and profits per partner. Almost all firms (92 percent) saw cost per lawyer increases, despite mergers often being viewed as a way to gain efficiencies. Those cost increases amounted, on average, to a 4 percent reduction in profits per partner.[18]

Nicholas Bruch, an ALM Intelligence analyst who studied 50 law firm mergers between 2000 and 2015, states: "The prevailing takeaway is that mergers are not successful at creating an environment of supercharged growth, and they are not very successful either at creating a merged firm that is drastically more efficiently run. In fact, it is probably the opposite."[19]

---

[18] Strom, Roy. (2017, March 7). The untold story behind Big Law mergers: Revenue slips, costs rise. *The Am Law Daily.*

[19] Ibid. Trans-Atlantic firm mergers also fail to meet partners' expectations. Bruch finds that most trans-Atlantic combinations "have not facilitated growth in head count after adjusting for additional mergers. In fact, a majority of the trans-Atlantic mergers analyzed by ALM Intelligence saw the firm shrink." He concludes that the supposed benefits "are exaggerated at least and, at worse, just plain wrong." Bruch, Nicholas. (2018, September 24). Trans-Atlantic mergers are on the rise: What do they really achieve? *The American Lawyer.*

A possible reason for these disappointing results is that the merged firms do not or cannot conduct an adequate investigation of each other's financial condition before the merger. Am Law 100 firms that merged with another firm between 1986 and 2011, for instance, appear to have been in the same financial condition as the firms that failed during that period.[20] This suggests that, for many law firms, the difference between emerging as a successful merger partner or descending into insolvency might be the extent of financial scrutiny undertaken by the suitors.

Lateral Partners

The predominant growth strategy for nearly all large law firms is hiring partners from other law firms.[21] Instead of emphasizing internal growth through business development training and improved client service, "law firms are focusing on the acquisition of lateral partners with portable books of business in an effort to increase the bottom line at a time of stagnant revenues."[22] The percentage of law firms citing "acquire laterals" as their top growth option has increased nearly every year, from 85 percent in 2010 to 96 percent in 2017.[23] This focus on lateral partners has resulted in an annual

---

[20] Henderson, *supra* note 5.

[21] Gluckman, Neil. (2016, May 18). Too many lawyers? Report faults firms for resisting layoffs. *The Am Law Daily*. Harper, Steven J. (2013, June 7). Proof of the profession's crisis. *The Am Law Daily*.

[22] Weiss, Debra Cassens. (2012, July 17). Sticky wages depress associate hiring: Big Law on track to become 'older and dumber.'" *ABA Journal*. See ALM Intelligence. (2012). Thinking like your client: Strategic planning in law firms (p. 21). New York: ALM Intelligence. (Ninety-six percent of law firms selected "acquiring laterals" as their growth option, among 21 possible options. Only 71 percent of firms selected "lawyer professional development," and only 65 percent selected "client relationship management." See also Lippe, Paul. (2013, January 22). Why not improve value instead of doubling down on bad practices? *ABA Journal* (Legal Rebels). (After reviewing law firms' strategic plans, Paul Lippe notes, "the typical 2011–2014 strategic plan that I reviewed contained six major strategic initiatives resulting in 32 specific action plans with at least 10 of those actions plans involving nothing more than lateral acquisitions. Absolutely no reference to building attorneys' skills, finding ways to do our kinds of matters at less cost, or even meaningfully taking action to improve client service.")

[23] Clay, Thomas S., & Seeger, Eric. (2017). 2017 *Law firms in transition* (p. 49). Newtown Square, PA: Altman Weil.

turnover rate of about five percent among law firm partners.[24] At a typical law firm, about one-half of all law firm partners practiced law as a partner at another firm before joining their current firm.[25]

Studies of lateral partner hiring demonstrate that most lateral partners do not meet firms' expectations, and lateral partners do not increase firm profitability.[26] About 40 percent of lateral partners leave within five years after joining a firm.[27] "These are extremely costly failures," notes ALM Intelligence analyst Steve Kovalan, "impacting firm finances, cultural stability, brand and client relationships."[28] Although 77 percent of law firms intend to hire more laterals for the specific purpose of improving profitability, there is no empirical evidence showing that lateral partners, on average, have improved law firms' financial performance.[29] As Aric Press, the former editor of *The American Lawyer*, explains, researchers have scoured 10 years of lateral partner data, "searching for a correlation between [lateral partner hiring] activity and improved economic performance."[30] The researchers, Press reports, "didn't find it."[31]

---

[24] Parnell, David. (2015). *The failing law firm: Symptoms and remedies* (pp. xi-xii, 11). Chicago: American Bar Association. See Weiss, Adam. (2015). *The lateral lawyer: Opportunities & pitfalls for the law firm partner.* Chicago: ABA Publishing.

[25] Lowe, Jeffrey A. (2016). *2016 partnership compensation survey* (p. 48). Washington, DC: Major, Lindsey, & Africa. See Simons, Hugh, & Ellenhorn, Michael A. (2018, January 28). Recent survey shows firms aren't doing right due diligence on laterals. *The American Lawyer.*

[26] Clay & Seeger, *supra* note 23 at iii. Li, Victor. (2017, April). Value proposition. *ABA Journal*, p. 32. See Citi Private Bank. (2017). *2018 Client Advisory: The legal market in 2018 and beyond* (p. 8). ("Firms reported that just 59 percent of the laterals hired during 2011–2016 were considered a success.") Flaherty, Scott. (2017, June 22). Hiring misfires show need for tougher law firm vetting. *The Am Law Daily.* ("'Fifty percent of all laterals will fail within five years. And that pretty much shows up across the board in every study that's been done,' said Michael Ellenhorn.")

[27] Simons & Ellenhorn, *supra* note 25.

[28] Li, *supra* note 26.

[29] Clay, Thomas S., & Seeger, Eric. (2018). *2018 law firms in transition* (p. 38). Willow Grove, PA: Altman Weil.

[30] Press, Aric. (2014, October 29). Special report: Big Law's reality check. *The American Lawyer.*

[31] Ibid.

In fact, the data indicates that "the most profitable firms tend to have the lowest rates of lateral hiring."[32]

Hiring lateral partners is beset with multiple problems and disappointments. The failure to deliver the anticipated revenue is the most common problem, but lateral partners present a host of other problems, including malpractice claims and personality and cultural "fit" issues. All firms report that they have experienced problems with lateral partners not bringing "the expected volume of portable business," and 72 percent report problems with lateral partners "being poor performers on billings and collections."[33] One of every three lateral partners brings in less than half of the projected revenue in their first year.[34] About 35 percent of law firms state that a malpractice issue has arisen with a lateral partner within five years after that partner joined the firm; a professional liability insurance carrier estimates that one in five malpractice claims "are directly related to lateral hires."[35] (Because lateral partners feel pressured to meet their revenue projections, they evidently accept more troublesome clients and attempt to handle matters beyond their level of expertise.) Two-thirds of law firms, moreover, have experienced problems with lateral partners "fitting in culturally," and 39 percent note problems with "treating associates with respect."[36]

The overall quality of lateral partners may be declining. As law firms attempt to increase profitability by easing poorly performing partners out of their firms, the number of subpar partners seeking positions in new firms may be increasing. The possibility of diminished quality in the lateral partner pool is indicated by a major change in the profile of lateral partners. During the 2000–2006 period, the average lateral partner moved from a firm of lower annual revenues to a firm of higher annual revenues.[37] Beginning

---

[32] Weiss, Debra Cassens. (2013, January 31). Does lateral hiring produce higher partner profits? Not according to the statistics. *ABA Journal*.

[33] Simons & Ellenhorn, *supra* note 25. See Rosen, Ellen. (2014, November 12). Report says wrong fit can be costly. *Bloomberg Law*.

[34] Cohen, Rebecca. (2016, December 12). Law firms struggle with lateral partner due diligence, report finds. *The Am Law Daily*.

[35] Simons & Ellenhorn, *supra* note 25.

[36] Simons & Ellenhorn, *supra* note 25.

[37] Henderson, *supra* note 5.

in 2008, this profile changed markedly, and the average lateral movement since then has been from a firm of higher annual revenues to a firm of lower annual revenues.[38] The lateral movement from relatively more successful law firms to relatively less successful law firms, law professor William Henderson contends, "suggests that large law firms are becoming tougher, more unforgiving places to work at least for the partners."[39] If Henderson is correct, law firms hiring lateral partners may perceive themselves to be upgrading their practices as they acquire partners from more prestigious firms when, in fact, they may be hosting those firms' performance problems.

The risks of lateral partner hiring mistakes are not mitigated by due diligence. Neither law firms nor lateral partners undertake an investigation commensurate with their risks. Law firms rarely interview the candidates' former colleagues, employ personality assessments, or complete background checks.[40] Lateral partners, for their part, engage in a process more reminiscent of Blanche's line in *A Streetcar Named Desire* ("Whoever you are, I have always depended on the kindness of strangers") than attorneys' reputed skepticism and thoroughness. As Jon Lindsey and Jeffrey Lowe, partners of the legal search firm Major, Lindsey, & Africa, write,

The financial due diligence performed by many lateral partner candidates remains shockingly inadequate: only 36.6% of all respondents reported reviewing their new firm's financial statements, leases or loan documents before joining, while only 40.4% reported meeting with the firm's CFO. Tellingly, only 60.7% of respondents even claimed to have reviewed the partnership agreement by which they would be bound before joining their new law firm.[41]

---

[38] Ibid.
[39] Ibid.
[40] Nardello, Dan. (2017, June 20). The case for lateral partner due diligence. *The Am Law Daily.* Simons & Ellenhorn, *supra* note 25.
[41] Lindsey, Jon, & Lowe, Jeffrey A. (2014). *Lateral partner satisfaction survey* (p. ii). Washington, DC: Major, Lindsey, & Africa.

If attorneys advised their clients to engage in the same degree of due diligence that attorneys exhibit in their own partnership decisions, Lindsey and Lowe assert, "multiple alarm bells would go off and malpractice insurers would expire of apoplexy."[42]

Star Partner Recruiting and Compensation

Closely related to law firms' emphasis on lateral partner hiring is their drive to recruit "star" partners from other firms—and their willingness to pay exceptionally high compensation to those star partners. Star partners with large books of ostensibly portable business receive annual compensation from their new law firms ranging from $3 million to more than $10 million. These compensation levels have now loosened the sense of loyalty and many other bonds that previously attached partners to their law firms. As a legal recruiter recently remarked, "What is really changing is what I call the bold, audacious hiring, away from the New York-based Wall Street firms. In the past, you just wouldn't think of those people as movable."[43]

The results of "chasing stars" are mixed, and overweighting this growth strategy has contributed to the demise of law firms like Dewey & LeBoeuf.[44] The star system, asserts Harvard Business School Professor Felix Oberholzer-Gee, "is not a great development if you are worried about profitability. Dewey is a great example that chasing after talent with the promise of super lucrative compensation doesn't work."[45] Oberholzer-Gee finds that law firms seeking

---

[42] Ibid. at 21.

[43] Strom, Ray, & Simmons, Christine. (2018, January 28). The top 5 strategies behind law firms' lateral hiring—and whether they work. *The American Lawyer.*

[44] Ibid. See Groysberg, Boris. (2010). *Chasing stars* (pp. 6, 8). Princeton, NJ: Princeton University Press. In the Groysberg study of 1,000 "stars" hired by competitors in the investment banking industry, researchers found that 85 percent of the stars asserted that their performance was "highly portable" and "independent of the companies they work for." But their performance with the new employers demonstrated that "exceptional performance is far less portable than is widely believed." Most stars "experienced an immediate degradation in performance." After five years with the new employer, "star analysts who changed employers underperformed comparable star analysts who stayed put."

[45] McQueen, M. P. (2015, November 23). Growth won't solve your firm's problems: Harvard Business prof. *The American Lawyer.*

rapid growth "often try to get big fast by luring top rainmakers away from, or merging with, other firms."[46] In this process, they "often promise such high compensation that the firm winds up paying the new partners any additional profit they bring."[47] Another problem, he notes, is that "the high pay used to entice 'star' laterals can cause a ripple effect of demand for higher pay from existing partners."[48]

Apart from the risks of overpaying star partners and provoking inflationary pressures from existing partners, a growth strategy centered on star partners may damage attorneys' morale and undermine a firm's culture. Hiring stars with supersize compensation packages conveys an implicit message to the current partners that, although their firm is sufficiently vibrant and profitable to attract stars, it does not have the internal capacity to develop them. As Robin Sparkman, the former Editor-in-Chief of *The American Lawyer*, writes:

> [B]ringing in highly paid rainmakers can have terrible downsides. At Dewey it led to an elitist group being paid (when they got paid) dramatically more than the rest of the partners. It's hard to believe that seriously overweighting pay is ever a good idea for any partnership. Law firms are not sports leagues. They are supposed to be a group of men and women who work together to serve their clients, their partners, and the well-being of the firm. Meeting those needs should mean that all partners' wallets get taken care of along the way—but in a manner that reflects the overall health and ethos of the firm.[49]

Although many firm leaders acknowledge that the star system can be damaging, Sparkman states, "they still believe in it."[50] For that reason, they continue to pay large premiums for outside partner talent

---

[46]   Ibid.
[47]   Ibid.
[48]   Ibid.
[49]   Sparkman, Robin. (2012, June 27). How to not be the next Dewey. *The American Lawyer*.
[50]   Ibid.

and revenue that may not meet their expectations or may simply fall short of their profitability projections due to the unanticipated costs of the star's supporting cast. "Wouldn't it be a lot cheaper to groom associates in a thoughtful, efficient way," Sparkman asks, "instead of constantly being on the lookout to buy partner talent?"[51]

Client Origination and Gross Billings Incentives

Law firms' partner compensation systems tend to be poorly designed and easily manipulated. They frequently reward gross client billings rather than profitability and provoke intense infighting and resentment over client origination credits and annual compensation decisions. Law firm compensation systems that have evolved incrementally over many years often worked well in their original iteration when firms were smaller and the partners were familiar with each other; but as the firms expanded, they neglected to reexamine their goals, values, and priorities and change their compensation systems accordingly. In their current form, many compensation systems create fiefdoms when law firms need collegiality and promote autonomy when law firms need collaboration.

The primary determinants of partner compensation are client origination, billings, collections, profitability, billable hours, and in some firms with lockstep compensation, the number of years as a partner.[52] Managing partners rate client origination as more important than profitability in partner compensation decisions. On a 1 (low) – 10 (high) scale, managing partners' median rating of the importance of an individual partner's client origination is 8, while the median rating of the importance of the profitability of a partner's origination is 6.[53] Law firms' emphasis on client origination and gross revenue derived from that client origination, instead of the profitability of the matters related to that origination, is unusual. After discussing compensation systems with many

---

[51] Ibid.

[52] See Aderant. (2015, October). *Your partner compensation system can be better: Here's how.*

[53] Clay & Seeger, *supra* note 23 at 28–29, 31. (Firms that report annual increases in their profits per equity partner place a higher priority on profitability of client origination than client origination itself.)

partners at several different law firms, consultant Ian Oxman commented, "One of the points that was surprising to me in attending these sessions we had is how few firms used profitability as a metric towards determining partner compensation."[54] Another consultant, Nicholas Gaffney, states that "it's hard to imagine any other business focusing primarily on revenue and not profit. The answer probably lies in the classic view held by many lawyers that law firms aren't businesses; they're professional service organizations where practitioners simply do good work and the rest works itself out."[55]

The rule of unintended consequences has a special affinity for law firms and their compensation systems. Perhaps that is because attorneys are adept at viewing a statutory scheme intended to achieve specific legislative objectives and then imagining how the statute might be construed to achieve other, unanticipated objectives. Compensation systems intended to reward partners for successful client origination and ongoing work for that client, for example, end up promoting client hoarding and deterring cross-selling of services within law firms. As Patrick Lamb, founder of Valorem Law Group and a BTI Consulting Group "Client Service All-Star MVP," explains,

---

[M]any firms have rewarded revenue generators so lavishly in comparison to the lawyers who do much of the work for the rainmaker's clients that they have fostered a "what's in it for me?" mentality on virtually every issue. Instead of looking first to the interests of clients, many partners first consider whether a course of conduct will provide career security or additional income. . . .

The result of this behavior is that no matter how large a firm might be, it is comprised of individual silos. The partner builds his or her team, but there rarely are multiple "star" partners working on the same matter, no matter how complicated. . . .

---

[54] Warren, Zach. (2015, October 22). Law firms embracing metrics in calculating partner compensation. *Legaltech News.*

[55] Gaffney, Nicholas. (2016, May 12). Finding the future of finance. *ABA Law Practice Today.*

> The amount of time spent tearing down "the other guy" or complaining about minor compensation differences is enormous and wasteful, and particularly offensive in light of the amounts partners, especially senior partners, are paid.[56]

Law firm consultant David Maister voices similar concerns about law firms' compensation systems. He finds that attorneys are "gaming the system through hoarding work and bickering over origination credits." Unless an activity is an explicit part of the compensation formula, partners avoid doing it. "As a result," Maister asserts, "many behaviors necessary for the firm's success cannot be enforced, because they are not in the formula. Firm leaders have bemoaned this situation for decades, but few have found a way to solve it."[57]

Law firms' inability to design and implement better compensation systems harms their profitability and sometimes leads to insolvency. Kent Zimmerman, a consultant with The Zeughauser Group, finds that "strong firms generally work hard to try to serve key clients across the firm, not in limited silos. Many strong firms credit their growth in the challenging years since 2008 to a laser-like focus on identifying and then growing key client relationships across the firm."[58] Firms that cannot move from a "me" culture to a "we" culture and capitalize on the broad range of expertise and talent in their firms are more likely to fail. In the study of failed law firms discussed in Chapter 1, the researchers concluded, "Client-hoarding creates an inherent conflict and significantly increases a firm's likelihood of failure. Whether generated by a firm's compensation system or by the lawyers' lack of confidence in each other, it is toxic."[59]

---

[56] Lamb, Patrick, McKenna, Patrick, Reeser, Edwin, & Carr, Jeffrey. (2009, November 11). Partner compensation and the new 'value' reality. *San Francisco Daily Journal*, p. 7.

[57] Maister, *supra* note 1.

[58] Zimmerman, Kent. (2012, June 8). Four steps every firm should consider in the wake of Dewey & LeBoeuf. *Chicago Daily Law Bulletin*.

[59] Raasch, Janet Ellen. (2007, September 30). Why do some law firms fail while others succeed?

Lawyers seem to have abandoned the compensation systems that fostered a sense of collegiality and professionalism decades ago. The "Cravath system," for instance, regarded all client business as "firm business" of Cravath, Swaine & Moore.[60] Origination credits, consequently, did not exist. The firm expressly stated that "business-getting ability is not a factor in the advancement of a man within the office at any level, except in so far as that ability arises out of competence in doing law work."[61] Collegiality was not merely desirable but required: "Every partner is expected to cooperate with every other in the firm's business, through whichever partner originating, and to contribute to all the work of the firm to the maximum of his ability."[62] Although managing partners today might characterize models like Cravath's as antiquated or Pollyannaish, the reality is that contemporary compensation systems often fail to promote collegiality, reward client service, encourage cross-selling, prioritize profitability over origination, and support nonbillable activities like associate attorney training and mentoring.

Rate Increases and Premium Pricing

As discussed in Chapter 2, law firm revenue increases are derived primarily from their hourly rate increases. Stated differently, law firms are not growing organically, and any income growth is dependent on their ability to raise the price of products for which demand has stagnated. This model is not sustainable in the long term. But since many law firm partners are retiring within a few years and rainmaker partners can quickly exit and then embrace another high-paying law firm, the model is serviceable for those partners, who control the bulk of all client billings, in the short term.

For partners and associate attorneys who intend to stay with their current law firms, the dependence on rate increases is hazardous.

---

[60] Henderson, William. (2008, July 29). How most law firms misapply the "Cravath system." Empirical Legal Studies Blog. Available at: http://www.elsblog.org/theempiricallegalstudi/2008/07/how-most-law-fi.html. See Cravath, Swaine & Moore LLP. Our philosophy. Available at: https://www.cravath.com/systemshistory.

[61] Ibid.

[62] Ibid.

Although rates have increased steadily and substantially exceed the inflation rate during the last 11 years, it is unlikely that clients will continue to underwrite their law firms.[63] Recent evidence indicates that clients, in fact, have already solidified their resistance to rate increases and have curtailed legal spending on law firms.[64] The growth rate of key financial indicators—revenue per lawyer, profits per lawyer, and profits per equity partner—slowed in the 2015–2017 period.[65] Financial analyses of law firms, moreover, indicate that rate increases are not correlated with superior financial performance. The data "suggests that lower rate growth may be translating into stronger revenue growth"; and "firms that are willing to slow their rate increases are seeing higher average growth in demand and revenue than firms that are raising rates more aggressively."[66] Rate increases, in short, are no longer a reliable engine of revenue growth.

An extreme version of rate increases—premium pricing—enables law firms to move beyond annual hourly rate increases and concentrate on practice areas where pricing is inelastic. In those practice areas, client demand is so high and the consequences so severe that clients will pay almost any hourly rate for expert attorneys. These practice areas warrant exceptionally high fees and free law firms from the pedestrian annual price increases that hobble their competitors. Presenting an opportunity to increase revenue and partner compensation explosively, premium pricing has become a critical element in many law firms' growth and recruiting strategies.

The basic problem with the premium pricing strategy is that, like many law firm strategies, it is easily replicated, rapidly disrupted, and generally short-lived. More than 25 years ago, Peter Drucker,

---

[63] See Georgetown Law Center for the Study of the Legal Profession, & Thomson Reuters Legal Executive Institute. (2018). *2018 report on the state of the legal market* (p. 7).

[64] Ibid. at 8,14.

[65] Bruch, Nicholas. (2017, December 19). The Am Law 100: Dark clouds on the horizon. *The American Lawyer*.

[66] Thomson Reuters. (2016, October). Does slower rate growth increase revenues?: A Peer Monitor special report. For a contrary position, see Simons, Hugh A. (2018, February 26). Why elite law should raise rates. *The American Lawyer*.

the founder of modern management theory, identified premium pricing as one of the "five deadly business sins":

The first and easily the most common sin is the worship of high profit margins and of "premium pricing." . . .

The worship of premium pricing always creates a market for the competitor. And high profit margins do not equal maximum profits. Total profit is profit margin multiplied by turnover. Maximum profit is thus obtained by the profit margin that yields the largest total profit flow, and that is usually the profit margin that produces optimum market standing.[67]

Drucker notes that companies like Xerox, GM, Chrysler, and Ford all decided at some point to concentrate on high-profit margin markets and leave the small-profit margin markets to seemingly insignificant competitors. Over time, however, those competitors produced less expensive products that more closely matched customer demands. To stay in business, the once dominant companies had to subsidize their customers with discounts, giving away "more in subsidies than it would have cost them to develop a competitive (and profitable)" product for the markets they eschewed.[68]

Law firms' current emphasis on premium markets and pricing seems to ignore Drucker's warnings and the painful experiences of Xerox, GM, Chrysler, and Ford. Those lessons have guided Japanese auto manufacturers' expansion but not the Am Law 50's strategies.[69] Toyota, Honda, and Nissan expanded into high-end, luxury

---

[67] Drucker, Peter F. (2005). *Managing in a time of great change* (pp. 45–46). New York: Penguin Group.

[68] Ibid. at 46.

[69] Both Peter Drucker and W. Edwards Deming had more influence on Japanese manufacturers than American law firms. Their ideas are an integral part of many Japanese companies' management systems, including Hoshin Kanri. GM chose to largely ignore Drucker's advice and lost more than one-half of its market share, while Toyota adopted Drucker's ideas and emerged as the world's largest automobile manufacturer. (Volkswagen displaced Toyota as the world's largest automaker in 2016.) See Halberstam, David. (1986). *The reckoning* (pp. 301-318). New York: William Morrow and Company.

markets with their Lexus, Acura, and Infiniti brands, but they still maintain and profit from their original, lower-end markets. The progenitor manufacturers also serve as sources of experimentation and innovation for their luxury brands. Many large law firms, in contradistinction, boast that they have moved out of low-profit, "commoditized" legal services and now focus almost exclusively on high-profit, "bespoke" services. Unlike the Japanese auto manufacturers that seek competitive advantages across all market segments, these law firms contend that offloading clients who currently lack the financial resources or the need to purchase their most complex and expensive products is an adroit, long-term strategy. It remains to be seen, however, whether clients once deemed insufficiently capitalized or sophisticated to warrant high-end legal services will retain elite law firms once the clients' balance sheets have improved and their legal needs have become more complex.

Law firms' emphasis on premium markets and pricing has a hint of arrogance that clients find off-putting, and it encourages attorneys to skip the trust-building process that underpins many durable attorney–client relationships. Norman Brothers, the Chief Legal Officer of United Parcel Service, Inc., describes this problem:

My own personal pet peeve is when firms come in and try to position themselves as a bet-the-company firm, so the sort of firm that you want to use when you have the really significant matter but probably not the sort of firm you want to use for the more routine matters. It goes back to my feeling that before you're going to be trusted with the big things, you need to show us that you really do the little things well and understand the blocking and tackling before we will feel comfortable giving you the really significant matters. Also, I think it plays into really understanding the company at the lowest level to put you in the best position to represent us on the more complex matters.[70]

---

[70] Lehman-Ewing, Paula. (2016, December 1). Packaging partners. *San Francisco Daily Journal*, p. 6.

As Brothers points out, clients may not embrace the new *uber-attorney* who has catapulted from neophyte to all-star without building a commensurate level of trust and confidence with the client. This trust-building process usually requires attorneys to inhabit lower hourly rate regions while they work with clients on matters of increasing complexity and consequence. Without the opportunity to work on the relatively less significant matters, it is unclear how the premium pricing model enables attorneys to advance from legal functionary to trusted advisor.

Morgan Lewis, one of the highest-grossing firms in the world, has not adopted the premium-pricing model. Its chair, Jami Wintz McKeon, acknowledges that "there are some law firms who have skinnied down and chase only the highest rate work." She, however, rejects the idea that large law firms should abandon relatively routine work to lower-cost providers, stating, "For us, it's relationship-driven. We do wide and deep."[71]

Client Relegation

Clients are frequently overlooked in law firms' drive for growth and higher profits per partner. Like software engineers who become enamored of product features that are fascinating to other engineers but frustrating and annoying to actual users, lawyers increasingly focus on financial performance metrics and compensation models that excite other lawyers but have questionable value to their clients. Law firms' shift from client service and satisfaction to attorney status and compensation has been slow but discernible:

- "There's a mismatch between the firm & the client as to what makes a star lawyer. For law firms, star qualities are generally considered to be those that contribute the most to generating the highest fees or the strongest profit margins, typically measured annually. This ability may seem totally at odds with client desires for lawyers who invest real time in building a

71 Rozen, Miriam. (2018, February 1). Reality check for law firms: It's not just about you anymore. *American Lawyer*.

relationship with their business, and consistently deliver a swift yet comprehensive response. Such dedicated client focus may prevent these star lawyers from managing huge books of business, however, perhaps placing them at odds with what the firm wants from them."[72] (Lisa Hart Shepherd, Chief Executive Officer, Acritas Research Ltd.)

- "The problem has been a lack of courage and discipline to create and deliver what clients in every industry ask for: a better-quality product and service for a better price—to provide increased value. Firms stopped investing in people and the future of the enterprise as an institution, and they did it long before the onset of the Great Recession. . . . Clients were clear in expressing what they wanted. Instead of giving it to them, the all-too-frequent leadership response was to raise rates, flog people to bill more, and internally reallocate profits."[73] (Edwin Reeser, former Managing Partner, Los Angeles, Sonnenschein Nath & Rosenthal.)

- "None of these strategies [lateral partners, outsized compensation, leverage] make a law firm more attractive in the eyes of the clients. . . . Rather, most large law firms seem to be managed for the short-term benefit of individual rainmaking partners. . . . The resulting collection of lawyers may produce little or no synergistic value for clients, but it may create internal perceptions of firm vitality and growth and buy managers more time to deal with the vicissitudes of the lateral market. . . . In the short term, the maintenance of relatively high profitability within these firms will convince stakeholders to stay the course—that is, to continue to pay out large profits and not invest too heavily in efforts to retool the underlying business model. These are the seeds of destruction."[74] (William Henderson, Indiana University Maurer School of Law.)

---

[72] Shepherd, Lisa Hart. (2016). What makes a star lawyer? Thomson Reuters.

[73] Reeser, Edwin. (2013, September 12). Big Law is looking for change in all the wrong places, Part II. *ABA Journal.*

[74] Henderson (2013), *supra* note 5.

The former dean of Northwestern University School of Law, David Van Zandt, characterizes the contemporary law firm as "a business built for the suppliers rather than the customers."[75] Lawyers, he asserts, have a "guild" mindset that turns their attention inward, encouraging their peers to determine the quality and value of their work instead of recognizing that their clients are the ultimate arbiters.[76] Clients expect both high quality and competitive pricing, but guilds typically believe that they can set their own standards and prices. "Guilds are always giving out awards and badges," Van Zandt observes, "and clients don't really care about that sort of thing."[77]

Reflective of law firms' isolation from their clients is their managing partners' belief that profits per partner will continue to grow while they minimize client inputs. Most managing partners project higher profits per partner; but when asked to identify activities that their firm is "proactively initiating to better understand what individual clients want," only 41 percent state that they have a "formal client interview program," and only 27 percent have a "formal client survey program."[78] When asked to designate which actions their firms are taking "to increase efficiency of legal service delivery," only one in four law firms report that they are "reengineering work processes."[79] As former California State Bar president Howard Miller notes, clients have a legitimate interest in improving attorney efficiency and reducing legal costs. "That is where we have let them down," he says. "Our court and lawyer processes are often embarrassingly oblivious to client concerns of time and cost."[80]

[75]   Ward, Stephanie Francis. (2009, August 24). David Van Zandt: Purple praise. *ABA Journal.*

[76]   Ibid.

[77]   Ibid.

[78]   Clay & Seeger (2018), *supra* note 29 at 10.

[79]   Ibid. at 56.

[80]   Miller, Howard B. (2010, February 2010). Structural or cyclical? *California Bar Journal*, p. 8.

Leverage

Leverage is the financial advantage law firms obtain from charging clients for associate attorneys' time at rates that exceed law firms' costs of compensating those associate attorneys. Under time-honored practices that exalt leverage, law firm profitability is seen as being directly proportional to partner/associate ratios.[81] A firm with one partner for every three associate attorneys (1:3) is presumed to be better managed and more profitable than a firm with, say, one partner for every two associate attorneys (1:2). Stripped to its essence, leverage presumes that it is invariably better to have fewer partners sharing the profits generated by more associate attorneys than it is to have more partners sharing the revenue generated by those partners and fewer associate attorneys.

As an arithmetic model, the logic of leverage may be hard to beat. But as a practical matter, leverage appears to have reached its limits in promoting profitability and presuming that partners can over-see a large number of inexperienced associate attorneys without jeopardizing work product quality and client relations.[82] Leverage is now criticized because it "makes high quality training, mentoring and monitoring infeasible" as each partner is required to monitor an ever-increasing number of associate attorneys.[83] Leverage also presents serious motivational challenges because it assumes that the "galley slaves," as one partner characterizes associate attorneys, will continue "to row at the same pace" despite diminishing opportunities for promotion to fleet captain.[84]

A high degree of inefficiency and opaqueness is built into the leverage model. It requires clients willing to pay a lower hourly rate for associate attorneys developing expertise instead of a higher hourly rate for partners possessing expertise. Now that clients are

---

[81]   See Denney, Robert W. (2011, October). Leverage: Out with the old, in with the new. *Law Practice Magazine, 37*(5).

[82]   See Ribstein, Larry E. (2010). The death of Big Law. *Wisconsin Law Review, 2010*(3), 749.

[83]   Henderson, *supra* note 5.

[84]   Kiser, Randall. (2010). *Beyond right and wrong: The power of effective decision making for attorneys and clients* (p. 186). Berlin, Heidelberg: Springer.

refusing to pay for entry-level associates and law firms are handling many engagements on a fixed-fee basis, the leverage model of profitability is questionable. As law firm management consultant Jim Hasset explains, "Suppose a $1,000-per-hour senior partner can solve a problem in one hour, but a $300-per-hour associate will require 10 hours to come to the same solution. If the firm is paid the same fixed fee regardless of who does the work, it is obvious that solving the problem at the unleveraged partner 'cost' of $1,000 is more profitable than at the leveraged associate cost of $3,000."[85]

Fixed fees fundamentally alter the economics of leverage and arguably require a new model for law firms. Jeffrey Carr, former general counsel of FMC Technologies, describes this new model:

The hallmarks of firms that have made the kind of client-focused commitment to alternative fees that will pay off for the client are those that have dramatically altered their leverage, focusing on experience and production instead of body count. In these firms, senior associates and young partners are the foundation on which a team is built because they are starting to have the experience needed to provide value. The benchmark firm will not be bringing in legions of rookies and then suffering through turnover at double-digit figures. The firm will invest heavily in the training of its people because it will be relying on them to produce results quicker and thus improve the firm's profit margins. . . . These firms will be relentlessly focused on lowering costs and streamlining work and work processes because these things also will add to the bottom line.[86]

Carr, who received the Association of Corporate Counsel's "Excellence in Corporate Practice" award in 2010, contends that "the

---

[85]   Hassett, Jim. (2015, March). Flawed finances. *MP*, p. 34.

[86]   Carr, Jeffrey, Lamb, Patrick, McKenna, Patrick J., & Reeser, Edwin B. (2009, September 29). Wannabes, pretenders and the real deal. *San Francisco Daily Journal*, p. 5.

relationship between business and its lawyers is on the cusp of tectonic change."[87]

Perhaps because of the increasing criticisms of leverage, 57 percent of law firm managing partners now report that "reduced leverage will be a permanent trend going forward."[88] (In 2009, only 12 percent of managing partners anticipated a decline in leverage.) Despite their recognition that reduced leverage is a trend, nearly one-half of managing partners expect their firms to employ more associates, both partner track and non-partner track, in the next five years.[89] Their expectations suggest that managing partners recognize but have not yet internalized the limits of leverage.

If law firms increase the number of associate attorneys and thereby extend the leverage model, they are taking risks not justified by recent analyses of law firm growth and profitability. In its study of law firms' financial performance during the 2014–2016 period, Thomson Reuters analyzed their growth in revenue per lawyer (RPL), total profit, and profit margins. Thomson Reuters selected these factors because they represent "pillars of law firm success: law firm value (RPL), bottom-line financial health (profit), and operational efficiency (profit margin)."[90] The law firms then were categorized as "Dynamic" (top 25 percent in composite financial performance) or "Static" (bottom 25 percent in composite financial performance). The Dynamic firms, Thomson Reuters discovered, actually had less leverage than the Static firms, indicating that leverage was not positively correlated with growth or profitability:

Leverage is considered one of the key levers of profitability for a law firm. The ability to push work down to the lowest-cost, capable timekeeper gives law firms the ability to push work to higher-margin timekeepers, maximizing the profit potential, or so goes the theory.

---

87   Ibid.
88   Clay & Seeger, *supra* note 23 at 53.
89   Ibid. at 51.
90   Thomson Reuters. (2017). *Dynamic law firms study* (p. 1).

But in a surprising finding in our analysis, we discovered that with few exceptions, on average, Static firms exercised greater leverage than their colleagues at Dynamic firms in nearly every measure of leverage we examined.[91]

"Conventional wisdom," the researchers report, "would have predicted that, due to generally higher profit margins and profit growth, the Dynamic firms would be found to be exercising better [higher] leverage. That this was not the case was a surprise."[92]

Short-Term Planning and Profitability

Law firms' emphasis on short-term planning and revenue growth often conflicts with the legal profession's core values of client service, professional development, access to the legal system, and public service. It reinforces public perceptions that lawyers are primarily motivated by money and shortchanges younger attorneys' careers by devaluing training, mentoring, and informal feedback and advice. Many activities that could have a lifelong impact on an associate attorney's performance are not rewarded in a supervising partner's year-end distribution but are an integral part of that partner's responsibilities. When law firms are fixated on short-term profitability, they compel partners to curtail those training and mentoring activities.

Short-term financial priorities foster a near-obsession with revenue and retard investments in talent development, process analysis, and technology. This short-term perspective is driven, in part, by partners' perceived need to recover financial losses sustained in the Great Recession and the sheer force of law firm demographics. As discussed in Chapter 2, roughly 20 percent of all current partners will retire by 2022, and about 40 percent of current partners will have retired by 2027.[93] Among veteran

---

[91] Ibid. at 3.
[92] Ibid. at 4.
[93] Triedman, Julie. (2016, August 29). Retiring partners pose big challenges for firms. *The American Lawyer*. See McQueen, M. P. (2015, July 30). A lateral boom of older lawyers. *The American Lawyer*. Weiss, Debra Cassens. (2014,

partners, the horizon is even shorter. Thirty-nine percent of partners with a tenure of 21 or more years, as of 2016, expected to
retire by 2021; and 80 percent of those partners expected to retire
by 2026.[94] Whether based on personal financial needs or impending retirements, short-term priorities appear to have displaced
long-term investments in law firms. "The short-term approach
of present-day law firm management in too many firms," states
Edwin Reeser, a former managing partner of Sonnenschein, Nath
& Rosenthal LLP's Los Angeles office, "appears to have more
in common with a smash-and-grab visit to a Tiffany's counter
than exercise of fiduciary duty for one's partners or a long-term
responsibility for colleagues' careers, let alone delivering a better
value proposition for clients."[95]

The shift to short-term perspectives and planning is palpable but
relatively recent. It has become so pervasive that many of the profession's most prominent commentators are warning of the serious
consequences of this trend:

- "When the Great Recession struck in 2008, most companies
  were able to do a 'great reset,' re-setting stakeholder expectations by cleaning up balance sheets, lowering short-term
  profit expectations and making the case for strategic investments. But the folks running law firms don't seem to feel they
  have the latitude to fess up that firms need to revamp to focus
  on client value, not near-term profits."[96] (Paul Lippe, founder,
  Legal OnRamp.)
- "Regrettably, most law firm leaders that I meet have only a
  few years left to serve and hope they can hold out until retirement before much that I predict engulfs them. Operating
  as managers rather than leaders, they are more focused on
  short-term profitability than long-term strategic health. For
  junior partners this is tragic because any major re-invention

---

October 22). As fewer law grads become lawyers, the profession shows its age.
ABA Journal.

[94]   Lindsey & Lowe, *supra* note 41 at 84.
[95]   Reeser (2013, September 12), *supra* note 73.
[96]   Lippe, Paul. (2012, March 27). Dewey or don't we: Abnormal or new normal?
ABA Journal.

and re-engineering of law firms has to be driven from the top. I find a great contrast here with the large accounting firms, where senior partners seem far more concerned about the prospects of their junior partners. Their philosophy—to regard themselves as temporary custodians of long-term and enduring businesses rather than short-term investors who want to bail out when the price is right—is one that could fruitfully be assumed by more equity partners."[97] (Richard Susskind, author of *Tomorrow's Lawyers*.)

- "In my travels over the last several years, I have talked to hundreds of lawyers, including many law firm partners. One of the strongest impressions I have drawn is that many partners are too immersed in their own practices to grasp the broader changes that are occurring in the profession. This is because maximizing short-term revenue has become a precondition of maintaining one's status and income. The little white space that remains is inadequate to think through their firms' business problems, much less how the principles of legal operations can improve the lives of clients and younger lawyers."[98] (William Henderson, Indiana University Maurer School of Law.)

When asked, "What has been the biggest negative change to the legal profession since the start of your career?," Larren Nashelsky, chair of Morrison & Foerster, replied, "The drive for short-term financial success that has dominated the profession, sometimes with tragic results. Even where firms are financially strong, competition among Big Law causes many good firms to lose their focus on the profession, their culture and their communities."[99] Nashelsky's concerns are supported by analyses showing that companies taking a short-term perspective invest less in research and development, generate fewer new jobs, and end up with lower revenue

---

[97] Susskind, Richard. (2013). *Tomorrow's Lawyers* (pp. 57–58). Oxford: Oxford University Press.

[98] Henderson, William. (2015, October). What the jobs are. *ABA Journal*, p. 43.

[99] (2013, May 15). The ATL interrogatories: 10 Questions with Larren Nashelsky of Morrison & Foerster. *Above the Law*.

and earnings growth than companies with a long-term vision and strategy—"short-termism really destroys value."[100]

Chapter Capsule

Law firms' current strategies are unlikely to improve their performance. By adopting strategies embraced but not adequately tested by their peers, law firms have followed a conventional path to growth and profitability that, at best, will yield conventional returns. Absent a determination to implement innovative strategies that reflect a law firm's distinct advantages and mitigate its disadvantages, law firms will continue to emulate strategies that have proven to be inadequate, if not counterproductive.

Empirical research demonstrates that law firms' "me-too" strategies—growth, mergers, lateral partners, star partner recruiting, client origination incentives, rate increases, premium pricing, and leverage—do not reliably increase profitability or provide other competitive advantages. These strategies appeal to law firms because they offer the possibility of increasing profitability without changing law firms' basic business model or requiring higher levels of client service. Because they do not fundamentally challenge or alter law firms' current practices, these strategies are more akin to expedient plans than genuine strategies.

Even if the strategies were sound, they would not produce the expected results because too many firms are following the same strategies. If nearly all firms intend to add lateral partners, for instance, they cannot increase their overall profitability by shuffling their partners and providing the newly acquired partners with higher compensation than they received at their predecessor firms. In this lawyerly version of musical chairs, every lateral partner has a seat, and each seat pays an ever-increasing amount to a fresh occupant. In a similar vein, nearly all firms are seeking practices that

---

[100] Barton, Dominic, Manyika, James, & Williamson, Sarah Keohane. (2017, February 7). Finally, evidence that managing for the long term pays off. *Harvard Business Review.* Cf. Kaplan, Steven N. (2017, June). Are U.S. companies too short-term oriented? Some thoughts. National Bureau of Economic Research Working Paper No. 23464.

support premium pricing, although it is clear that premium pricing invariably attracts new competitors and technological advances.

Law firm leaders acknowledge that strategies like lateral partner hiring have not yielded the intended results, but they continue to double down on these failed strategies. Firm leaders seem to assume that they will be better at implementing a strategy that has been unsuccessful at other firms. Even when a strategy has proven to be unsuccessful at their own firms, firm leaders are reluctant to abandon it. This occurs because these leaders, like other business leaders, engage in "consensual neglect"—the tendency to "ignore events that undermine their current strategy and double down on the initial decision in order to justify their prior actions."[101]

---

[101] Vermeulen, Freek, & Sivanathan, Niro. (2017, November–December). Stop doubling down on your failing strategy. *Harvard Business Review*.

5
Culture

The concept of law firm "culture" makes some attorneys uneasy. It strikes them as being abstract, illusive, transient, and, in any event, unrelated to the practice of law. Since culture seems to lack the tangibility and rationality associated with lawyerly analysis, attorneys' discussions about law firm culture tend to be brief, awkward, and unavailing.[1] That's unfortunate because, as Ben Heineman, the former general counsel of General Electric Company, asserts, "Creating a common culture based on professional values of service, collegiality, loyalty, quality, integration, and cooperation is probably the greatest challenge for today's law firm leader."[2]

Attorneys' understanding of law firm culture is hampered by their apprehension that culture is subjective in nature—highly dependent on individual perceptions and group interactions and thus precariously linked to personal feelings and emotions. As consultant David Maister explains, lawyers are trained to be dispassionate and tend to be uncomfortable with feelings and sociability. "This

---

[1] Lawyers and executives share an unease about culture. Harvard Business School professor Boris Groysberg and his colleagues find that "it is far more common for leaders seeking to build high-performing organizations to be confounded by culture. Indeed, many either let it go unmanaged or relegate it to the HR function, where it becomes a secondary concern for the business." Groysberg, Boris, Lee, Jeremiah, Price, Jesse, & Cheng, J. Yo-Jud. (2018, January–February). The leader's guide to corporate culture. *Harvard Business Review*, p. 46.

[2] Heineman, Ben W., & Lee, William F. (2010, May 20). Trust, justice and the BigLaw Way. *The American Lawyer*.

doesn't mean they don't like people," Maister elaborates. "It just means that, statistically speaking, lawyers prefer focusing on the job at hand rather than investing in relationships with those they are working with (other partners or associates) or for (clients)."[3] One lawyer, for example, says he leaves his personal feelings at home; and "when he hung up his jacket on the back of his door in the morning, with it went his personality, both of which he put on at the end of the day as he left the office."[4]

Although law firm culture may seem to be subjective or amorphous, it actually is palpable, measurable, and, for most firms, determinative. Those attorneys who think that firm culture is uncomfortably affective or relatively unimportant might be surprised to learn that firm culture is the main reason partners cite for leaving their firms—and the most important factor in their selection of a new firm. When asked to identify the reasons why they left their former firm, the most common response among surveyed partners is "did not like firm culture," followed by "compensation" and "firm financial health."[5] When asked to list the most important factors in choosing their current firm, partners rank "firm culture" above all other factors.[6] "Practice area support," "firm management," "firm financial health," and "personality of partners" are ranked below firm culture in importance.[7] As these surveys indicate, culture matters to attorneys and strongly influences where they choose to practice.

Culture also is a key factor in profitability. Although people tend to assume that financial success contributes to a strong company culture, the process actually works in reverse: a strong company culture causes financial success.[8] "We found that culture causes

---

3   Maister, David. (2006, April). Are law firms manageable? *The American Lawyer*.

4   Ibid.

5   Lindsey, Jon, & Lowe, Jeffrey A. (2014). *Lateral partner satisfaction survey* (p. 12). Major, Lindsey, & Africa.

6   Ibid. at 14.

7   Ibid.

8   Boyce, Anthony S., Nieminen, Levi R. G., Gillespie, Michael A., Ryan, Ann Marie, & Denison, Daniel R. (2015, April). Which comes first, organizational culture or performance? A longitudinal study of causal priority with automobile dealerships. *Journal of Organizational Behavior*, 36(3), 339. Denison

performance, not vice versa," concludes Michael Gillespie, a psychology professor and co-author of a recent study.[9] Companies that promote a culture of engagement, purpose, and motivation, therefore, generally achieve higher customer satisfaction rates and higher profits than companies without a positive culture.[10] Culture not only reflects an organization's values; it drives individual performance with goals implementing those values, and it guides behavior through the shared beliefs, norms, and objectives that constitute the organization's culture.[11]

Analyses of law firm financial performance specifically demonstrate that leaders who communicate a common purpose and promote a shared culture are "dramatically more likely to preside over extraordinarily successful firms."[12] But it may take a few years for a positive culture to produce superior results. Unless law firms are patient, they may become frustrated with competitors' relative profitability and mistakenly conclude that their attention to firm culture is useless. For patient law firms, however, culture is a distinct competitive advantage not easily or quickly replicated by other law firms.

Law firm cultures that produce a durable competitive advantage incorporate the six features listed below. A firm may be profitable,

---

Consulting, LLC (2011). Which comes first: Culture or performance? *Denison Research Notes, 5*(2). See Gagnon, Chris, John, Elizabeth, & Theunissen, Rob. (2017, September). Organizational health: A fast track to performance improvement. *McKinsey Quarterly.*

[9] Dizik, Alina. (2016, February 21). The relationship between corporate culture and performance. *The Wall Street Journal.*

[10] Ibid. See Denison Consulting, LLC (2012). Proving the link: ROA, sales growth, market to book. *Denison Research Notes, 7*(2). Kotter, J. P., & Heskett, J. L. (1992). *Corporate Culture and Performance.* New York: The Free Press. Harding, D., & Rouse, T. (2007). Human due diligence. *Harvard Business Review, 85* (4), 124–131. Rosenthal, J., & Masarech, M. A. (2003). High-performance cultures: How values can drive business results. *Journal of Organizational Excellence, 22*(2), 3–18. Hurley, Robert F. (2012). *The decision to trust* (p. 148). San Francisco: Jossey-Bass.

[11] Groysberg, Lee, Price, & Cheng, *supra* note 1 at 45.

[12] Belser, Burkey. (2012, June 28). Why firms fail: A diagnosis of the death of Dewey LeBoeuf. Available at: http://greenfieldbelser.com/big-ideas/why-firms-fail-a-diagnosis-of-the-death-of-dewey-leboeuf.

but it will not be durable unless its culture embodies these beliefs, values, practices, and expectations:

- *Shared objectives*—common values, expectations, and goals for attorney conduct and firm direction
- *Commitment to clients*—a belief in client primacy and the evaluation of client services and firm strategies based on what is best for clients
- *Accountability*—an insistence on accountability for client and firm outcomes
- *Trust and collegiality*—a uniform practice of treating other attorneys with respect and building relationships based on trust and candor
- *Continuous learning and improvement*—a commitment to ongoing evaluation and improvement of client service and firm leadership, supported by a culture that facilitates constructive criticism and feedback.
- *Social purpose*—a sense of responsibility to society and a sense of meaning derived from that connection with society

These key features of law firm culture are analyzed in the following sections. To provide a context for this analysis, the first section defines culture and identifies its components, dimensions, and ramifications. The remaining sections describe the six features, explain their importance, and show how they are developed.

Definition and Concepts

What is firm culture? Every attorney will have a different way of defining firm culture, but in its most fundamental form a firm's culture expresses, "This is who we are, what we believe, what we do, and what makes us different from other firms." It tells attorneys, clients, and the rest of the world what it means to be part of that law firm. It also tells the world what the firm is not. It impliedly expresses what the firm will not do or tolerate, discouraging dissimilar people from becoming affiliated with it. Dan DiPietro, former chair of Citi Private Bank's Law Firm Group, posits this definition: "culture equals the values, beliefs and behaviors partners share in common. It doesn't mean partners always agree; it doesn't mean they share the same political views; but it does mean they agree on the basics: the hierarchy of values, what is really important, how we treat one another."[13]

Across nearly all companies and organizations, culture has four major attributes:

- *Shared.* By definition, culture is a social phenomenon. "It resides in shared behaviors, values and assumptions and is most commonly experienced through the norms and expectations of a group—that is, the unwritten rules."[14]
- *Pervasive.* Culture implicitly governs the interactions within an organization and defines the range of appropriate reactions to people and events outside the organization. It permeates and shapes behavior, mindsets, motivations, assumptions, and the "mental models of how to interpret and respond to the world around you."[15]
- *Enduring.* Culture affects beliefs and determines behavior for extended periods. Culture is lasting, while strategy is temporal; as Peter Drucker is reputed to have said, "Culture eats strategy for breakfast." Because people tend to stay with organizations whose culture is consistent with their values, "culture becomes a self-reinforcing social pattern that grows increasingly resistant to change and outside influences."[16]
- *Implicit.* Culture is largely a collection of beliefs, attitudes, principles, and rules that derive their strength from humans' highly evolved capacity to discern norms without express communication. Culture frequently operates as a "silent language."[17]

These concepts are integrated into organizational behavior expert Karl Weick's theory that culture is a collection of *expectations* about

---

13 DiPietro, Dan. (2015, February 18). Does culture matter at law firms? *Bloomberg Law.*

14 The four features of culture and the quotations appearing in the four bulleted points are from Groysberg, Lee, Price, & Cheng, *supra* note 1 at 46.

15 Ibid.

16 Ibid.

17 Ibid.

appropriate attitudes and behaviors. Culture, states Weick, is "what we expect around here. Cultures affect both what people expect from one another internally (these expectations are often called norms) and what people expect from their dealings with the external environment of customers, competitors, suppliers, shareholders, and other stakeholders."[18]

Firm culture may evolve in response to changed conditions and unexpected outcomes, but it always contains core constituents that reflect the distinct values, priorities, and experiences of the firm and its attorneys. In durable firms, those core constituents invariably possess a moral character. Edwin Reeser, a former managing partner of Sonnenschein Nath & Rosenthal's Los Angeles office, describes this moral character and explains how responsible law firm leaders inculcate it throughout the law firm:

> Specifically, a very definite, clear and uncompromising definition of a moral "right" thing, which is communicated to all and embraced and adhered to by all, with rigor. It is through the pursuit and achievement of the "right" thing that the culture of a firm is built, and the team commitment by people to each other and for each other can be framed to achieve everything else that matters in the enterprise. Without that group commitment to the value-based mission at the beginning of the enterprise endeavor, nothing can be soundly built or grow, and without it applied steadily to the end nothing of real value can be sustained or survive. Leadership must tend to this culture relentlessly, such that it is embodied in everything the firm does, and thus by everyone in what they do.[19]

The hallmark of struggling firms, Reeser contends, is the neglect of this moral component and the failure to "unequivocally

---

[18]   Weick, Karl E. (2007). *Managing the unexpected* (p. 115). San Francisco: John Wiley & Sons.

[19]   Reeser, Edwin. (2009, August 31). The lost art of leadership. *San Francisco Daily Journal.*

demonstrate to everyone in the firm" that its culture is the utmost priority.[20]

Because culture has a moral component and incorporates a law firm's values and principles, its core constituents do not vary with the vicissitudes of the economy or fluctuations in a firm's profitability. A durable law firm's values, standards, principles, and integrity are tested but not compromised in periods of economic distress. In that sense, culture can be understood as what's left of a firm after the euphoria of ever-increasing income has disappeared.[21] In many firms, nothing is left after an economic downturn because income was the only adhesive; and in the absence of a deliberately developed and widely embraced culture, law firms function merely as "transitory associations of individuals who happen to practice law under the same roof for a particular period of time."[22] When Dewey & LeBoeuf filed its bankruptcy petition in 2012, it had become a transitory association, an archetype of a firm without a culture. Referring to Dewey & LeBoeuf's leaders, a former partner comments, "[Steven] Davis and [Stephen] DiCarmine understood that the firm was all about the money. What they could never understand is, if that's all that holds a firm together, you have nothing left when the money runs out."[23]

Law firm culture is immensely difficult to build, yet it is easily corrupted or destroyed when firms encounter partner defections, malpractice claims, financial setbacks, and leadership crises. These events test the firm's culture because they incite a primitive impulse to single out, blame, and expel individuals seen as untrustworthy. As Gary Smith, CEO of the telecommunications company Ciena, explains, "Culture takes an awful lot of time and effort, and it can be destroyed very quickly, because it's built on trust and respect. You're respecting the individual and what they do, and you're trusting them, and they're doing the same for you." Adverse events signal a threat to the firm's culture, suggesting that someone has violated

20 Ibid.
21 See Lattman, Peter. (2012, September 24). Culture keeps firms together in trying times. *The New York Times*.
22 Li, Victor. (2015, August). The end of partnership? *ABA Journal*.
23 Triedman, Julie, Randazzo, Sara, & Baxter, Brian. (2012, June 27). House of cards. *The American Lawyer*.

its underlying sense of trust. In law firms with fragile cultures, the immediate urge to punish and exclude individuals overcomes the prospective value of finding collective solutions within the firm's culture of teamwork, engagement, responsiveness, agility, and continuity.[24]

The development, maintenance, and repair of law firm culture require an ongoing investment in human relationships that, as David Maister noted at the beginning of this chapter, attorneys are reluctant to make. Like any major investment in people, education, or skills development, this commitment to culture requires a large expenditure of resources without the assurance that every increment of expense will produce a commensurate return. At each stage of development, the efforts to build culture may be difficult to justify on a strict cost-benefit basis. Because it is a deeply human endeavor, building culture is inevitably a nonlinear, inefficient process that yields uneven results with different people in a law firm—even when the process is succeeding overall. Despite these difficulties, building and safeguarding culture is imperative. Culture is the only bond that enables firms to survive with their attorneys engaged and their reputations intact.

Shared Objectives

The threshold requirement for law firm culture is a shared set of objectives, values, ethics, standards, norms, and priorities. Many of those qualities can be inferred from a firm's history, stories, and leaders, but unless the essential qualities are expressly identified and formally endorsed, law firms may be surprised to learn that their attorneys' experiences have produced disparate views of the firm and what it stands for. Although culture is often viewed as the "unwritten rules" of an organization, there is no advantage in keeping those rules tacit.

Daniel Pink, author of the best seller *Drive*, recommends a simple exercise to determine whether an organization shares a

---

[24] Groysberg, Lee, Price, & Cheng, *supra* note 1 at 44–49. Groysberg identifies and explains eight culture styles: caring, purpose, learning, enjoyment, results, authority, safety, and order.

common purpose. He suggests that leaders ask each person to write a one-sentence answer to the question, "What is our organization's purpose?"[25] This exercise, Pink has discovered, provides "a glimpse into the soul of your enterprise" and frequently shows "some people believing one thing, others something completely different." Although leaders usually are convinced that they have clearly defined the culture and mission, in reality "most organizations do a pretty shabby job of assessing this aspect of their business."[26]

A law firm's culture does not have to be encapsulated in a mission or vision statement, but the exercise of writing the statement and circulating it for approval among key decision makers serves multiple purposes. Because the statement necessarily implicates culture, it often exposes disparities in objectives, values, and priorities that have been suppressed for years, if not decades. These disparities, unless addressed candidly, carefully, and promptly, exact an enormous toll on the firm—sapping motivation, decreasing productivity, and leading eventually to partner and practice group defections. Quite often, these disparities are not so much conflicts between "good" and "bad" or "professional" and "unprofessional" cultures but rather conflicts that reflect a lack of consensus about the firm's culture and a lack of trust among its partners. These conflicts manifest as disagreements about priorities, risk taking, short-term versus long-term planning, status, and power. The mission or vision statement brings these conflicts to the surface, revealing dissimilar perceptions of the firm's culture or exposing other sources of friction among partners.

The exercise of drafting and circulating the statement also serves to highlight values that are essential to attorneys' sense of purpose but may not have been fully recognized, understood, or promoted. Since culture usually functions at a subliminal level and attorneys are not always aware of the norms that direct their behavior, the statement enables them to better understand the meaning of their work and how they can more precisely direct their performance to conform to the firm's standards and expectations. On occasion, the statement also alerts attorneys to the fact that their level

---

[25] Pink, Daniel. (2009). *Drive: The surprising truth about what motivates us* (p. 171). New York: Riverhead Books.
[26] Ibid.

of commitment to the firm or their perception of an attorney's role and responsibilities is inconsistent with the firm's requirements.

A mission or vision statement, in its most basic form, is a credible expression of "what the partners aspire to build together as partners for the firm's practice."[27] That statement should meet the following requirements, according to law firm consultant Peter Zeughauser:[28]

- Identify and communicate the firm's position and brand in the legal marketplace
- Distinguish the firm from competitors in a way that is attractive to clients, prospective clients, lawyers the firm wants to keep, and lawyers the firm would like to attract
- Offer a value proposition distinct from competitors
- Direct the firm's goals, strategies, and action items
- Provide a guide for firm decision making and for aligning the firm's structure and systems
- Affect choices about how to allocate limited resources (time and money)

Although the mission or vision statement is not a comprehensive summary of the firm's culture, it performs a valuable function in revealing key features of the firm's culture and how those features might affect the firm's future plans and strategies. The statement assists attorneys and law firms in not only identifying the firm's values but also determining their priorities among those values.

Commitment to Clients

Service to clients is the primary value and objective in effective, durable law firms. This statement seems self-evident to clients and the general public, but it is neither endorsed nor practiced in many law firms. Surveys indicate that many, perhaps most, law

---

[27] Zeughauser Group. (2015, August 29). Five drivers of success: What enables law firms to pull away. PowerPoint slide presentation at Association of Defense Counsel of Northern California and Nevada Seminar, Monterey, California. [on file with author.]

[28] Ibid.

firms regard client service as a secondary priority in their pursuit of growth and income.[29] Most law firms, for instance, do not have a formal client interview program to evaluate their performance and discern how they could improve their client service.[30] Only one in four law firms conducts client surveys.[31] When asked how serious they are about "changing their legal service delivery model to provide greater value to clients," law firms' median rating on a 0 (not at all serious)–10 (doing everything they can) scale is 5. Their corporate clients give them a median rating of 3 on this question, and this rating has not improved in the last five years.[32] Consistent with this low rating of law firms' responsiveness, 43 percent of chief legal officers report that they are planning or considering termination of an outside law firm.[33]

The low priority accorded to clients is not unique to large law firms or even U.S. law firms. Attorneys in small firms (1–29 attorneys) select "overall profits" instead of "client satisfaction ratings" as their primary measure of success.[34] Only 34 percent of small law firms "track client satisfaction ratings as a metric within their law firms."[35] In the United Kingdom, lawyers are similarly disconnected from their clients. Thirty-nine percent of lawyers in a United Kingdom survey report that their level of client service is "well above average," but only 13 percent of their clients think their service is at that level.[36] Despite their high self-ratings on client service, 77 percent of the attorneys agree with the statement, "Lawyers don't always appreciate that they are operating in a service industry."[37] Attorneys' reluctance to see themselves as operating in a service industry may

---

[29] See generally Harper, Steven. (2012, November 9). Big law firm management puzzles. *The Am Law Daily*. ALM Legal Intelligence. (2012). Thinking like your client: Law firm strategic planning.

[30] Clay, Thomas S., & Seeger, Eric. (2017) *2017 law firms in transition* (p. 8). Newtown Square, PA: Altman Weil.

[31] Ibid.

[32] Ibid. at 12.

[33] Association of Corporate Counsel. (2018) *ACC Chief Legal Officers 2018 survey* (p. 4).

[34] Thomson Reuters. (2017). *2017 State of U.S. small law firms* (p. 2).

[35] Ibid. at 4.

[36] LexisNexis. (2016). *The bellwether report 2016: The riddle of perception* (p. 30).

[37] Ibid. at 21.

explain why they think that clients would rank "efficiency" as their ninth most important priority in dealing with lawyers, while the clients, in fact, rank efficiency as their second most important priority (after "clear understanding of my particular needs").[38]

A different perspective on clients—in which client service is deeply embedded in the firm's culture—is evident at Sullivan & Cromwell, an esteemed and highly profitable Am Law 10 firm. Its chairman, Joseph Shenker, articulates its philosophy and practices:

> The key to this is a firm culture in which all lawyers recognize they are part of one team, and one person's success rebounds to the benefit of the firm, and thus, everyone. In that way our clients are best served. And we believe that when our clients are best served, the firm will be best served over the long-term—which is the primary time framework we think about. Thus, . . . everyone realizes that their most important job is to ensure the client has the benefit of *all* the areas of our expertise that are necessary; all the practice areas and jurisdictions that are relevant to its issues.
>
> We try to have all of our lawyers across all practice areas and geographies know each other and work together in as many ways as possible, using both physical gatherings as well as our technology infrastructure, so that when a client comes to us with a problem or an issue, all of our talents are quickly brought together to address it. No matter how big or small the client is, we never speak of them as "my" client, we think of them as "our" client.[39]

This dedication to serving clients' interests is paramount and changeless. As Shenker notes, "From the firm's inception, our ethos has always been the same: Every client and every matter requires our highest and best focus, with no shortcuts."[40]

---

[38] Ibid. at 29.

[39] Parnell, David. (2014, October 23). Joseph Shenker of Sullivan & Cromwell, on standing the test of time. *Forbes.* Available at: https://www.forbes.com/sites/davidparnell/2014/10/23/joseph-c-shenker-sullivan-cromwell-on-standing-the-test-of-time/3/#1d3f3d596c84. (When Shenker was elected partner at 29 years of age, he was Sullivan & Cromwell's youngest-ever partner.)

[40] Ibid.

Skeptical attorneys may question whether any law firm is genuinely committed to serving clients and whether firms consistently provide the commitment and quality of service they espouse. The condensed answer is that, in the absence of a firm culture that expressly and continuously advances clients' interests over attorneys' interests, attorneys will persistently disappoint their clients; and when a firm's culture articulates and demonstrates a steadfast commitment to clients' interests, nearly every attorney will strive to conform with that culture.[41] Attorneys, like most people in organizations, are constantly searching for behavioral cues and models of conduct. They find those cues and models in a firm's culture and the icons and guardians of that culture. When firms fail to provide positive cues and exemplary models that express a culture of client primacy, they severely damage three critical elements of firm success: their attorneys, their clients, and their reputation.

Accountability

Accountability, an essential element of law firm culture, has two dimensions: attorneys' accountability to their law firm's clients and law firm leaders' accountability to the firm's partners and employees. In weak law firms, attorneys distance themselves from client outcomes, and leaders focus more on extrinsic reasons for the law firm's problems than the ideas, decisions, and actions for which they should be accountable. In effective law firms, in contradistinction, the attorneys assume primary responsibility for client outcomes, despite numerous factors seemingly beyond their control; and their leaders evaluate their performance relative to explicit objectives, despite unanticipated, adverse conditions. The ability to blame other factors has little or no effect on the performance of attorneys and leaders in effective law firms. They drive results by concentrating on the factors over which they can exert control.[42] Those attorneys and leaders may

---

[41] See Martin, Roger. (2007). *The opposable mind* (p. 36). Boston: Harvard Business School Press. ("Employees believed only what they saw. If we were seen showing greater concern for profit, prestige, quotas, rather than for customers and employees, there'd be no belief in our values, no whole-hearted commitment.")

[42] See generally Ericsson, K. Anders. (Ed.). (2009). *Development of professional expertise.* New York: Cambridge University Press. Rhodewealt, Frederick, &

have an exaggerated sense of responsibility and accountability, but it compels them to achieve opportunities and goals prematurely forfeited by their competitors.[43]

A lack of accountability for outcomes is injected into attorneys' training at an early stage. Unless this lack of accountability is corrected by a law firm's culture, it permanently damages attorney-client relationships and impairs law firm leadership. In the first year of law school, students enroll in Civil Procedure courses and learn about the constitutional guarantees of "due process." Over time, the study of law convinces students that they are duty bound to ensure that the proper procedures and processes are followed, and this belief fosters a misconception that attorneys' responsibilities vanish at the terminus of a procedural route—regardless of the client's intended destination. Although clients hire attorneys to achieve a desired result, attorneys tend to see their role as knowing and ensuring compliance with procedural requirements. When procedures fail to produce the outcomes clients expect, attorneys frequently recommend or resort to more procedures rather than correct their mindsets or strategies. As Paul Lippe observes, "Lawyers very often suggest more process as the cure for what ails us. It's kind of our preferred playbook, and we resist being held accountable if the process yields an outcome we can no longer defend."[44]

A sense of accountability for outcomes distinguishes novices from expert performers in nearly all endeavors. Novices see themselves as being responsible only for the information they

---

Vohs, Kathleen D. Defensive strategies, motivation and the self: A self-regulatory process view. In Elliot, Andrew J., & Dweck, Carol S. (Eds.). *Handbook of competence and motivation* (p. 548). New York: The Guilford Press.

[43] See Schultheiss, Oliver C., & Brunstein, Joachim C. An implicit motive perspective on competence. In Elliot & Dweck, *supra* note 42 at 45. (Achievement-motivated individuals "prefer personal responsibility for performance and thus show a greater interest in, and better performance on, tasks that are under their direct control than on tasks whose outcomes depend on chance.") Simons, Robert. (2005, July–August). Designing high-performance jobs. *Harvard Business Review.* ("By explicitly setting the span of accountability wider than the span of control, executives can force their managerial subordinates to become entrepreneurs. In fact, entrepreneurship has been defined . . . as 'the process by which individuals—either on their own or inside organizations—pursue opportunities without regard to the resources they currently control.'")

[44] Lippe, Paul. (2013, April 11). Was Rutgers GC blamed for properly managing a process to the wrong outcome? *ABA Journal.*

provide, but experts hold themselves responsible "for the complete professional task, including treatment."[45] While a novice provides a unit of information, a professional assumes responsibility for the entire spectrum of care: diagnosis, inference, and treatment.[46] Absent a firm culture instilling a sense of accountability, many attorneys default to a narrow spectrum of services more typical of novice performance: presenting information to clients, acknowledging responsibility for the correctness of that information, and absolving themselves of responsibility for resolving the problem for which the information was requested.

Organizations that adopt a culture of accountability and assume responsibility for outcomes actually produce superior financial results. Researchers find that organizations that attribute adverse outcomes to internal causes, instead of blaming them on external factors, "will come out ahead not only in public perception, but also in terms of the profit line."[47] An extensive analysis of companies' annual reports over a 21-year period indicates that companies that attribute failures to internal and controllable factors "had higher stock prices one year later than those that pointed to external and uncontrollable factors."[48] Accepting responsibility, ironically, "makes the organization appear to have greater control over its own resources and future" and leads clients and the public "to assume that the organization has a plan to modify the internal features of the organization that may have led to the problems in the first place."[49] For law firms, this research demonstrates that accepting responsibility and requiring accountability heighten client retention, while displacing responsibility and accountability onto other agents, even when fully supported by the facts, convinces clients that their problems with the firm will be recurring.

---

[45] Mieg, Harald A. (2006). Social and sociological factors in the development of expertise. In Ericsson, K. Anders, Charness, Neil, Feltovich, Paul J., & Hoffman, Robert R. (Eds.). *The Cambridge handbook of expertise and expert performance* (p. 753). New York: Cambridge University Press.

[46] Ibid at 751.

[47] Cialdini, Robert. (2008). *Yes* (p. 120). New York: Free Press.

[48] Ibid. at 122. See Lee, F., Peterson, C., & Tiedens, L.A. (2004). Mea culpa: Predicting stock prices from organizational attributions. *Personality and Social Psychology Bulletin, 30,* 1636.

[49] Cialdini, *supra* note 47 at 122.

As mentioned in the beginning of this section, a sense of accountability extends not only to a law firm's clients but also to the law firm's partners and employees. Law firm leaders are accountable to partners and employees for the firm's results, and they are accountable for implementing a system that identifies the intended results and shows whether they are achieving them. Imposing a sense of accountability on law firm leaders is unusual, as Zeughauser explains:

Most chairmen are elevated to their positions after successful careers as practitioners. Few have meaningful management experience before being thrust into the role of running what is, in essence, a mid-cap business. Seldom (if ever) have they been the subject of a management review or meaningfully reviewed anyone else's management performance. Upon taking the job, they inherit a staff of high-salaried non-lawyer professionals who have gotten written job descriptions only in recent years, if at all. The chances are that the enterprise as a whole has no written business plan. . . .

Successful or not, few chairmen are reviewed, and even fewer are compensated based on anyone's evaluation of their performance against a set of goals and objectives. Even though today's firms are unquestionably—to use the common refrain—run "more like businesses" than ever before, they still typically lack any sort of human resources infrastructure at the partner level, and they don't often have boards of directors. Even when policy committees and the like are formed to fill the strategy-setting and advisory role of a board, they—like the partners they serve—are largely unaccountable to the other owners in any meaningful way.[50]

Zeughauser's insights indicate that lack of accountability is the default setting for law firm leaders. Unless law firms make a

---

[50] Zeughauser, Peter. (2006, December). Leading by serving: Successful chairmen focus on their responsibilities to clients, lawyers, the public and the legal system. *The American Lawyer.*

deliberate effort to establish clear objectives and hold their leaders accountable for meeting them, law firm leaders themselves are unlikely to assume that responsibility. This lack of accountability defies all models of contemporary leadership.[51] Every attorney in a leadership position, whether primarily responsible for a client matter or the law firm itself, should continually answer four questions: What can we expect of you? What should we hold you accountable for? What are you trying to accomplish? By what time will you accomplish it?[52]

Trust and Collegiality

Writing in 1859, Charles Dickens described an evening meeting of solicitors as "a bad dinner in a party of four, whereof each individual mistrusts the other three."[53] Dickens could not have foreseen modern personality assessments showing that attorneys score high in skepticism and low in interpersonal sensitivity and sociability, but he seems to have captured a perennial suspiciousness that characterizes many attorney interactions.[54] With the benefit of personality assessments, we now have learned that attorneys in large law firms display a series of traits that might undermine trust, candor, and teamwork in their firms.[55] The Hogan personality assessments

---

[51] See Ricks, Thomas E. (2012, October). What ever happened to accountability? *Harvard Business Review.*

[52] Drucker, Peter. (1985). *Innovation and entrepreneurship* (pp. 199–200). New York: Harper Business.

[53] Gest, John Marshall. (1905, July). The law and lawyers of Charles Dickens. *The American Law Register* (1898–1907), *53*(7), 405. Published by The University of Pennsylvania Law Review.

[54] See Foster, Jeff, Richard, Larry, Rohrer, Lisa, & Sirkin, Mark. (2010). *Understanding lawyers: The personality traits of successful practitioners.* Hildebrandt Baker Robbins. Hartmann, Markus, Mordan, Bill, Schoenfelder, Thomas E., & Sweeney, Patrick. (2011, July/August). The perfect legal personality. *ACC Docket.* Levin, Mark, & MacEwen, Bruce. (2014). *Assessing lawyer traits & finding a fit for success.* Richard, Lawrence E. (2001–2002). Psychological type and job satisfaction among practicing lawyers in the United States. *Capital University Law Review, 29,* 979. Richard, Larry, & Rohrer, Lisa. (2011, July/August). A breed apart? *The American Lawyer,* p. 43. Richard, Larry. (2008). Herding cats: The lawyer personality revealed. *LAWPRO, 7*(1), 2–5.

[55] Foster, Richard, Rohrer, & Sirkin, *supra* note 54. See Richard (2008), *supra* note 54.

administered to 1,800 associate attorneys and partners in four large law firms, for instance, indicate that attorneys possess a unique set of behavioral tendencies:[56]

- *Skeptical*—"a tendency to be argumentative as well as suspicious of others" and "cynical, mistrustful, and overly sensitive to criticisms"
- *Leisurely*—resists authority and "tends to be independent, ignore others' requests, and becomes irritable if they persist"
- *Excitable*—becomes "tense and overly critical"
- *Reserved*—"tough, remote, detached, and hard to reach" and "a tendency to distance themselves from others and become uncommunicative"

The attorneys also score low on altruism, suggesting that they "place more value on their own work than in helping others" and may not have a strong interest in "building a better workplace."[57]

Effective law firms recognize that attorneys' independence, detachment, autonomy, and argumentativeness may be assets in advocating on behalf of clients but turn out to be liabilities in operating and managing law firms. The very traits that may protect and advance clients' interests under competitive conditions can be destructive when working with law firm colleagues. In his consulting work for law firms, Maister finds that attorneys' skepticism and distrust lead them to "place the worst possible construction on the outcome of any idea or proposal, and on the motives, intentions, and likely behaviors of those they are dealing with."[58] As a consequence, Maister observes, attorneys tend to suspect and then attack their colleagues' ideas about firm direction, operations, and strategies, and "within a short time, most ideas, no matter who initiates them, will be destroyed, dismissed, or postponed for future examination."[59] Unless these personality traits are corrected by firm culture, they create a permanent low-trust

---

[56]   Foster, Richard, Rohrer, & Sirkin, *supra* note 54.
[57]   Ibid.
[58]   Maister, *supra* note 3.
[59]   Ibid.

environment where skepticism and cynicism defeat collaboration and progress.

Trust is required at multiple levels of a law firm's operations because attorney performance, client service, and law firm management are undermined by suspicion, skepticism, and doubt.[60] Partners, for instance, have to trust that another partner will be competent, responsive, and efficient when working with a mutual client; that the firm's leaders are accurately assessing its financial condition and implementing plans to provide security and future opportunities for professional growth; that workloads will be equitably balanced among partners and disproportionate efforts will be recognized, appreciated, and compensated; and that other partners will be candid in communicating dissatisfaction with a partner's performance and will provide an opportunity to correct deficiencies before de-equitizing or expelling them.[61] This emphasis on trust is particularly important when firms are expanding rapidly. "There's a lot of research to support the idea that when firms grow very quickly through mergers or through lateral partner acquisitions," states Heidi Gardner, a Distinguished Fellow at Harvard Law School's Center on the Legal Profession, "it leads to a deterioration in things like trust between partners."[62]

Culture is a proven antidote to distrust and an effective instrument for converting attorneys' distrust to collaboration.[63] People who work in organizations whose culture instills a sense of trust show dramatically lower stress levels and significantly higher levels of productivity, engagement, enjoyment, empathy, commitment, satisfaction, and loyalty.[64] High-trust cultures also are correlated

---

[60] See Kuhlman, David C. (2013). *Leading firms*. New York: SelectBooks. Maister, David H., Green, Charles H., & Galford, Robert M. (2000). *The trusted advisor*. New York: Free Press.

[61] See Normand-Hochman, Rebecca (Ed.). (2015). *Leadership for lawyers*. Surrey, UK: Globe Law and Business Ltd.

[62] Li, Victor. (2015, August). The end of partnership? *ABA Journal*.

[63] See Hurley, Robert F. *The decision to trust*. (2012). San Francisco: Jossey-Bass. Karlgaard, Rich. (2014). *The soft edge*. San Francisco: Jossey-Bass. Reina, Dennis, & Reina, Michelle. (2015). *Trust and betrayal in the workplace: Building effective relationships in your organization*. San Francisco: Berrett-Koehler.

[64] Zak, Paul. (2017, January–February). The neuroscience of trust. *Harvard Business Review*. Karlgaard, *supra* note 63.

with higher employee salaries and company profitability.[65] To foster a high-trust culture, law firms can adopt many of the methods proven to be successful in other business organizations:

- *Increase communication.* Law firms tend to be hierarchical organizations controlling information on a "need to know" basis. To foster a culture of trust, law firms must communicate more frequently with their attorneys. This is particularly important to attorneys in the Millennial generation. Orrick, for instance, holds regular "town hall" meetings with two-way feedback.[66] The discipline of establishing more frequent communication forces leaders to be more purposeful about their activities because they are expected to discuss them regularly. It also encourages leaders to become more attentive to others' perspectives since they are presented more often.
- *Share information broadly.* Most employees in companies report that they do not receive sufficient information about their company's goals, strategies, and tactics.[67] Regular communication among firm leaders, partners, associate attorneys, and non-attorney employees provides a broader scope of information and increases engagement and motivation. When leaders choose not to share information, they are ignoring the fact that, absent information from leaders, people are compelled to make inferences and assumptions. "Obviously, there is some information that must be kept to an inner circle," state leadership experts Warren Bennis and Joan Goldsmith, "but leaders hold it to a minimum, and to the extent possible, share data that will enable their colleagues to make informed decisions and act responsibly."[68]
- *Deliberately build relationships.* Law firms with high-trust cultures regularly conduct events to encourage communication

---

[65]   Zak, Paul. (2017). *Trust factor: The science of creating high-performance companies*. Nashville, TN: AMACOM Books.

[66]   McLellan, Lizzy. (2017, October 23). Millennials won't destroy your law firm. Can they save it? *The American Lawyer*.

[67]   Zak, *supra* note 64 at 89.

[68]   Bennis, Warren, & Goldsmith, Joan. (2010). *Learning to lead* (p. xix). New York: Basic Books.

among attorneys and to increase familiarity with the firm's leaders. These events may be lunches, after-work parties, team-building activities, formal and informal professional development courses, firm retreats, practice group offsites, and brief presentations in which attorneys describe their expertise to other attorneys, either individually or in a practice group meeting.[69] Research shows that "the higher the number of formal or informal connections between a person and their colleagues, the more they are committed to both their job and their organization."[70]

- *Speak with "good purpose."* Speaking with good purpose means that "a leader communicates constructively and directly to the people involved."[71] Being constructive means that leaders have a genuine, positive intent to resolve an issue, and communicating directly means that leaders "do not go around people," "do not generate rumors," and do not communicate "behind peoples' backs."[72] Attorneys in large law firms may have a particularly difficult time communicating directly with people because their personality assessments reveal a general tendency "to shy away from others when under pressure."[73] Their coping styles "overwhelmingly favor" what psychologists call a "Moving Away" strategy—a consistent effort to distance oneself from a source of conflict and stress instead of dealing with it in a direct and straightforward manner. To overcome this tendency, lawyers have to be aware of their propensities and adopt a new discipline of direct yet tactful communication.

- *Enforce a "no jerks" policy.* "When hiring," Gardner cautions, "leaders need to resist the temptation to bring in 'high-performing jerks' who might be a toxic influence on a collaborative culture." She warns leaders, "As long as you

---

[69] Gardner, Heidi. (2017). The business case for smart collaboration in today's law firms. *Legal Business World*.

[70] Gardner, Heidi. Leading the campaign for greater collaboration within law firms. In Normand-Hochman, *supra* note 61 at 13.

[71] Hurley, *supra* note 63 at 109.

[72] Ibid.

[73] Foster, Richard, Rohrer, & Sirkin, *supra* note 54.

compromise on a candidate's character to get the one with the biggest book of business, you can't build a firm where people widely trust other partners enough to invite them along on client work." A fourth-year associate attorney at Baker & Hostetler, responding to an *American Lawyer* survey about advice young lawyers would give to their firms' managing partners, expresses this concern succinctly: "Do not hire assholes as partners."[74]

Continuous Learning and Improvement

The Japanese term "kaizen"—loosely translated as "change for the better" or "continuous improvement"—has become familiar to some North American attorneys, as its applications have expanded from automobile manufacturing to service businesses. Ironically, the companion concept of "hansei"—meaning introspection and the acknowledgment of one's mistakes—has been largely ignored and is rarely used in North America. Yet it is difficult to imagine how continuous improvement occurs without serious self-evaluation. This point is brought home by Tadashi Yamashina, the leader of the Toyota Technical Center: "Without hansei it is impossible to have kaizen."[75] Hansei is integral to continuous improvement because hansei includes not only the process of introspection but also the responsibility of solving a problem or changing one's performance. "Hansei is a mindset, an attitude," Yamashina adds. "Hansei and kaizen go hand in hand."[76]

In most American law firms, kaizen is an intermittent consideration, and hansei is an isolated event. Law firms infrequently examine and reevaluate their processes to determine how they could be improved, and introspection is a practice seen as more appropriate for mystics than lawyers. In its survey of 386 U.S. law firms, Altman-Weil found that most law firms have not changed their pricing or efficiency "to stay competitive in the post-recession

---

[74] McLellan, Lizzy. (2017, September 1). Associates say the darndest things: Their funny advice to managing partners. *The American Lawyer*.

[75] Liker, Jeffey (2004). *The Toyota way* (p. 257). New York: McGraw-Hill.

[76] Ibid.

economy."[77] At no time during the last five years have a majority of law firms reported changing their pricing or efficiency to stay competitive.[78] Most law firms, moreover, do not regularly evaluate their performance; only 20 percent of law firms in the Altman-Weil survey report that they conduct post-matter reviews.[79] This lack of innovation, evaluation, and improvement is harmful and incongruous, as Stephen Poor, chair emeritus of Seyfarth Shaw, explains: "True long-term success requires businesses to improve continually and reimagine how they operate in the face of changing competition and market forces. Yet this innovative urge, which drives so much of the rest of the American economy, is largely absent from large law firms."[80]

Highly effective law firms distinguish themselves from ordinary law firms by a culture of continuous learning and improvement. They develop and maintain this culture carefully and tactfully because it requires an exceptional degree of candor, openness, collegiality, and tenacity in evaluating and improving individual and organizational performance. Attorneys in law firms that consistently merit client loyalty and approbation display an unusually high level of humility and receptiveness in learning from each other, challenging their ideas, and guarding against complacency, as illustrated by these esteemed partners' comments:

- "I see this pattern throughout our firm of an optimistic yet realistic approach to litigation, to solving legal problems. It's really digging deep, doing our homework, thinking about a problem from all different perspectives, and we really value talking to each other and trying to come to the right result based on everybody's input."[81]—Theodore Boutrous, Jr., Gibson Dunn & Crutcher

---

[77] Clay & Seeger, *supra* note 30 at 13.
[78] Ibid.
[79] Clay, Thomas S., & Seeger, Eric. (2018) *2018 Law firms in transition* (p. 10). Willow Grove, PA: Altman Weil.
[80] Poor, J. Stephen. (2012, May 7). Re-engineering the business of law. *The New York Times*.
[81] LaRoe, Ginny. (2015, December 21). Litigation department of the year, winner: Gibson Dunn. *The American Lawyer*.

- "[N]ever be complacent. Question everything you're doing. Just because something has been successful up to this point doesn't mean it will continue to work. Every enterprise, not just law firms, is vulnerable to becoming a victim of its own success. If you're a market leader there's an inbred inertia not to change, so there's a built-in tendency to do nothing. You see that time and time again in every industry where the people at the top get complacent and they're not the innovators. Innovation rarely comes from the market leader because they don't see a need to innovate and that's how they get overtaken. We've seen that in the last year in the legal industry, some of the best firms in the country are suffering now, struggling and figuring out 'how do we change our culture?'"[82]—John Quinn, Managing Partner, Quinn Emanuel Urquhart & Sullivan

- "It's like a group of brain surgeons sharing their individual secrets on how to do the most difficult operations. . . . Watching [trial attorney John Keker] operate from the very beginning made it clear to me that, in order to be really effective as an advocate, you have to understand your strengths and how you as an individual connect with other people. It's a very human thing."[83]—Jon Streeter, former partner, Keker, Van Ness & Peters, and current Associate Justice of the California Court of Appeal

These attorneys and their law firms illustrate the importance and benefits of continuous learning and improvement. Despite notable achievements throughout their careers, these attorneys continue to question their own assumptions and seek and incorporate other attorneys' insights and opinions. They defy the conventional tendency among professionals to "stop learning and simply depend on accumulated wisdom and expertise to see them through—often while thinking they are continuing to learn."[84]

---

[82] Becker, Amanda. (2009, June 24). Managing partner A-list: John Quinn. *San Francisco Daily Journal.*

[83] Spees, Amy K. (2005, February 22). A mouse among elephants. *San Francisco Daily Journal,* p. 15.

[84] Russo, J. Edward, & Schoemaker, Paul. (2002). *Winning decisions* (p. 198). New York: Random House. See Argyris, Chris. (1991). Teaching smart people how to

Law firms that seek to initiate or renew a culture of continual learning and improvement will benefit from nine practices: (1) eliciting other attorneys' opinions, listening attentively to them, and asking questions to clarify and refine their ideas; (2) providing and requesting regular, constructive feedback on all major projects; (3) admitting mistakes to promote humility and candor and accelerate improvements; (4) maintaining confidentiality and acting with discretion to encourage openness and establish trust; (5) deemphasizing hierarchy and status so that less senior attorneys feel comfortable expressing their views; (6) encouraging productive conflict so that attorneys learn how to express and debate opinions without being personally attached to them; (7) upgrading attorney and team performance by focusing on outcomes and possible changes rather than affixing blame; (8) requiring "after action reviews" of matters to determine how the firm's representation could have been improved; and (9) establishing intervals, deadlines, and procedures for reevaluating law firm systems, processes, and goals.[85]

Social Purpose

In the late 1950s, Peter Drucker introduced the term "knowledge workers" to describe the new executive and professional class that derived its value from information and a specialized ability to employ critical and creative thinking to solve problems.[86] Although the general public understood that a new class of workers had

---

learn. *Harvard Business Review, 69*(3), 99. Argyris, Chris. (1994, July–August). Good communication that blocks learning. *Harvard Business Review.*

[85] See Cook, Randy, & Jenkins, Alison. (2014, December 9). Building a problem-solving culture that lasts. McKinsey & Company. Detert, James R., & Burris, Ethan R. (2016, January–February). Can your employees really speak freely? *Harvard Business Review.* Edmondson, Amy C. (2012). *Teaming.* San Francisco: Jossey-Bass. Garvin, David A., Edmondson, Amy C., & Gino, Francesca. (2008, March). Is yours a learning organization? *Harvard Business Review.* Gino, Francesca, & Staats, Bradley. (2015, November). Why organizations don't learn. *Harvard Business Review.* Hurley, *supra* note 63. Zak, *supra* note 64.

[86] See Turriago-Hoyos, Alvaro, Thoene, Ulf, & Arjoon, Surendra. (2016, March 23). Knowledge workers and virtues in Peter Drucker's management theory. *SAGE Open.* Wartzman, Rick. (2014, October 16). What Peter Drucker knew about 2020. *Harvard Business Review.*

emerged in the "Knowledge Society," employers have been reluctant to acknowledge and adapt to two distinct features of knowledge workers: (1) companies need knowledge workers more than knowledge workers need companies; and (2) knowledge workers need and expect a sense of social purpose. The first fact has been largely ignored by law firms, contributing to their high attorney dissatisfaction and attrition rates; and the second fact is the subject of this section.

Drucker recognized that knowledge workers' motivations were complex and significantly different from those of laborers and farmers in previous generations of workers. As Drucker noted, knowledge workers "need to know the organization's mission and to believe in it."[87] Financial compensation is important but not sufficient for knowledge workers, Drucker asserted, and their employers cannot expect work or loyalty simply by satisfying knowledge workers' financial needs and ambitions. "It will have to be done by satisfying their values," Drucker declared.[88] Rosabeth Moss Kanter, a professor at Harvard Business School, summarizes Drucker's thoughts on knowledge workers and social purpose this way: "Knowledge workers cannot be controlled; they must be motivated. Such employees must see a purpose more meaningful than personal profit."[89]

Attorneys, like all knowledge workers, seek a larger purpose for their work. Unfortunately, many attorneys do not find that larger purpose—or even a minor sense of purpose—in their practices. Only 16 percent of lawyers report that their "ability to contribute to the social good" matched their expectations, and 25 percent state that their expectations were "not at all" met.[90] When asked how well their expectations matched their experience in six practice aspects (intellectual challenge, financial remuneration, career satisfaction,

---

[87] Wartzman, *supra* note 86.

[88] Ibid.

[89] Kanter, Rosabeth Moss. (2009, November). Drucker today: What would Peter say? *Harvard Business Review.* Kanter adds, "When the game is only about money, disparities in society get worse as the favored grab the largest share."

[90] Linder, Douglas, & Levit, Nancy. (2014). *The good lawyer* (p. 219). New York: Oxford University Press. See Rhode, Deborah. (2000). *Ethics in practice* (p. 5). New York: Oxford University Press.

ability to help others, quality of life, and contribution to social good), attorneys reported the widest disparity between expectations and experience in their ability to help others and their contribution to the social good.[91] Attorneys practicing in large firms were twice as likely as attorneys practicing in small firms to state that their expectations about helping others and contributing to the social good were "not at all" met.[92] When asked why they might leave their current firms, about one in four midlevel associate attorneys at Am Law 200 firms said that "it would be for more fulfilling work."[93]

During the last two decades, many large law firms have responded to attorneys' need for a sense of purpose and meaning by raising associate attorney salaries, increasing partners' income, and then paying for these compensation increases by requiring more billable hours. When this response did not increase attorney engagement, productivity, satisfaction, or retention rates, those firms instituted more rounds of compensation increases followed by higher billable hour requirements. This process has created a downward cycle of disaffection marked by more compensation injections, higher billable hour requirements, increased dissatisfaction, a heightened sense of alienation, and yet more compensation increases.

Following a series of compensation increases that began in 2016, the majority of attorneys report that they are either "not engaged" or "actively disengaged" from their work.[94] When asked specifically whether they like what they do and whether they are motivated to achieve their goals, 46 percent of attorneys say they are "struggling"

---

[91] American Bar Association. (2000). *ABA Young Lawyers Division survey: Career satisfaction.* (Based on attorneys choosing "not at all" in response to the survey.)

[92] Ibid.

[93] McLellan, Lizzy. (2017, September 1). Salary hikes keep associates happy. *The American Lawyer.*

[94] Gallup & AccessLex Institute. (2018). *Examining value, measuring engagement* (p. 15). Research consistently demonstrates that extrinsic rewards do not increase engagement, satisfaction, or performance. See Brafman, Ori, & Brafman, Rom. (2008). *Sway.* New York: Doubleday. Deci, Edward. (1995). *Why we do what we do.* New York: Penguin Group. Pink, Daniel H. (2009). *Drive.* New York: Riverhead Books. Ryan, Richard, & Brown, Kirk. (2007). Legislating competence. In Elliot, Andrew J., & Dweck, Carol S. (Eds.). *Handbook of competence and motivation* (pp. 354–372). New York: The Guilford Press.

or "suffering" in their efforts to achieve that level of well-being.[95] The futility of expecting more income to increase attorney satisfaction is demonstrated by the fact that Cozen O'Connor was the top-rated firm in a recent survey of 5,346 midlevel associate attorneys. The associates ranked Am Law 200 firms on various measures of attorney satisfaction (e.g., challenging work, firm management openness, and communication about paths to partnership); and Cozen O'Connor scored a near-perfect 4.864 on a 0–5 rating scale. The firm's score for compensation, however, was the lowest among the top five firms.[96] Compensation, apparently, had little effect on attorney satisfaction.

Although most attorneys find that pro bono work "is extremely gratifying," they do not believe that their law firms support pro bono work and other forms of public service.[97] Most attorneys report that their employer either "discourages pro bono activities" or "neither encourages nor discourages pro bono activities."[98] When asked to rank 15 "motivating factors" for their pro bono work, attorneys place "helping people in need" at the top and "recognition from employer" at the bottom.[99]

Attorneys' perceptions that their law firms do not support pro bono work and other forms of community service are substantiated by the Institute for the Advancement of the American Legal System (IAALS) survey of 24,000 attorneys. As indicated in Table 5.1, the IAALS survey shows that attorneys place a remarkably low priority on new attorneys' participation in voluntary activities like pro bono work and local bar association activities. These volunteer opportunities provide a sense of purpose and enable attorneys to see how their work fits into a broader societal quest to promote justice, the rule of law, and equal access to the courts.

---

[95]   Gallup & AccessLex Institute, *supra* note 94 at 17.

[96]   McLellan, *supra* note 93.

[97]   American Bar Association Standing Committee on Pro Bono and Public Service. (2013, March). *Supporting justice III: A report on the pro bono work of America's lawyers* (p. 21). Chicago: American Bar Association.

[98]   Ibid. at 28.

[99]   American Bar Association. (2018 April). *Supporting justice: A fourth report on the pro bono work of American's lawyers* (p. 19). Chicago: American Bar Association. See American Bar Association (2013, March), *supra* note 97 at 21. (Only 43 percent of attorneys report that their firm has "a culture of volunteering.")

Table 5.1   Importance of Public Service, Pro Bono Work, and
Other Voluntary Activities

Quality/Skill	Necessary Immediately for a New Attorney's Success (%)	Necessary over Time for a New Attorney's Success (%)	Necessary Immediately or over Time for a New Attorney's Success (%)
Have a passion for public service	24.8	14.2	39
Engage in pro bono work	10.2	17.1	27.3
Volunteer or take on influential positions in the community	4.5	19.9	24.4
Be involved in a bar association	11.0	12.8	23.8

Source: IAALS, Foundations for Practice (2016).

To counter attorneys' malaise and instill a sense of meaning in their work, law firms need to renew a commitment to public service that has been neglected or lost in their drive to increase revenue. They must establish, articulate, and materially support a culture of public service. This commitment to public service is an integral part of law firms' function in American society; they have a time-honored duty of "protecting individual and societal rights, including ensuring that the weak, unknowing, and indigent have the same legal protections and access to the courts as the strong, knowing, and moneyed."[100]

Ben Heineman, the former general counsel of General Electric, and William Lee, a partner at WilmerHale, reiterate this commitment to public service by noting that "one of the great failures of American society is the inequality in the provision of legal services—the unequal access to equal justice under law."[101] They urge law firms

[100] Zeughauser, *supra* note 50.
[101] Heineman, Ben W., Jr., & Lee, William F. (2010, May 20). Truth, justice and the Big Law way. *The American Lawyer.*

to "address this issue (and many do), even if it means less revenue, through meaningful commitments, in terms of real time devoted to pro bono activities. This mission has to be at the core of professional obligations."[102]

Chapter Capsule

Louis Gerstner, the CEO of IBM from 1993 to 2002, did not fully appreciate the importance of culture when he first joined the company. He initially saw culture as "just one among several important elements in any organization's makeup and success—along with vision, strategy, marketing, financials, and the like."[103] During his highly successful tenure, Gerstner's opinion of culture evolved: "I came to see, in my time at IBM, that culture isn't just one aspect of the game, it is the game. In the end, an organization is nothing more than the collective capacity of its people to create value."[104]

For law firms, too, culture determines their collective capacity to create value for their attorneys, employees, clients, and community. It is an overarching set of attitudes and principles that expresses what is uniquely important to a firm and how it expects to be seen by its members and everyone who interacts with its members. A law firm's culture thus determines its values, defines its purpose, guides its decisions, and animates its actions. It may enhance a firm's financial performance, but its influence exists independent of its financial performance and organizational changes.

The culture in durable law firms has six core features: (1) shared values, objectives, and expectations for attorney conduct and firm direction; (2) a commitment to clients that underpins all decisions and ensures that a firm's actions and strategies are based on what is best for clients; (3) accountability for client and firm

---

[102] Ibid. Luis J. Rodriguez, a former president of the California State Bar, states: "We are the one profession born to speak for a cause, an idea, an individual who does not have a voice, whether we work in the public or the private sector." Hernandez, America. (2015, November 23). Judges extol virtues of pro bono work. *San Francisco Daily Journal*, p. 3.

[103] Gerstner, Louis V., Jr. (2002). *Who says elephants can't dance?* (p. 181). New York: HarperBusiness.

[104] Ibid. at 182.

outcomes, imposing responsibility on attorneys for clients' results, not just legal processes, and holding law firm leaders responsible for their decisions and strategies; (4) collegial relationships based on respect, trust, appreciation, and candor; (5) continuous learning and improvement, driven by rigorous, ongoing evaluation, continuous feedback, constructive criticism, and effective professional development programs; and (6) a social purpose and sense of responsibility to society, imbuing attorneys' work with meaning and integrating attorneys into a noble tradition of public service, pro bono work, and ethical conduct.

6

Character

Although law firms market their attorneys as dedicated professionals, many law firms more closely resemble manufacturing plants with rigid production goals than professional firms committed to client service. In the IAALS survey of 24,000 attorneys, for instance, attorneys in private practice rated the need to "adhere to proper timekeeping and billing practices" considerably above "loyalty and dedication," "passion for work," and "commitment to justice/rule of law" in importance.[1] The surveyed attorneys also placed a higher value on "prioritize and manage multiple tasks" than "increase value to clients or stakeholders," "maintain positive professional relationships," and "have an internalized commitment to developing toward excellence."[2]

Consistent with this emphasis on production and billing, private practice attorneys ranked "effectively use technology" as more important than "focus on improving the work process," "budget resources appropriately," and "leverage technology to increase value."[3] The ability to "adapt work habits to meet demands and

---

[1] Gerkman, Alli, & Cornett, Logan. (2016, July). *Foundations for practice: The whole lawyer and the character quotient.* Denver, CO: Institute for the Advancement of the American Legal System. (These results are compiled from the "Explore the Data" feature on the IAALS website. The dataset is accessible at: http://iaals.du.edu/foundations/explore/all. The results are based on the responses of attorneys in private practice.)

[2] Ibid.

[3] Ibid.

expectations" also was rated above "seek opportunities for professional growth," "demonstrate leadership," and "work effectively on a team."[4] Attorneys' utilitarian approach to the practice of law is again reflected in their ranking of the abilities to "work autonomously" and be "confident" and "persuasive" above the ability to "objectively assess the soundness of a deal or a proposed solution" and the attributes of "prudence" and "a strong moral compass."

The IAALS survey indicates that many attorneys and their law firms place a higher priority on functionality than client service, loyalty, collegiality, value, and professional development. These findings are consistent with personality assessments of attorneys showing that they score relatively low in altruism, sociability, interpersonal sensitivity, and prudence.[5] The below-average score on altruism is particularly worrisome because it indicates that lawyers have a relatively low interest in "providing good customer service," and they "place more value on their own work than in helping others."[6] Although this self-centeredness could be advantageous in some endeavors, it is a major liability in a service profession.

If law firms are serious about client service and satisfaction, they will need to be more deliberate in their attorney selection processes and more committed to their talent development programs. If law firms also intend to build the requisite leadership skills in the next generations of attorneys, they need to start modeling, teaching, and supporting the desired skills now—before the imminent retirement of thousands of law firm leaders. Although law firms have been financially successful for decades, the trends described in Chapter 2 suggest that the current level of prosperity will be unsustainable unless law firms identify and develop an attorney skill set that is markedly different from the template presently used to select, evaluate, and promote attorneys.

To enhance client service and prioritize attorneys' problem-solving and interpersonal skills, this chapter examines six critical,

---

[4]   Ibid.
[5]   Foster, Jeff, Richard, Larry, Rohrer, Lisa, & Sirkin, Mark. (2010). *Understanding lawyers: The personality traits of successful practitioners.* Hildebrandt Baker Robbins.
[6]   Ibid.

presently neglected qualities. Law firms would benefit from incorporating these qualities into their attorney selection criteria and talent development programs:

- *Likeability*—the habit of instilling trust and projecting warmth to resolve conflicts, promote creative problem solving, and achieve shared goals
- *Humility*—the capacity to recognize the limitations of one's knowledge and skills and to seek advice and information from others before those limitations harm clients and colleagues
- *Engagement*—the ability to focus attention on client matters and direct one's skills to achieve client objectives, despite personal distractions and workplace impediments
- *Realism*—the discipline of seeing and responding to people, events, and conditions as they are instead of how we would like them to be
- *Openness*—a willingness to comprehend and respond to feedback and a receptiveness to new information and ideas
- *Resilience*—the ability to learn and recover from criticism, difficulties, changes, setbacks, and failures

This chapter discusses each of these qualities and concludes with an examination of the "dark traits"—those qualities that consistently degrade attorney performance and must be identified and avoided in hiring and promotion decisions.

Likeability

Being likeable ranks fairly low among many attorneys' priorities. About one in three attorneys thinks that sociability is not required for an attorney's success, and one in five attorneys asserts that retaining existing clients is not even relevant to an attorney's success.[7] Since a large percentage of attorneys believe that being friendly, agreeable, and affable is unimportant and that maintaining current client relationships is inconsequential, it's doubtful that

---

[7]   Gerkman & Cornett, *supra* note 1. This data is derived from the "Explore the Data" feature on the IAALS website at: http://iaals.du.edu/foundations/explore.

they will put much effort into being likeable. This is unfortunate for both attorneys and clients because their relationship is inescapably and invariably personal. The value of that relationship is dependent on the sense of trust, respect, and affinity that underpins likeability.

In the initial phase of an attorney–client relationship, likeability is more important than competence.[8] Although attorneys try to impress new clients with their competence, clients are seeking answers to three threshold questions: Can I trust you? Do you care about me? Are you committed to my success?[9] Because the ability to accurately assess a person's trustworthiness has been essential to human survival for many centuries, human brains evaluate trustworthiness rapidly and at an intuitive level.[10] That evaluation is largely determined by the client's perception of the attorney's personality and character, not the client's perception of the attorney's competence.[11] "Before people decide what they think of your message," states business administration professor Amy Cuddy, "they decide what they think of you."[12]

Likeability has two key components: trust and warmth. Management professor David Schoorman defines trust as "the willingness of a party to be vulnerable to the actions of another party based on the expectation that the other will perform a particular action important to the trustor, irrespective of the ability to monitor and control that other party."[13] This definition, with its emphasis on vulnerability,

8   Capps, Rob. (2012, November 20). First impressions: The science of meeting people. *Wired.* Cuddy, Amy J.C. (2009, February). Just because I'm nice, don't assume I'm dumb. *Harvard Business Review.* Cuddy, Amy J. C., Kohut, Matthew, & Neffinger, John. (2013, July–August). Connect, then lead. *Harvard Business Review.*

9   Cuddy (2009), *supra* note 8. Kelley, Tom. (2001). *The art of innovation* (p. 85). New York: Doubleday.

10 Williams, Lawrence E., & Bargh, John A. (2008, October 24). Experiencing physical warmth promotes interpersonal warmth. *Science, 322*(5901), 606. Cuddy, Kohut, & Neffinger (2013), *supra* note 8.

11 Balachandra, Lakshmi. (2011, August 2). Pitching trustworthiness: Cues for trust in early-stage investment decision-making. Doctoral dissertation, Carroll School of Management, Boston College. (2017, May–June). How venture capitalists really assess a pitch. *Harvard Business Review.* Cuddy, Kohut, & Neffinger (2013), *supra* note 8.

12 Cuddy, Kohut, & Neffinger (2013), *supra* note 8.

13 Mayer, Roger C., Davis, James H., & Schoorman, F. David. (1995, July). An integrative model of organizational trust. *The Academy of Management Review, 20*(3), 709, 712.

expectations, and one party's inability to supervise and direct another party's actions, epitomizes the attorney–client relationship. The second element of likeability (warmth) is considered "the most powerful personality trait in social judgment."[14] It is defined as being concerned, caring, generous, friendly, and helpful—the qualities necessary to determine another person's intentions.[15]

Being trustworthy and projecting warmth are not optional accessories in the attorney–client relationship. Although many attorneys prefer to take a clinical approach to their clients—examining, probing, and circumflexing clients' legal matters with the utmost detachment—they will not establish enduring, profitable relationships with their clients unless they meet the threshold requirement of likeability. Clients do not trust attorneys they do not like, and they do not like attorneys they do not trust. They also do not like attorneys they perceive to be cold—indifferent to clients' needs, unconcerned about their well-being, and seemingly devoid of empathy. If compelled to work with an attorney who is competent but disliked, clients will exhibit a high level of resentment and antipathy.[16]

Those attorneys who can instill and maintain a sense of trust and warmth in their client relationships have more influence on client behavior, are more effective in persuading people to accept their ideas, achieve better financial results, and are more likely to attain leadership positions.[17] Cuddy describes the importance of warmth and how it affects perceptions of trust:

A growing body of research suggests that the way to influence—and to lead—is to begin with warmth. Warmth is the conduit

---

14 Williams & Bargh, *supra* note 10.
15 Ibid. See Bayes, M. A. (1972). Behavioral cues of interpersonal warmth. *Journal of Consulting and Clinical Psychology, 39*(2), 333–339.
16 Cuddy, Kohut, & Neffinger (2013), *supra* note 8. Capps, *supra* note 8.
17 Meier, Michael. (2017, April 10). Why warmth is the underappreciated skill leaders need. *Kellogg Insight*. Shellenbarger, Sue. (2014, March 25). Why likability matters more at work. *The Wall Street Journal*. Zenger, Jack, & Folkman, Joseph. (2013, March 2). I'm the boss! Why should I care if you like me? *Harvard Business Review*. Hirschman, Karen L., & Greeley, Ann T. (2009). Trial teams and the power of diversity. *Litigation, 35*(3). 3. Cuddy, Kohut, & Neffinger (2013), *supra* note 8.

of influence: It facilitates trust and the communication and absorption of ideas. Even a few small nonverbal signals—a nod, a smile, an open gesture—can show people that you're pleased to be in their company and attentive to their concerns. Prioritizing warmth helps you connect immediately with those around you, demonstrating that you hear them, understand them, and can be trusted by them.[18]

Cuddy finds that people often overlook the importance of showing that they are trustworthy before demonstrating how competent they are. "We're sure of our own intentions," she notes, "and thus don't feel the need to prove that we're trustworthy—despite the fact that evidence of trustworthiness is the first thing we look for in others."[19]

Humility

Projecting confidence, taking initiative, and being decisive are highly prized attributes in attorneys. Ninety-four percent of attorneys report that those attributes are required for an attorney's success.[20] The more deliberative attributes of prudence, patience, and humility are ranked significantly below the "action hero" attributes of confidence, initiative, and decisiveness.[21] These priorities are consistent with a society that values doing over thinking, telling over asking, and presuming over inquiring.[22]

These priorities also are consistent with leadership archetypes that highlight extroversion, certainty, and positiveness.[23] A Harvard Business School student, for instance, recalls being advised, "Speak

---

[18]   Cuddy, Kohut, & Neffinger (2013), *supra* note 8.
[19]   Ibid.
[20]   Gerkman & Cornett, *supra* note 1 (based on the percentage of attorneys stating that the quality is necessary in the short term or must be acquired over time).
[21]   Ibid.
[22]   Schein, Edgar H. (2013). *Humble inquiry*. San Francisco: Berrett-Koehler Publishers.
[23]   See Brown, Heidi K. (2017). *The introverted lawyer*. Chicago: American Bar Association.

with conviction. Even if you believe something only fifty-five percent, say it as if you believe it a hundred percent."[24] Another student remembers the admonition, "Don't think about the perfect
answers. It's better to get out there and say something than to never
get your voice in."[25] This emphasis on extroversion is supported by
studies showing that outgoing people are more popular than withdrawn people; and that people who are evasive but speak eloquently
are more trusted than people who are honest but ineloquent.[26] In
American society, people prefer confident, articulate overtalkers,
and they're uneasy with restrained, contemplative introverts.[27]
Those societal preferences are replicated and frequently amplified
in law firm hiring and partner promotion decisions.[28]

Ignored in the national admiration and promotion of highly
confident, decisive people is the extensive research showing they
are not particularly good decision makers.[29] As Nobel laureate
Daniel Kahneman explains, "Subjective confidence in a judgment

---

[24] Cain, Susan. (2012). *Quiet* (p. 47). New York: Broadway Books. See Broughton,
Philip Delves. (2009). *Ahead of the curve: Two years at Harvard Business School.*
New York: Penguin Books.

[25] Ibid.

[26] Rogers, Todd, & Norton, Michael I. (2010, November). Defend your research:
People often trust eloquence more than honesty. *Harvard Business Review.*
Fiske, Susan T. (2009). *Social beings: Core motives in social psychology* (p. 155).
Hoboken, NJ: John Wiley & Sons.

[27] See Brown, *supra* note 23. Cain, *supra* note 24.

[28] Brown, Heidi. (2018, August). Talented but overlooked: We should transform
hiring and mentoring of introverted lawyers. *ABA Journal.*

[29] See Fischhoff, Baruch. (1982). Debiasing. In Kahneman, Daniel, Slovic, Paul,
& Tversky, Amos (Eds.). *Judgment under uncertainty: Heuristics and biases*
(p. 440). Cambridge: The Press Syndicate of the University of Cambridge.
Goodman-Delahunty, Jane, Granhag, Par Anders, Hartwig, Maria, & Loftus,
Elizabeth. (2010). Insightful or wishful: Lawyers' ability to predict case out-
comes. *Psychology, Public Policy, and Law, 16*(2), 147. Kahneman, Daniel,
& Tversky, Amos. (1995). Conflict resolution: A cognitive perspective. In
Kahneman, Daniel, & Tversky, Amos (Eds.). (2000). *Choices, values, and frames*
(p. 474). Cambridge: The Press Syndicate of the University of Cambridge. Plous,
Scott. (1993). *The psychology of judgment and decision making* (p. 71). New York:
McGraw-Hill. Sternlight, Jean R., & Robbennolt, Jennifer. (2008). Good lawyers
should be good psychologists: Insights for interviewing and counseling clients.
Ohio State Journal on Dispute Resolution, 23, 437, 485, fn. 188. ("Research has
demonstrated a generally weak correlation between confidence and accuracy,
although the relationship can be stronger under some circumstances.")

is not a reasoned evaluation of the probability that this judgment is correct. Confidence is a feeling, which reflects the coherence of the information and the cognitive ease of processing it."[30] When someone projects confidence, Kahneman cautions, it tells you that "an individual has constructed a coherent story in his mind, not necessarily that the story is true."[31] The high frequency of decision-making errors made by confident people is reflected in the adages, "strong but wrong" and "often in error, never in doubt."[32] Poorly performing law firm leaders often fit this profile of confident but mistaken decision makers. Law firm consultant Patrick McKenna notes, "what is most distinctive about these leaders is their self-assurance which often gives them a certain presence— they are the first to speak in a group, and they do with great confidence . . . even when they are wrong."[33]

Being a quick and confident decision maker appears to be detrimental in solving complex problems, the type of problems that comprise the vast majority of legal matters. Management professor James March observes a tension between knowledge and action in decision making. He finds that more knowledge makes decision making more difficult because it "increases questions at a faster rate than it increases answers."[34] As a consequence, March states, "decisive actions come more readily from the ignorant than from the wise, more easily from the short-sighted than from those who anticipate the long run."[35] For quick, decisive people, speed and

---

[30]   Kahneman, Daniel. (2011). *Thinking fast and slow* (p. 212). New York: Farrar, Straus, & Giroux.

[31]   Ibid.

[32]   Kiser, Randall. (2010). *Beyond right and wrong: The power of effective decision making for attorneys and clients* (p. 292). Berlin, Heidelberg: Springer.

[33]   McKenna, Patrick J. (2010). Where leaders stumble. See Schragle-Law, Susan, Samii, Massood, & Sharma, Nidhi. (2007). Leadership style of Indian managers: A comparative analysis. Paper presented at the Dynamics of Globalization Conference, Academy of International Business Northeast U.S. Annual Conference, October 18–20, 2007, at Portsmouth, New Hampshire. ("Humility is not a common attribute of American leadership but can be found more frequently in Indian companies.")

[34]   March, James G. (1994). *A primer on decision making* (p. 265). New York: The Free Press.

[35]   Ibid.

cognitive closure are more important than being informed, accurate, and perspicacious.[36]

Dietrich Dorner, a psychology professor and recipient of the prestigious Gottfried Wilhelm Leibniz Prize, is an expert on complex decision making. His research focuses on decisions characterized by intransparency, incorrect and incomplete information, mistaken assumptions, competing objectives, inaccurate predictions, ongoing changes in behavior and circumstances, and opaque, complicated interactions among actors and conditions—challenges similar to those attorneys encounter every day.[37] In a simulation of complex decision making, Dorner detected an inverse relationship between action and inquiry and decisiveness and information gathering:

> [T]he bad participants [whose decisions resulted in lower profits] made significantly more decisions . . . than did the good participants [whose decisions resulted in higher profits] . . . the bad participants asked significantly fewer questions than did the good ones. In short, the bad participants displayed . . . a reluctance to gather information and an eagerness to act. By contrast, the good participants were initially cautious about acting and tried to secure a solid base of information. What we plainly see here, then, is an inverse relationship between information gathering and readiness to act. The less information gathered, the greater the readiness to act. And vice versa.[38]

In this simulation, the participants who displayed prudence, patience, and reticence achieved superior results, despite the

---

36   See De Dreu, Carsten K. W. (2003). Time pressure and closing of the mind in negotiation. *Organizational Behavior and Human Decision Processes, 91*(2), 280–295. Partnoy, Frank. (2012). *Wait: The art and science of delay.* New York: PublicAffairs. Sullivan, Paul. (2012). *Clutch.* New York: Portfolio.

37   Dorner, Dietrich. (1996). *The logic of failure* (pp. 37–47). New York: Metropolitan Books.

38   Ibid. at 101.

conventional wisdom that good decision makers are confident, bold, and expeditious. Dorner's analysis indicates that the contemporary emphasis on confidence and decisiveness may be misplaced since those attributes are correlated with inadequate decision-making processes and adverse outcomes.[39]

The critical quality missing in lawyers' emphasis on confidence, initiative, and decisiveness is humility. Although humility may appear to be antithetical to effective attorney behavior, it actually is an essential feature of good judgment and effective performance. Humble people, for instance, are more objective in evaluating their own performance, more receptive to feedback, and more likely to acknowledge their mistakes.[40] William Bablitch, a former Wisconsin Supreme Court Justice, describes humility as "an awareness of what we do not know, and awareness that what we think we know might well be incorrect."[41] He regards humility as a particularly important quality in the practice of law because "the law has a funny way of jumping up and biting you right where it hurts at the most unexpected times."[42] If attorneys and their law firms start to value humility as much as they value confidence, they might begin to anticipate and prevent a few of those bites.

Engagement

In early 2018, Gallup, Inc. released the results of its first study of attorney engagement. That study shows that most attorneys are not engaged in their work.[43] Forty-nine percent of the surveyed attorneys state that they are "not engaged," and an additional eight

---

[39] Psychology professor Tomas Chamorro-Premuzic states, "There is no bigger cliché in business psychology than the idea that high self-confidence is key to career success. It is time to debunk this myth. In fact, *low* self-confidence is more likely to make you successful." Chamorro-Premuzic, Tomas. (2012, July 6). Less-confident people are more successful. *Harvard Business Review.*

[40] Rhode, Deborah L. (2013). *Lawyers as leaders* (p. 12). New York: Oxford University Press. Chamorro-Premuzic, *supra* note 39.

[41] Brown, Heidi, *supra* note 23 at 40.

[42] Ibid. at 40–41.

[43] Gallup & AccessLex Institute. (2018). *Examining value, measuring engagement* (p. 15).

percent consider themselves to be "actively disengaged."[44] Only 43 percent of attorneys consider themselves to be engaged.[45]

Gallup's engagement surveys measure considerably more than individual job satisfaction and have become strong indicators of general company performance. The surveys assess 12 elements of engagement, including workplace opportunities, expectations, interactions, recognition, mission, purpose, and training.[46] As Gallup explains, "engagement is more than job satisfaction. It encompasses employees being intellectually and emotionally connected to their organizations and work teams because when they are at work, they can do what they do best, they like what they do and they have someone who cares about their development."[47]

During the last 30 years, Gallup has refined and tested the 12 engagement elements and has determined that they are reliably correlated with company sales and profitability; customer loyalty; employee turnover, absenteeism, and productivity; and product quality.[48] The correlation between engagement and company performance indicates that law firms with low engagement levels will experience poor client retention rates, low attorney productivity, decreased income and profitability, and inferior work product quality. Increasing attorney engagement, therefore, is an urgent,

---

[44] Ibid. "Disengaged" means those who "are not emotionally connected to their workplaces and are less likely to put in discretionary effort." "Actively disengaged" means those who "are emotionally disconnected from their work and workplace and jeopardize their teams' performance." Gallup. What is Gallup's Employee Engagement Index, and what does it measure? Actively disengaged employees "are unhappy and unproductive at work and liable to spread negativity to coworkers." Crabtree, Steve. (2013, October 8). Worldwide, 13% of employees are engaged at work.

[45] Gallup & AccessLex Institute, *supra* note 43 at 15.

[46] Gallup. (2009, August). *Q12 Meta-analysis: The relationship between engagement at work and organizational outcomes.*

[47] Gallup & AccessLex Institute, *supra* note 43 at 15.

[48] Gallup, *supra* note 46. See Burger, Jeff, & Giger, Andrew. (2014, June 5). Want to increase hospital revenues? Engage your physicians. ("Physicians who were fully engaged or engaged were 26% more productive than physicians who were not engaged or who were actively disengaged. This increase equates to an average of $460,000 in patient revenue per physician per year." Gallup also found that engaged physicians gave the hospital an average of "51% more inpatient referrals than physicians who were not engaged or who were actively disengaged.")

firm-wide responsibility with serious consequences ranging from revenue declines to attorney attrition.

Although the attorney engagement levels are consistent with those of other advanced degree holders and other business organizations, they fall short of the 70 percent engagement level achieved in outstanding organizations like Hyatt, USAA, Adventist Health System, Nationwide Insurance, and PNC Bank.[49] The outstanding organizations also have very few actively disengaged employees. For every 14 engaged employees, the outstanding organizations have only one "actively disengaged" employee.[50] The ratio among the surveyed attorneys is significantly bleaker; for every five engaged attorneys, there is one actively disengaged attorney.

It might be tempting to dismiss attorneys' low engagement levels as being consistent with those of average companies. That approach is mistaken for at least three reasons: (1) unlike employees in average companies, attorneys have fiduciary duties to their clients; (2) unlike employees in average companies, attorneys are required to comply with rules of professional conduct imposing duties of competence, diligence, promptness, and attentiveness; and (3) unlike average companies, midsize and large law firms have the financial resources to recruit, select, and develop highly engaged employees. Considering their sophistication, resources, and the complexity of their services, law firms should display engagement levels similar to or better than those of the outstanding companies with 70 percent engagement levels. This would require law firms to boost the current engagement level by about 60 percent.

---

[49] Gallup & AccessLex Institute, *supra* note 43. Gallup. (2017). *State of the American workplace* (p. 71). The attorneys' engagement levels also are slightly below those of recent Gallup clients. In 2017, the companies that had received the Gallup Great Workplace Awards for five years or more were ABC Supply Co., Inc., Adventist Health System, Bon Secours Health System, Compassion International, DTE Energy, Hawaii Pacific Health, Hendrick Health System, Hyatt Corporation, Mars Inc., Nationwide Insurance, PNC Bank, Self Regional Healthcare, Stryker Corporation, Taj Hotels Resorts and Palaces, and Winegardner & Hammons Hotel Group. Gallup. (2017). Current and previous Gallup Great Workplace Award winners.

[50] Gallup (2017), *supra* note 49 at 71, 73.

Law school graduates, when compared with other advanced degree holders, also score remarkably low on four of Gallup's five measures of well-being:[51]

- *Purpose well-being*—"liking what you do each day and being motivated to achieve your goals." Forty-six percent of law school graduates were "struggling" or "suffering" in their efforts to enjoy their work and feel motivated.
- *Social well-being*—"having strong and supportive relationships and love in your life." Forty-five percent of law school graduates were "struggling" or "suffering" in trying to establish and maintain fulfilling, supportive personal relationships.
- *Financial well-being*—"managing your economic life to reduce stress and increase security." Most law school graduates (52 percent) were "struggling" or "suffering" in handling the stress caused by their financial affairs and trying to improve their financial condition.
- *Physical well-being*—"having good health and enough energy to get things done daily." Sixty-five percent of law school graduates were "struggling" or "suffering" to maintain their health to perform their daily activities.

Law school graduates score higher than other graduate degree holders in a single category: community well-being, which is defined as "liking where you live, feeling safe and having pride in your community."[52] Overall, Gallup reports, only 13 percent of law school graduates "are thriving in all five elements—purpose, social, financial, community, and physical. This matches the percentage among those with a bachelor's degree only, though it falls short of the 17 percent among those with another type of advanced degree."[53]

Attorneys' low engagement levels and low scores on four well-being measures are a profession-wide threat to clients, and they represent a failure of law firm leadership and talent development

---

[51] Data and definitions in the bulleted points are derived from Gallup & Access-Lex Institute, *supra* note 43 at 17–18.
[52] Ibid.
[53] Ibid. at 17.

practices. They also pose a risk to long-term law firm profitability and growth. When only 43 percent of attorneys are engaged in their work, clients are being charged for unfocused, inefficient work and are bearing the consequences of inattentive, sloppy lawyering. Attorneys who feel compelled to meet minimum billable requirements, while being distracted, bored, and uninterested in their client matters, do not provide value commensurate with their hourly rates or service consistent with the ethical duties of competence and diligence.

Realism

A popular perception of attorneys is that they are tough, objective thinkers and decision makers. They are trained in law school, according to popular perception, to become detached, hardnosed evaluators and to analyze and apply legal principles rigorously and dispassionately. Consistent with those perceptions, the public regards attorneys as "high-competence, low-warmth" professionals.[54]

Personality assessments of attorneys, however, present a different view of their thought processes. Those assessments show that attorneys score high in "abstract reasoning"—the ability to conceptualize complex problems and the potential to solve them.[55] People who score low on abstract thinking "tend to be more concrete in their thinking" and "prefer to deal with more tangible or practical problems."[56] Attorneys also display a strong preference for an "intuitive" style of thinking over a "sensing" style.[57] This means that they are conceptual and theoretical; they focus on "big picture" possibilities, look for patterns in facts, and "are more comfortable paying

---

[54] Fiske, Susan, & Dupree, Cydney. (2014, September 16). Gaining trust as well as respect in communicating to motivated audiences about science topics. *Proceedings of the National Academy of Sciences, 111*(4), 13595.

[55] Richard, Larry. (2002). Herding cats: The lawyer personality revealed. *Report to Legal Management. 29*(11), 1. Corporate counsel, when tested separately, also score high on abstract reasoning. Hartmann, Markus, Mordan, Bill, Schoenfelder, Thomas E., & Sweeney, Patrick. (2011, July/August). The perfect legal personality. *ACC Docket*, pp. 29–42.

[56] Caliper. Caliper profile user's guide.

[57] Richard, Larry. (1993, July). The lawyer types. *ABA Journal*, p. 76.

attention to the abstract impressions they perceive."[58] People who prefer a "sensing" style to an intuitive style emphasize facts and data and value testable, practical applications.[59]

Attorneys' preference for abstract reasoning and intuitive thought processes strongly affects how they perceive and attempt to solve problems and how they relate to colleagues and adversaries. Law students whose personality assessments show a typical intuitive preference, for instance, tend to rely on theories and arguments, ignore or minimize facts and data, and ask fewer questions than students with a sensing style.[60] In reviewing their behavior following a negotiation exercise, the law students with intuitive styles disclose a host of errors that highlight the shortcomings of their intuitive thinking:

- "The mistake was made because I had already been thinking about my arguments before I actually attempted to understand the facts. Therefore, when I actually went to the facts I was looking at them in light of how they could support my arguments."[61]
- "I did too much interpreting or, rather, reading 'between the lines.' In effect I let my imagination get the best of me. . . ."[62]
- "I always tended to dive into a situation before considering all of the possible facts. I would take the information that I knew and apply it to the exclusion of other sources of information. It was never a conscious decision on my part."[63]
- "Hell, I'm the worst numbers person there is. . . . Give me some abstract solutions, then I'll be on Cloud Nine. We can hash out the details later."[64]

---

[58] Ibid. Myers, Isabel Briggs. (1993). *Introduction to type* (5th ed.) (p. 7). Palo Alto, CA: Consulting Psychologists Press.

[59] Ibid.

[60] Peters, Don. (1993). Forever Jung: Psychological type theory, the Myers-Briggs Type Indicator and learning negotiation. *Drake Law Review, 42*(1), 1–121.

[61] Ibid. at 48.

[62] Ibid.

[63] Ibid.

[64] Ibid. at 49.

The law students with an intuitive style overlooked important factual details, made arguments contradicted by uncontested facts, reached conclusions based on incomplete information, forgot their client names, and miscalculated their own scores.[65]

Since most attorneys prefer abstract reasoning and display an intuitive style, they may not thoroughly evaluate their clients' positions and may develop excessively optimistic predictions about likely outcomes. Studies of attorneys' litigation case assessments and predictions about pending matters, for example, demonstrate a consistent pattern of optimistic overconfidence.[66] Despite the popular perception of attorneys as doggedly pursuing facts and providing tough, unvarnished advice, they frequently succumb to motivated reasoning, egocentrism, confirmation bias, and other cognitive illusions and biases.[67]

Attorneys' lack of realism generally assumes eight forms in client matters: (1) defining a problem incompletely by focusing on the most vivid or easily observed factors;[68] (2) ignoring complexity and simplifying analysis by dividing legal problems into discrete practice areas;[69] (3) focusing on the aspect of a legal problem that is familiar and squarely within an attorney's area of expertise while minimizing other aspects;[70] (4) relying on superficially analogous

---

[65]   Ibid. at 38–51.

[66]   Goodman-Delahunty, Granhag, Hartwig, & Loftus, *supra* note 29. Gross, Samuel, & Syverud, Kent. (1991). Getting to no: A study of settlement negotiations and the selection of cases for trial. *Michigan Law Review, 90,* 319. Gross, Samuel, & Syverud, Kent. (1996). Don't try: Civil jury verdicts in a system geared to settlement. *UCLA Law Review, 44,* 1, 42–43. Kiser, Randall, Asher, Martin, & McShane, Blakeley. (2008). Let's not make a deal: An empirical study of decision making in unsuccessful settlement negotiations. *Journal of Empirical Legal Studies, 5*(3), 551–591. Kiser, Randall. (2010). *Beyond right and wrong: The power of effective decision making for attorneys and clients* (pp. 42–46). New York: Springer. Rachlinski, Jeffrey. (1996). Gains, losses and the psychology of litigation. *Southern California Law Review, 70,* 113.

[67]   See Haidt, Jonathan. *The righteous mind* (p. 94). New York: Random House.

[68]   Hallinan, Joseph T. (2009). *Why we make mistakes* (p. 208). New York: Broadway Books.

[69]   See Kronman, Anthony. (1993). *The lost lawyer* (pp. 275–276). Cambridge, MA: Belknap Press.

[70]   See Cullen, Robert. (2010). *The leading lawyer* (p. 1). St. Paul, MN: West. Cullen quotes Ben Heineman Jr., the former general counsel for General Electric:

cases and prior practice experiences while failing to detect factual distinctions and nuances in new matters;[71] (5) providing advice that is consistent with what the client wants to believe or what other attorneys in the firm have already conveyed to the client;[72] (6) depicting a range of possible actions and consequences rather than determining likely actions and consequences;[73] (7) responding to difficult client questions by answering easier but related questions;[74] and (8) disregarding or misinterpreting subsequent developments so that prior advice, positions, and strategies appear to be correct, adequate, and foresightful.[75]

These eight deficiencies reflect a lack of realism, facilitated by abstract reasoning and intuitive thinking. Lawyers and law firms committed to serving their clients in the long term will need to recognize and mitigate the hazards in these cognitive styles. They will have to shift their attention from concepts to facts, from theories to practicalities, and from possibilities to probabilities as they attempt to develop accurate assessments, predictions, and recommendations. Both attorneys and their clients will need to experience what Jim Collins calls "an honest confrontation of the brutal facts."[76]

"Lawyers are taught to be very powerful analytically, but they are not always taught to ask large questions and to understand what tools are necessary to answer those questions."

[71] See Pollack, John. (2014). *Shortcuts*. New York: Gotham Books. ("No matter how seductive an analogy may be, be sure to examine several others before deciding which one might be most useful.")

[72] See, Kiser, Randall. (2011). *How leading lawyers think: Expert insights into judgment and advocacy* (pp. 32–33, 152–154). Heidelberg, New York: Springer.

[73] See Herrmann, Mark. (2013, July 1). What outside counsel don't understand. *Above the Law*.

[74] Kahneman, Daniel. (2007). A short course in thinking about thinking. Edge Master Class 2007. Ben-Shahar, Omri, & Schneider, Carl. E. (2010, June 7). Disclosed to death. *Forbes*. ("When you look at the way people make decisions, even very skilled people, it isn't by gathering huge amounts of information and then trying to analyze it. Instead, they tackle complicated decisions by reducing their focus to a few easy-to-understand factors.")

[75] See Kiser (2011), *supra* note 72 at 237, 238.

[76] Collins, Jim. (2001). *Good to great* (p. 88). New York: HarperCollins.

Openness

The "Big Five" personality traits are extraversion, agreeableness, conscientiousness, neuroticism, and openness.[77] Psychological research beginning in the 1960s indicates that these are the core personality traits, although many psychologists now argue that a sixth trait (humility–honesty) should be added to assess moral and ethical factors such as deceit, insincerity, and exploitation.[78]

This section focuses on openness, a trait defined as "a willingness to consider new ideas and try new things" and "the recurrent need to enlarge and examine experience."[79] Open people have a wide range of interests and "easily make more remote and creative connections between ideas."[80] Closed people, in contrast, are "more set in their ways and prefer familiarity to learning new things."[81] Openness is correlated with intelligence, divergent

---

[77] John, O. P., Naumann, L. P., & Soto, C. J. (2008). Paradigm shift to the integrative Big-Five trait taxonomy: History, measurement, and conceptual issues. In John, O. P., Robins, R. W., & Pervin, L. A. (Eds.). *Handbook of personality: Theory and research* (pp. 114–158). New York: The Guilford Press. See Allen, Timothy A., & DeYoung, Colin G. Personality, neuroscience and the Five Factor Model. In Widiger, Thomas A. (Ed.). (2017). *Oxford handbook of the Five Factor Model* (p. 319). New York: Oxford University Press.

[78] See Bono, J. E., & Judge, T. A. (2004). Personality and transformational and transactional leadership: A meta-analysis. *Journal of Applied Psychology, 89,* 901–910. Lee, Kibeom, & Ashton, Michael C. (2012). *The H factor of personality. Assessment.* Waterloo, Ontario: Wilfrid Laurier University Press. Thielmann, I., Hilbig, B. E., Zettler, I., & Moshagen, M. (2017, December 24). On measuring the sixth basic personality dimension: A comparison between HEXACO honesty-humility and Big Six honesty–propriety. Woodley, H. J., Bourdage, J. S., Ogunfowora, B., & Nguyen, B. (2016, January 8). Examining equity sensitivity: An investigation using the Big Five and HEXACO models of personality *Frontiers in Psychology, 6,* 2000.

[79] McCrae, Robert R., & Costa, Paul. Conceptions and correlates of openness to experience. In Hogan, Robert, Johnson, John, & Briggs, Stephen (Eds.). (1997). *Handbook of Personality Psychology* (pp. 825–847). London: Academic Press. Camps, Jeroen, Stouten, Jeroen, & Euwema, Martin. (2016, February 10). The relation between supervisors' Big Five personality traits and employees' experiences of abusive supervision. *Frontiers in Psychology, 7,* 112. Costa, P. T., Jr., & McCrae, R. R. (1992). *Revised NEO Personality Inventory (NEO-PI-R) and NEO Five-Factor (NEO-FFI) Inventory professional manual.* Odessa, FL: Psychological Assessment Resources.

[80] Sutin, Angelina R. (2017). Openness. In Widiger, Thomas E., *supra* note 77 at 86.

[81] Ibid.

thinking, tolerance for ambiguity, creativity, ingenuity, introspection, and resourcefulness—all traits that could contribute to effective problem solving for clients.[82]

Openness is not a trait generally associated with attorneys. They, in fact, score lower than a comparison group of managers and other professionals in inquisitiveness ("the degree to which a person seems imaginative, adventurous, and analytical") and imagination (the tendency "to think and act in interesting, unusual, or even eccentric ways").[83] They also score low in idea orientation ("thinking creatively and generating new ways to solve problems") and flexibility (willingness to modify one's approach "as changing conditions or circumstances require").[84] Earlier studies of attorney personality show that they "prefer work involving structure, schedules, closure on decisions, planning, follow through, and a 'cut to the chase' approach."[85]

Attorneys' lack of openness manifests as a resistance to eliciting new information; a reluctance to reconsider facts, methods, and opinions; and, for some attorneys, a lifelong opposition to developing a broader, more proficient skill set. The dangers posed by this lack of openness are obscured and normalized by the legal profession's inclination to elevate argument, skepticism, and criticism to a fine art. As law firm consultant David Maister points out, attorneys are "professional skeptics," trained to "find counterexamples of or

---

[82]   Schretlen, David J., van der Hulst, Egberdina-Józefa, Pearlson, Godfrey D., & Gordon, Barry. (2010) A neuropsychological study of personality: Trait openness in relation to intelligence, fluency, and executive functioning, *Journal of Clinical and Experimental Neuropsychology*, 32(10), 1068–1073. Sutin, *supra* note 80. Costa & McCrae, *supra* note 79.

[83]   Foster, Richard, Rohrer, & Sirkin, *supra* note 5. The attorneys, however, scored higher in Learning Approach ("The degree to which a person enjoys academic activities and values education as an end in itself") than the comparison sample.

[84]   Hartman, Mordan, Schoenfelder & Sweeney, *supra* note 55.

[85]   Daicoff, Susan. (1997). Lawyer know thyself: A review of empirical research on attorney attributes bearing on professionalism. *The American University Law Review*, 46, 1337, 1394. For an illuminating study of how the need for cognitive closure affects law students' evaluations of a case and its likely outcome, see Stark, James H., & Milyavsky, Maxim. (2018). Towards a better understanding of lawyers' judgmental biases in client representation: The role of need for cognitive closure. Manuscript submitted for publication.

exceptions to any proposition."[86] For attorneys, contesting, criticizing, and prevailing in arguments "is a deadly serious business—a challenge to their core ability."[87] The risk of perpetual criticism is that attorneys may develop a form of "skilled incompetence," a highly specialized, counterproductive way of relating that is acceptable among colleagues but incapable of producing constructive results for law firms and their clients.[88] Attorneys engage in skilled incompetence because it is a defensive routine that gives them a feeling of safety, even though it prevents them from properly managing their firms and effectively serving their clients.[89]

Charles Munger, a founder of Munger, Tolles & Olson and the vice-chairman of the highly successful holding company Berkshire Hathaway, has deliberately avoided the lack of openness that characterizes many attorneys' thinking. He describes how his openness and willingness to learn have affected his life:

> I constantly see people rise in life who are not the smartest, sometimes not even the most diligent, but they are learning machines. They go to bed every night a little wiser than they were when they got up, and boy, does that help, particularly when you have a long run ahead of you. . . . Nothing has served me better in my long life than continuously learning. I went through life constantly practicing (because if you don't practice it, you lose it)

---

[86]   Maister, David. (2006, April). Are law firms manageable? *The American Lawyer*.

[87]   Ibid.

[88]   Chris Argyris first used the term "skilled incompetence." See Argyris, Chris. (1986, September). Skilled incompetence. *Harvard Business Review*. Argyris, Chris. (1993, October). Beware of skilled incompetence. *R&D Innovator*, 2, 10. For a brief discussion of the correlation between active open-mindedness and favorable decision-making results, see Baron, Jonathan. (2000). *Thinking and deciding* (3rd ed.) (pp. 203–204). New York: Cambridge: Cambridge University Press.

[89]   Argyris (1986), *supra* note 88. See Ericsson, K. Anders. The acquisition of expert performance as problem solving. In Davidson, Janet E., & Sternberg, Robert J. (2003). *The psychology of problem solving* (p. 63). Cambridge: The Press Syndicate of the University of Cambridge. ("One of the most crucial challenges for aspiring expert performers is to avoid the arrested development associated with generalized automaticity of performance and to acquire cognitive skills to support continued learning and improvement.")

the multi-disciplinary approach, and I can't tell you what that's done for me. It's made life more fun, it's made me more constructive, it's made me more helpful to others, and it's made me enormously rich. You name it, that attitude really helps.[90]

Munger attributes much of his success to thinking differently from his peers. "I tried to do something," he says, "about this terrible ignorance I left the Harvard Law School with."[91]

Resilience

Resilience—a term associated with "grit," "tenacity," and "adaptability"—is the ability to learn and recover from criticism, difficulties, changes, setbacks, and failures.[92] Resilient people generally have three key qualities: they are brutally realistic; they motivate themselves with an overarching sense of meaning; and they adapt to challenges by improvising.[93] Research regarding resilience indicates that "you can bounce back from hardship with just one or two of these qualities, but you will only be truly resilient with all three."[94] Resilience is tested and displayed in a variety of personal and professional circumstances, including handling crises; dealing with stress; solving problems creatively; adapting to unpredictable work challenges; learning new tasks, technologies, and procedures; changing behavior to respond to different types of people; and being aware of and reacting appropriately to different cultures.[95]

---

[90] Griffin, Tren. (2015). *Charlie Munger: The complete investor* (p. 49). New York: Columbia University Press.

[91] Charlie Munger on the psychology of human misjudgment. (1995). (Speech at Harvard University).

[92] See Ovans, Andrea. (2015, January 5). What resilience means, and why it matters. *Harvard Business Review*.

[93] Coutu, Diane. (2002, May). How resilience works. *Harvard Business Review*. See Southwick, Steven, & Charney, Dennis. (2012). *Resilience* (p. 7). New York: Cambridge University Press. Gonzales, Laurence. (2003). *Deep survival: Who lives, who dies and why* (p. 25). New York: W. W. Norton.

[94] Coutu, *supra* note 93.

[95] Shadrick, Scott B., & Lussier, James W. Training complex cognitive skills: A theme-based approach to the development of battlefield skills. In Ericsson,

Attorneys generally lack resilience. Nearly all attorneys in private practice and corporate legal departments score below average in resilience, as psychologist/attorney Larry Richard reports:

People who are low on Resilience tend to be defensive, resist taking in feedback, and can be hypersensitive to criticism. In the hundreds of cases we've gathered, nearly all of the lawyers we've profiled (90% of them) score in the lower half of this trait, with the average being 30%. The range is quite wide, with quite a number of lawyers scoring in the bottom tenth percentile.

What does this tell us? Despite the outward confidence and even boldness that characterizes most lawyers, we may be a bit more sensitive under the surface. These lower scores suggest a self-protective quality.[96]

Attorneys' lack of resilience is evident in most practice settings. Attorneys in large law firms score high on security (the need for "certainty, predictability, and risk-free environments") and cautiousness (the tendency "to be overly worried about making mistakes and criticism"). They score low on adjustment ("the degree to which a person is steady in the face of pressure").[97] Even the most successful attorneys show a lack of resilience. Attorneys who advance to partner in less than eight years, for example, "have a hard time seeing the upside of a difficult situation, are apprehensive about challenging situations, and often find it difficult to bounce back after setbacks."[98] These exceptionally successful attorneys are more likely to feel apprehensive when faced with challenging situations than their colleagues who advance to partnership in nine or ten years.[99]

K. Anders. (2009). *Development of professional expertise* (p. 287). New York: Cambridge University Press.

[96] Richard, Larry. (2008). Herding cats: The lawyer personality revealed. *LAW-PRO*, 7(1), 2–5.

[97] Foster, Richard, Rohrer, & Sirkin, *supra* note 5.

[98] Berman, Lori, Bock, Heather, & Aiken, Juliet. (2016). *Accelerating lawyer success* (p. 18). Chicago: American Bar Association.

[99] Ibid.

Corporate counsel also score considerably below average in resilience, ego strength, and flexibility.[100] These scores indicate that corporate counsel may not "handle rejection and accept criticism in a manner that is positive and growth-oriented," and they may not be willing to "modify their approach as changing conditions or circumstances require."[101]

The attorneys most successful in attracting clients do not fit the usual attorney profile. They are resilient and display high ego strength. Richard's studies of rainmaker partners indicate that they have higher levels of resilience, empathy, and ego drive than service partners.[102] The rainmaker partners also score relatively high on risk taking, confidence, and sociability and relatively low on cautiousness and skepticism.[103] Other studies demonstrate that rainmaker partners are distinguished by four traits: engagement (the desire to be engaged in a work-related activity); dominance (the tendency to exercise power and influence over other people); motivating others (managing a team through delegation, trust, listening, encouragement, and empowerment); and risk taking (a willingness to question established methods and break with the past to achieve higher performance).[104] Rainmaker partners describe their risk taking as "putting themselves out there" and "playing in traffic."[105] A study of the most successful Canadian attorneys under 40 years of age also detected a relatively high level of resiliency, adaptability, and responsibility. Two-thirds of those superstars overcame adversity in their formative years—"death or serious illness of parent and financial hardship and language difficulties experienced with parents who immigrated to Canada, imposing 'responsibility where younger siblings and others relied upon them.'"[106]

---

[100] Hartman, Mordan, Schoenfelder & Sweeney, *supra* note 55.

[101] Ibid.

[102] Richard (2008), *supra* note 96.

[103] Ibid.

[104] Drake, Monique, & Parker-Stephen, Evan. (2013). *The rainmaking study*. Lawyer Metrics.

[105] Ibid.

[106] Kiser, Randall. (2017). *Soft skills for the effective lawyer* (p. 300). New York: Cambridge University Press. Taylor, Irene E. (2004, November). Top 40 under 40, *LEXPERT Magazine*. Those attorneys scored high in engagement, persistence, dominance, and confidence in success and relatively low in "Reduced

For law firms, the practical consequences of their attorneys' low resilience are fewer new clients because low-resilience attorneys are not rainmakers; less adaptation and innovation in firm strategies, processes, and technology; and an ongoing exodus of clients who had expected distinct, creative solutions for their problems. For the low-resilience attorneys themselves, the consequences include nominal adaptation to novel fact situations and evolving client needs; diminished interest in recent legal developments, new data, and creative methods; more reliance on conventional perspectives, habitual responses, and established procedures; strong defensiveness and minimal improvements following negative feedback; and disregard of new information that conflicts with previous assumptions, positions, and predictions. This maladaptive behavior may be fatal to some law firms because their clients expect and require resilience, flexibility, and adaptation. As Michael Rynowecer, president of BTI Consulting Group, explains:

> We have seen nothing more harmful to a law firm than an unwillingness or inability to tailor its offerings to better meet the needs and demands of clients. Even with requests as seemingly innocuous as changes in billing format or frequency, clients see a law firm's failure to comply with their wishes as a blatant disregard for their needs. The ability to be flexible and nimble is highly underrated in the legal world. Yet it can be the single attribute that distinguishes you from the competition. Clients see flexible firms as quicker to respond, better skilled at understanding business drivers and more client-focused— all the key ingredients to achieving superior levels of client satisfaction.[107]

Flexibility," which measures the extent to which an individual will make mistakes because of narrowing attention too much (i.e., excessive focus)." A low score on reduced flexibility is "strongly indicative of the probability of career success."

[107] Rynowecer, Michael B. (2006). The declining client satisfaction antidote. Washington, DC: BTI Consulting Group.

If law firms intend to increase client satisfaction and staunch the flow of legal work to corporate legal departments and alternative legal service providers, they will need to identify, develop, and promote attorneys who epitomize resilience. They also need to teach attorneys to augment their risk aversion with resilience because many problems simply cannot be identified and avoided in advance but can be mitigated or solved by flexible, inventive, and adaptive thinking. The stereotype of attorneys as "rigid of mind, rigid of manner, rigid of person" may be well deserved, but it is increasingly hazardous for law firms and their clients.[108]

The Dark Traits

In her humorous commencement address at Harvard Law School in 2014, actress Mindy Kaling remarked, "You are better educated and you are going to go out into the world and people are going to listen to what you say, whether you are good or evil, and that probably scares you because some of you look really young. And I'm afraid a couple of you probably are evil." She quickly added, "That's just the odds."[109]

The odds, in fact, indicate that considerably more than two of the approximately 800 Harvard Law School students being awarded a JD, LLM, or SJD degree will be evil or at least inclined to engage in antisocial behavior. Extensive studies conducted by Hogan Assessments indicate that most people display at least 3 of the 11 recognized "dark traits," and "about 40% score high enough on one or two to put them at risk for disruption in their careers—even if they're currently successful and effective."[110] The result, states business psychology professor Tomas Chamorro-Premuzic, "is pervasive dysfunctional behavior at work."[111]

The 11 dark traits are shown in Table 6.1. Many of these traits exist in a benign form but frequently assume an extreme, malevolent form

---

[108] Moll, Richard W. (1990). *The lure of the law* (p. 171). New York: Penguin Group.
[109] Strauss, Valerie. (2014, May 29). Mindy Kaling to Harvard law grads: "I'm afraid a couple of you probably are evil. That's just the odds." *The Washington Post.*
[110] Chamorro-Premuzic, Tomas. (2017, September–October). Could your personality derail your career? *Harvard Business Review*, p. 138.
[111] Ibid.

Table 6.1   Hogan Dark Traits Typology

Trait	Short Definition	Clinical Form	Symptoms
Excitable	Moody, unstable, easily annoyed	Bipolar	Volatility, outbursts, lack of persistence
Skeptical	Cynical, distrustful, overly sensitive to criticism	Paranoid	Lacks trust, quarrelsome
Cautious	Indecisive, anxious about making mistakes and criticism	Avoidant	Risk-averse, indecisive, resistant to change
Reserved	Remote, detached, indifferent to others' feelings	Schizoid	Insensitive, poor communications
Leisurely	Independent, apparently cooperative but privately uncooperative	Avoidant	Passive-aggressive, stubborn, procrastinating, and uncooperative
Bold	Sense of entitlement, inflated sense of self-worth	Narcissistic	Arrogance, inability to admit mistakes or give other people credit
Mischievous	Manipulative, excitement-seeking	Psychopathic	Impulsive, difficulty maintaining relationships and learning from experience
Colorful	Attention-seeking, dramatic, interruptive	Histrionic	Preoccupation with being noticed, inability to focus, socially obtuse
Imaginative	Eccentric or unusual thinking and acting	Schizotypal	Seems creative but lacks judgment, poor quality ideas
Diligent	Conscientious, detail-oriented, perfectionist	Obsessive-compulsive	Micromanages and disempowers people
Dutiful	Eager to please, reluctant to express disagreement	Dependent	Conflict-avoidant, submissive, reluctant to support co-workers

Sources: Chamorro-Premuzic, Tomas. (2017). Could your personality derail your career? Foster, Jeff, Richard, Larry, Rohrer, Lisa, & Sirkin, Mark. (2010). Understanding lawyers: The personality traits of successful practitioners. Kaiser, Rob. (2016). Dealing with the dark side.

in people who lack self-awareness and fail to change their behavior.[112] The tendency to ignore or deny one's dark traits increases as people gain power within an organization, and some leaders mistakenly attribute their success to these traits.[113]

Certain dark traits cause more damage to careers than others. The five traits most closely correlated with poor attitudes and negative performance ratings in leadership, decision making, and interpersonal skills are excitable, skeptical, cautious, reserved, and leisurely.[114] On all five of these traits attorneys score above a comparison group of managers and professionals in high-level positions.[115] Attorneys' scores suggest they have a stronger tendency to engage in behavior that pushes people away and decreases trust. They also may display passive-aggressive behavior—"pretending to have a relaxed, polite attitude while actually resisting cooperation or even engaging in backstabbing."[116]

Psychologist Delroy Paulhus presents a simpler, but nevertheless useful, model of socially offensive traits that he calls "dark" personalities. He identifies four socially averse personalities:

- *Narcissists*—"grandiose self-promoters who continually crave attention"[117]
- *Machiavellians*—master manipulators who attempt to achieve money, power, and competitiveness through deception, duplicity, and intimidation[118]
- *Sadists*—people who verbally or physically hurt other people for enjoyment[119]

---

[112] See Kaiser, Rob. (2016, January). Dealing with the dark side. *Talent Quarterly*, 37–42.

[113] Chamorro-Premuzic, *supra* note 110 at 138–139.

[114] Ibid. at 140.

[115] Foster, Richard, Rohrer, & Sirkin, *supra* note 5.

[116] Chamorro-Premuzic, *supra* note 110 at 139.

[117] Paulhus, Delroy. (2014, December). Toward a taxonomy of dark personalities. *Current Directions in Psychological Science, 23*(6), 421.

[118] Jones, Daniel N., & Paulhus, Delroy. Machiavellianism. In Leary, M. H., & Hoyle, R. H. (2009). *Handbook of individual differences in social behavior* (p. 93). New York: The Guilford Press.

[119] Paulhus, *supra* note 117 at 421.

- *Subclinical psychopaths*—malevolent people who cause serious harm to others "in an impulsive fit of callous thrill-seeking"[120]

The common feature in each of these dark personalities is callousness—a lack of empathy.[121] But each personality type manifests a lack of empathy in a different way: narcissists lack empathy because they are self-absorbed and are constantly seeking public attention; Machiavellians are strategic in appearing to be concerned about people while taking advantage of them and being emotionally detached from them; sadists affirmatively seek opportunities to harm others; and psychopaths are impulsive and give little or no thought to hurting others.[122] Ironically, many dark personalities come across well in interviews and are achievement-oriented and successful; they excel at self-promotion, duplicity, and aggressiveness.[123]

Attorneys score relatively low on empathy—a central feature of dark personalities.[124] Empathy is considered a "Non-fit for Law" personality trait because attorneys who score relatively high on empathy are more likely to leave their first law firm job and the practice of law.[125] The lack of empathy not only affects attorneys' interpersonal relationships with clients and other attorneys; it may result in substandard client service because the dark personality traits are correlated with low scores on conscientiousness.[126]

Large law firm attorneys also score low on two traits closely related to empathy: sociability (the degree to which a person needs and enjoys social interactions) and interpersonal sensitivity (the degree to which a person is socially sensitive, tactful,

---

[120] Ibid. at 422.

[121] Ibid.

[122] Jones & Paulhus, *supra* note 118 at 97. Paulhus, *supra* note 117 at 422. Paulhus, Delroy L., & Williams, Kevin M. (2002). The dark triad of personality: Narcissism, Machiavellianism, and psychopathy. *Journal of Research in Personality*, *36*, 556–563.

[123] Paulhus & Williams, *supra* note 122 at 557.

[124] Levin, Mark, & MacEwen, Bruce. (2014). *Assessing lawyer traits & finding a fit for success: Introducing the Sheffield Legal Assessment.*

[125] Ibid. at 10.

[126] Paulhus, *supra* note 117 at 423.

and perceptive).[127] On the Hogan Personality Inventory, large law firm attorneys' "lowest average score is on Interpersonal Sensitivity (40th percentile), indicating that lawyers are task-oriented and tend to speak their minds but may also come across as cold, critical, and argumentative."[128] Combined with their low scores on altruism, attorneys' low scores on sociability and interpersonal sensitivity suggest that law firms have unwittingly selected a large number of attorneys who may be insensitive, incommunicative, and indifferent.

Chapter Capsule

Law firms' emphasis on production and billing sometimes eclipses clients' need for loyalty, dedication, competence, efficiency, and value. This emphasis on revenue generation also may displace attorneys' ethical duty to continually upgrade their legal skills and enhance their performance; law firms' need for collegiality, collaboration, and leadership skills; and American society's call for attorneys who are committed to justice, the rule of law, and access to the legal system. If law firms are serious about improving client service and restoring the public's trust in their intentions and priorities, they will modify their attorney selection criteria and professional development programs to include six critical qualities: engagement, likeability, humility, realism, openness, and resilience.

Although each of the six qualities is essential to client satisfaction and professional growth, the threshold quality may be engagement. If most attorneys are not engaged in their work, as the Gallup report indicates, the other five qualities may never be developed or put into practice. The low levels of attorney engagement should be an acute embarrassment to law firms, as they signal inefficient client service, inattentive legal analysis, poor work product quality, and abysmal oversight, training, counseling, and mentoring.

Taj Hotels Resorts and Palaces consistently scores high on Gallup's engagement surveys. It is a six-time recipient of the Gallup Great Workplace Award. In its employee training programs, new

---

[127] Foster, Richard, Rohrer & Sirkin, *supra* note 5 at 4.
[128] Ibid at 6.

employees learn that they are the customer's ambassador, not the company's ambassador. They are "assured that the company's leadership, right up to the CEO, will support any employee decision that puts guests front and center and that shows that employees did everything possible to delight them."[129] In 2008, when terrorists started throwing grenades and firing automatic weapons inside the Taj Mahal Palace hotel in Mumbai, the Taj Group employees escorted the guests in a banquet room out first. In another large room, the employees formed a human cordon around the guests to protect them from the advancing terrorists. Eleven Taj Group employees sacrificed their lives to enable about 1,200 guests to escape. Each of these employees could have escaped in the initial minutes of the siege because they were familiar with the escape routes. If any lesson for law firms emerges from this horrific event it is this: engagement matters, and when dedication to customers permeates an organization's training programs and every interaction with its customer, people will demonstrate an astonishing level of selflessness and professionalism.

---

[129] Deshpande, Rohit, & Raina, Anjali. (2011, December). The ordinary heroes of the Taj. *Harvard Business Review.*

7

Practices

In 2008, Google launched Project Oxygen to determine the most important qualities of its best managers. It conducted qualitative interviews with its managers and analyzed exit-interview data, turnover and retention rates, employee surveys, team performance metrics, manager ratings and reviews, and Great Manager Award nominations going back to its incorporation in 1998.[1] After conducting statistical analyses of the data, Google identified the eight most important qualities of its highest performing managers:

1. Is a good coach
2. Empowers the team and does not micromanage
3. Expresses interest in and concern for each team member's success and personal well-being
4. Is productive and results-oriented
5. Is a good communicator—listens and shares information
6. Supports career development and discusses performance
7. Has a clear vision and strategy for the team
8. Has key technical skills to help advise the team[2]

---

[1] Strauss, Valerie. (2017, December 20). The surprising thing Google learned about its employees—and what it means for today's students. *The Washington Post*. Garvin, David A. (2013, December). How Google sold its engineers on management. *Harvard Business Review*.

[2] Harrell, Melissa, & Barbato, Lauren. (2018, February 27). Great managers still matter: The evolution of Google's Project Oxygen. *re:Work*. Garvin, *supra* note 1.

Although many Google executives had expected technical skills to be ranked above soft skills, only one technical skill (No. 8) survived the multivariate statistical analysis. These results are consistent with multiple studies demonstrating that soft skills are paramount in nearly all organizations—including law firms.[3]

In February 2018, after reevaluating and updating its data, Google added two new behaviors to the most important qualities list: "collaborates across Google" and "is a strong decision maker."[4] These qualities were selected because "Googlers wanted to see more effective cross-organization collaboration and stronger decision making practices from leaders."[5] Again, these results are consistent with other studies, including studies of law firms.[6]

The first eight qualities identified in the Google study and corroborated in other studies are self-explanatory; but the two new qualities (collaboration and decision making) are more complex and warrant further explanation. For that reason, the first sections of this chapter discuss collaboration and decision making and how those practices apply to lawyers. The remaining sections of this chapter examine three additional practices that facilitate outstanding performance: readiness, civility, and diversity.

Collaboration

Collaboration in law firms refers to cross-practice efforts to solve complex client problems. The purpose of collaboration is to

---

3   See Accenture. (2015). #ListenLearnLead Global Research. Brafford, Anne. (2017). *Positive professionals: Creating high-performing profitable firms through the science of engagement.* Chicago: American Bar Association. Edmondson, Amy C. (2012). *Teaming.* San Francisco: Jossey-Bass. Kiser, Randall. (2017). *Soft skills for the effective lawyer.* New York: Cambridge University Press. Muir, Ronda. (2017). *Beyond smart: Lawyering with emotional intelligence.* Chicago: American Bar Association. Seppala, Emma. (2015, March 18). Positive teams are more productive. *Harvard Business Review.*

4   Harrell & Barbato, *supra* note 2.

5   Ibid.

6   See Dubey, Prashant, & Kripalani, Eva. (2013). *The generalist counsel* (p. 57). New York: Oxford University Press. Gardner, Heidi K. (2017). *Smart collaboration.* Boston: Harvard Business Review Press. Krieger, Stefan H., & Neumann, Jr., Richard K. (2007). *Essential lawyering skills* (pp. 8–9). New York: Aspen Publishers.

integrate attorneys' expertise in various practice areas "to bear on problems that, increasingly, are so complicated and so sophisticated that no single expert—no matter how smart or hardworking— is in a position to solve them."[7] The term "collaboration" is often confused with "cross-selling," which is an episodic referral or handoff of a discrete client matter to another attorney within a firm.[8] Collaboration is different from cross-selling because collaboration usually requires an ongoing team effort that results not only in superior service to the client but also an enhancement of the team's ability to work together. Through regular interactions, the team members improve their efficiency by learning more about each other's expertise, work habits, analytical abilities, and decision-making propensities.[9]

Resistance to Collaboration

Many attorneys are reluctant to collaborate with colleagues in different practice areas. "From our surveys of hundreds of professionals across many firms and countries," states Heidi Gardner, author of *Smart Collaboration*, "we know that one of the biggest barriers to collaboration is distrust of others' competence. Partners have concerns that colleagues will not uphold high enough levels of quality and responsiveness."[10] Other impediments to collaboration include partners' lack of knowledge of other partners' expertise and experience; partners' apprehension about losing control of their client relationships when more attorneys assume critical roles in serving the client; partners' concerns about another attorney's motives and the possibility of client poaching and stealing client origination credits; and compensation system incentives that reward client hoarding, give undue weight to origination credits, and essentially penalize partners who collaborate with relationship partners.[11]

---

7   Gardner (2017), *supra* note 6 at 1.
8   Gardner, Heidi K. (2015, March). When senior managers won't collaborate. *Harvard Business Review*.
9   Gardner (2017), *supra* note 6 at 2.
10   Gardner, Heidi K. (2015). Leading the campaign for greater collaboration within law firms. In Normand-Hochman, Rebecca (Ed.). *Leadership for lawyers* (p. 17). Surrey, UK: Globe Law and Business Ltd.
11   Gardner (2017), *supra* note 6 at 78–84.

This last factor—compensation system incentives—may be the largest impediment to collaboration. As Patrick Lamb, a founding member of Valorem Law Group, explains, "The best way to guarantee that the first question on everyone's mind is how can we get better results for this client (and hence for the firm) would be to remove the ability of any partner to influence his or her compensation by a course of behavior different than the collaborative behavior the firm sought to maximize."[12]

Clients are aware of the distrust among partners and the internecine battles that deter collaboration and cause partners to give more attention to their internal conflicts than their client matters. In a survey of senior in-house lawyers working with international law firms, for instance, about one-half of the lawyers said they are aware of "inter-firm political wrangling" and that those conflicts "had a detrimental impact on the firm's ability to deliver a good service."[13] Seventy-seven percent of those lawyers said that "inter-firm politics" resulted in poor communication between teams, and 62 percent felt that internal politics led to "blocking relationships to preserve income for one particular office."[14] In some offices, they noted, "income secured for the local office is always valued more than referred revenue."[15]

Benefits of Collaboration

When attorneys overcome their reluctance to collaborate with colleagues in other practice areas, the financial benefits are substantial. Attorneys also report that the heightened complexity of the collaborative work is more intellectually stimulating than the tasks they otherwise would be performing in a siloed practice. Based on her studies of multiple law firms, Gardner identifies these specific benefits of collaboration:

---

[12] Lamb, Patrick, McKenna, Patrick K., Reeser, Edwin, & Carr, Jeffrey. (2009, November 11). Partner compensation and the new "value" reality. *San Francisco Daily Journal*, p. 7.

[13] (2018, February). Political wrangling and office rivalries impairing client service at global firms, in-house lawyers say. *Legal Week*. Legal Week Intelligence. (2018). Global legal services in a disruptive world, p. 10.

[14] LegalWeek Intelligence, *supra* note 13.

[15] Ibid.

- *Hourly rate increases.* Collaborative work enables attorneys to shift from providing technical legal expertise to strategic direction.[16] "Across all law firms we studied," Gardner reports, "we found that the more cross-discipline projects partners worked on, and the more complex each one was, the more their hourly rates increased in following years."[17]

- *Revenue increases.* When a client starts working with two practice groups instead of a single practice group, annual revenue from that client triples.[18] As the client works with more practice groups, income from that client increases dramatically.[19] The reason for this revenue increase is relatively straightforward, as explained by an account manager: "Getting more of our people in front of the client more often created a virtuous cycle because we became the top-of-mind adviser. When a new issue came up, we were the go-to team."[20]

- *"Stickier" clients.* When clients work with multiple partners, they are more likely to stay with the firm when the relationship partner departs. Only 28 percent of clients working with a single relationship partner state that they would remain with their current law firm if that partner departed. But 90 percent of clients working with multiple partners state that they would stay with their current law firm if the relationship partner departed.[21]

- *Better client service.* Cross-practice teams bring more perspectives to problem solving, generate more innovative solutions to client problems, and prevent more avoidable errors.[22] They also are more likely to be recommended by clients to their peers.[23]

---

[16] Gardner, Heidi K. (2015, June 1). Harvard study part II: Collaboration strategies for rainmakers. *Bloomberg Law.*

[17] Ibid.

[18] Gardner (2017), *supra* note 6 at 23.

[19] Ibid. at 22.

[20] Ibid. at 23.

[21] Ibid. at 30–31.

[22] Ibid. at 33, 218.

[23] Ibid. at 33.

- *Intellectual stimulation.* Providing clients with expertise in a single practice area is becoming a commoditized service vulnerable to hourly rate decreases and severe discounting in flat fee negotiations.[24] Collaborative work, by its very nature, requires cross-practice expertise, advice, strategy, and coordination. This work commands higher hourly rates and provides a heightened level of intellectual stimulation. "If I'm doing work just in my specialty," a partner states, "then I'm almost certainly talking to clients with a narrow scope and more limited responsibility. Once I move into more sophisticated work, I move up toward the C-suite, and that's when conversations get interesting."[25]

- *Increased referrals.* Attorneys who collaborate with partners in other practice groups benefit from more referrals. "On average," Gardner states, "one in six partners you work with for the first time will refer you more work in the next year."[26]

Methods of Promoting Collaboration

Recognizing the tremendous benefits of collaboration, many firms are making a concerted effort to promote cross-practice communication and inform attorneys of the wide range of expertise available for their clients. Specific methods of promoting collaboration include formal programs, law firm retreats, informal meetings, and social activities where attorneys meet colleagues from other practice areas and learn about their specialization areas; consultations with trusted firm attorneys about other attorneys' knowledge, work habits, and communication styles to make sure a planned collaboration will be successful; meetings with and educational programs for clients to better understand their businesses and discern legal

---

[24] Gardner (2015), *supra* note 16. (The increases in hourly rates "all statistically controlled for alternative predictors of rates such as a partner's practice, office, seniority, gender and other variables; we still find that cross-practice collaboration experience is a very robust determinant of a partner's ability to raise rates faster than his peers in the same firm who do more siloed work.")

[25] Gardner, Heidi K. (2015, June 26). Harvard study lays out keys to collaboration among lawyers. *Bloomberg Law.*

[26] Gardner, Heidi K. (2017, March 8). The business case for smart collaboration in today's law firm. *Legal Business World.*

needs beyond those currently served by the firm; and modifications of compensation systems to reward client origination as well as collaboration.[27] To stimulate and reward collaboration, partners' annual memoranda to the compensation committee should answer this question: "Over the past year, which partner outside of your practice, helped you build your practice the most?"[28]

Even when law firms lack specific programs to promote collaboration, partners often succeed in expanding their work into cross-practice services because collaboration does not require firm-wide approval or intervention. The collaboration process is relatively simple, and the rewards are consistently strong, as Gardner finds: "Subsequent year revenue from a rainmaker's *existing* clients increases the more she involves partners from both her own and other practices. For *new* clients, cross-practice collaboration is an even stronger predictor of long-term revenue growth."[29] Once attorneys take the initiative to collaborate and build a sense of trust in working with colleagues in other practices, they discover that their work is more engaging, their colleagues are more productive, and their clients are more profitable.

Decision Making

In the Google study discussed earlier in this chapter, the employees said they wanted to see "stronger decision making practices from leaders." This need for better decision-making practices extends far beyond Google and is evident in most businesses. In a survey of 2,207 executives, for instance, "only 28 percent said that the quality of strategic decisions in their companies was generally good, 60 percent thought that bad decisions were about as frequent as good ones, and the remaining 12 percent thought good decisions were altogether infrequent."[30] This section addresses these

---

27   Gardner, Heidi K. (2017, January-February). Getting your stars to collaborate. *Harvard Business Review*. Gardner (2017), *supra* note 6 at 85–94.

28   Farone, Deborah, & DiPietro, Dan. (2018, October 23). The deep value of law firm alignment. *The American Lawyer*.

29   Gardner (2015), *supra* note 8. [Emphasis in original].

30   Lovallo, Dan, & Sibony, Olivier. (2010, March). The case for behavioral strategy. *McKinsey Quarterly*.

deficiencies in decision making and serves as a "quick-start" guide to upgrading professional and personal decision-making practices. It briefly describes the scope and phases of decision making and then shows how attorneys can improve their decision-making practices in each of those phases.

Broadly defined, "decision making" includes problem detection, identification, and definition; option generation, evaluation, and synthesis; forecasting and simulation; choice; and reflection. These activities occur in four iterative phases: preparing to make decisions, making decisions, implementing decisions, and evaluating decisions. The challenges presented in those phases and techniques and practices to surmount those challenges are discussed below.

Preparing to Make Decisions

Effective decision makers start with the question, "What type of decision maker am I?" This inquiry enables attorneys to initially assess their personal decision-making biases—whether they tend to be risk-averse, cautious decision makers or risk-taking, opportunity-seeking decision makers.[31]

Most attorneys are risk-averse decision makers, and they focus on what to avoid instead of what to achieve. The disadvantage of being risk averse is that, as discussed in the preceding chapter, attorneys overlook new ways of approaching and solving problems, lack creativity and imagination, balk at taking risks, and are reluctant to experiment. Risk-averse decision makers may need to compensate for their biases by experimenting with small-scale, contained risks, working with a risk-seeking decision maker to balance their perspectives, and focusing on their overall goals instead of problems they wish to avoid.[32]

The next question effective decision makers ask themselves is, "Has my decision-making style evolved with my career?"[33] Attorneys

---

[31] See Tasler, Nick. (2008). *The impulse factor*. New York: Fireside.
[32] Ibid.
[33] See Brousseau, Kenneth, Driver, Michael, Hourihan, Gary, & Larsson, Rikard. (2006, February). The seasoned executive's decision-making style. *Harvard Business Review*, pp. 111–112.

tend to develop a decision-making style early in their careers and maintain that style throughout their careers. Unfortunately, they may neglect to modify their decision-making style as professional challenges evolve and responsibilities increase.

Entry-level attorneys tend to simplify facts and law to fit into the templates they learned in law school and the relatively narrow set of decision-making models they have experienced. As a result, they can be clear-headed, efficient, decisive—and, sometimes, deadly wrong. They focus on immediate tasks and decisions and display a preference for single-option solutions. The seasoned attorney, however, develops a more sophisticated decision-making style that is incorporative, creative, analytical, open, interactive, participative, and collaborative.[34] The seasoned attorney also recognizes that it is acceptable and sometimes necessary to employ different leadership and decision-making styles. The leadership style may exhibit certitude, while the decision-making style may be more amenable to subtlety, ambiguity, and modification.

The last question to be answered is, "*How* will this decision be made?"[35] In the haste to make decisions, people concentrate on who will make the decision, when the decision will be made, and what the decision will be. This approach omits the quality controls required for effective decision making. By asking how a decision will be made, attorneys can pause to identify their objectives and specify the decision-making criteria. Critical questions at this phase include:

- How will the decision be defined?
- How will the issues be identified?
- How will the stakeholders be determined?
- How will the objectives for the decision be defined?
- How will the decision be evaluated?[36]

---

[34] Ibid.
[35] See Yates, J. Frank. (2003). *Decision management: How to assure better decisions in your company.* San Francisco: Jossey-Bass.
[36] Ibid.

Making Decisions

As attorneys shift from preparing to make decisions to actually making decisions, they can improve their decisions by adopting the four techniques and practices described below.

The first step in making decisions is to elicit multiple opinions. Although a single attorney is not particularly effective in predicting a trial outcome or the direction of the legal services industry, the aggregate opinions of multiple attorneys are remarkably accurate. As attorney/jury consultant Jonas Jacobson noted in his study of attorneys' ability to predict jury verdicts, "the fastest, cheapest, and likely the most common method to supplement an attorney's personal estimate is simply to solicit the opinions of other attorneys."[37]

When attorneys in Jacobson's study obtained a second opinion about a jury verdict from another attorney, their estimates showed a higher level of accuracy; and when they were required to discuss the case with another attorney and agree upon a single estimate, their estimate showed "significant accuracy gain."[38] The average of the attorneys' estimates of the verdict amount was far more accurate than the vast majority of single estimates.

Closely related to the practice of eliciting multiple opinions is the "art of humble inquiry." Management professor Edgar Schein describes this as "the fine art of drawing someone out, of asking questions to which you do not already know the answer, of building a relationship based on curiosity and interest in the other person."[39] He notes that our business roles emphasize "telling" and "doing," and in our efforts to appear knowledgeable and productive, we often fail to elicit the information necessary to make sound decisions. "All my teaching and consulting experience," Schein relates, "has taught me that what builds a relationship, what solves problems, what moves things forward is asking the right questions."[40]

---

[37] Jacobson, Jonas, Dobbs-Marsh, Jasmine, Liberman, Varda, & Minson, Julia A. (2011). Predicting civil jury verdicts: How attorneys use (and misuse) a second opinion. *Journal of Empirical Legal Studies, 8*, 99–119.

[38] Ibid.

[39] Schein, Edgar. (2013). *Humble inquiry* (p. 2). San Francisco: Berrett-Koehler.

[40] Ibid. at 4.

Once attorneys have obtained a broad range of opinions and information, they need to generate multiple problem-solving alternatives.[41] This requires considerably more cognitive effort than most people are willing to devote to problem solving, as their tendency is to generate a single alternative and frame decisions as either/or and go/no-go scenarios. In requiring multiple alternatives, attorneys not only force themselves, their colleagues, and their clients to think more expansively; they also start to break down the one person/one idea/one proposal model that aligns a person with a single alternative and makes it difficult to reject an alternative without rejecting its proponent as well. Multiple alternatives tend to depersonalize decision making, enhance creativity, sharpen focus on objectives, and yield superior outcomes. If decision makers cannot or refuse to generate multiple alternatives, their thinking can be stimulated by asking, "What would you do if your current options disappeared?"[42]

A final step in making decisions is to conduct a "premortem." Decision scientist Gary Klein describes a premortem as the "hypothetical opposite of a postmortem."[43] In a premortem, a project team imagines that a few months have elapsed and a proposed decision or project was implemented but failed miserably. Each team member "is asked to independently write down every reason they can think of for the failure—especially the kinds of things they ordinarily wouldn't mention as potential problems, for fear of being impolitic."[44] The team discusses each possible reason for the failure and modifies the plans to anticipate and avoid possible setbacks and failures. The premortem, Klein explains, "doesn't just help teams to identify potential problems early on. It also reduces the kind of damn-the-torpedoes attitude often assumed by people who are overinvested in a project."[45]

---

[41] See Heath, Chip, & Heath, Dan. (2013). *Decisive.* New York: Crown Business.
[42] Ibid.
[43] Klein, Gary. (2007, September). Performing a project premortem. *Harvard Business Review.*
[44] Ibid.
[45] Ibid.

Implementing Decisions

After a decision is made, three techniques are helpful in implementing the decision. First, whenever possible, test the decision on a small scale. For law firm management decisions, this means implementing the decision within a single department, practice group, or geographical region. For litigation matters, this means testing the theory or argument with mock juries, focus groups, or at least among other attorneys and support staff whose sensibilities may more closely reflect those of jurors. Attorneys are notoriously poor predictors of how other people will respond to their ideas and arguments, and testing an idea or argument on a small scale enables attorneys to detect problems that otherwise go unnoticed until the problems reach an irreversible proportion. As Ed Catmull, the president of Pixar Animation Studios and Walt Disney Animation Studios explains, it is "better to have train wrecks with miniature trains than with real ones."[46]

Second, after simulating decisions on a small scale, expert decision makers attempt to understand how people will respond to those decisions by understanding and respecting human emotions. Although legal education and training attempt to strip decisions of their emotional content, both neuroscience and the history of human decision making demonstrate that people are fundamentally emotional decision makers. They feel first and think second.[47]

The most effective decision makers acknowledge the realities of human decision making and develop a remarkable ability to toggle back and forth between emotional and deliberative thinking. Functional magnetic resonance imaging (fMRI) scans of executives who function at the highest levels of strategic thinking, for instance, show "more activity in parts of the brain linked with emotion and intuition. Their nervous systems may even repress rational thought to free those areas up."[48]

Third, in implementing decisions, effective decision makers are receptive to modifying and abandoning their plans. In futurist

---

[46]   Catmull, Ed. (2014). *Creativity, Inc.* (p. 210). New York: Random House.

[47]   Rock, David. (2009). *Your brain at work.* New York: HarperCollins.

[48]   Gilkey, Roderick, Caceda, Ricardo, & Kilts, Clinton. (2010, September). When emotional reasoning trumps IQ. *Harvard Business Review.*

Paul Saffo's lexicon, they have "strong opinions weakly held."[49] Strong opinions, Saffo relates, "give you the capacity to reach conclusions quickly, but holding them weakly allows you to discard them the moment you encounter conflicting evidence."[50] He urges decision makers to "engage in creative doubt. Look for information that doesn't fit, or indicators that [are] pointing in an entirely different direction."[51] This capacity for fluid decision making distinguishes novice decision makers from expert decision makers and enables decision makers to modify plans on the fly, preserving the best elements of the original plan while modifying it to incorporate new information.

Evaluating Decisions

The key to evaluating and learning from decisions is "deliberate practice," a concept developed by psychology professor K. Anders Ericsson, an international expert on expertise.[52] His extensive research on expert performance in activities as diverse as sports, surgery, music, chess, and science indicates that personal development depends on a continuous cycle of performing, evaluating, setting new and harder goals, and executing. Deliberate practice, he explains, "involves two kinds of learning: improving the skills you already have and extending the reach and range of your skills."[53]

Practice alone does not improve performance. As Ericsson states, "not all practice makes perfect."[54] What distinguishes the expert performers from ordinary performers is deliberate practice: "We've observed that when a course of action doesn't work out as expected, the expert players will go back to their prior analysis to assess where they went wrong and how to avoid future errors. They continually work to eliminate their weaknesses."[55] As applied to

---

[49] Saffo, Paul. (2017, July-August). Six rules for effective forecasting. *Harvard Business Review.*

[50] Ibid.

[51] Saffo, Paul. (2008, July 26). Strong opinions weakly held.

[52] Ericsson, Eric. (2016). *Peak: Secrets for the new science of expertise.* New York: Houghton Mifflin Harcourt.

[53] Ericsson, K. Anders, Prietula, Michael J., & Cokely, Edward T. (2007, July-August). The making of an expert. *Harvard Business Review.*

[54] Ibid.

[55] Ibid.

decision making, deliberate practice requires a continuous cycle of establishing objectives and criteria for decision making, making decisions, implementing decisions, and then seeking feedback and obtaining objective information to evaluate those decisions.

Many attorneys neglect deliberate practice because they lack resilience, their firms do not conduct formal evaluation programs, and time spent on evaluating and improving performance is non-billable. Only one in five law firms conducts post-matter reviews, but the practice of conducting these reviews varies widely with firm size.[56] Twenty-eight percent of law firms with 250 or more attorneys conduct post-matter reviews, while only 17 percent of firms with fewer than 250 lawyers conduct them.[57]

Self-evaluation is integral to deliberate practice, and learning from mistakes is an essential component of self-evaluation. Although people often say that they learn from their mistakes, the reality is that they tend to learn from their successes and ignore their mistakes. But expert decision makers like Charles Munger regard mistakes as the best learning opportunities. As Munger says, "I like people admitting they were complete stupid horses' asses. I know I'll perform better if I rub my nose in my mistakes. This is a wonderful trick to learn."[58]

Readiness

"Readiness" means that individuals and organizations are aware of possible changes, receptive to modifying their perceptions and behavior, and confident that they will respond promptly and intelligently to planned changes as well as unanticipated conditions, events, and actions. Psychologists define readiness as both a commitment to change and an ability to implement change—being "psychologically and behaviorally prepared to take action."[59]

---

[56] Clay, Thomas S., & Seeger, Eric A. (2018). *2018 Law firms in transition* (p. 10). Willow Grove, PA: Altman Weil.

[57] Ibid.

[58] Griffin, Tren. (2015). *Charlie Munger* (p. 51). New York: Columbia Business School Publishing.

[59] See Weiner, Bryan J. (2009). A theory of organizational readiness for change. *Implementation Science, 4,* 67.

Our understanding of readiness has been advanced by High Reliability Organizations (HROs). These organizations—typified by aircraft carriers, air traffic control centers, nuclear-powered submarines, wildland firefighting crews, and hospital rapid response teams—must deliver a sustained, failure-free performance.[60] They operate in complex, high-risk environments that preclude trial-and-error training because any error would "result in absolutely unacceptable consequences."[61] In an environment where any error might be the last trial, every aspect of their operations must be mindful, safe, and expert.

Although HROs appear to be unique organizations, they actually are quite similar to law firms. Both HROs and law firms rely on highly skilled people to deliver error-free performances in complex situations presenting intense time pressures; multiple actors with varying levels of expertise; insufficient, contradictory, and unreliable information; competing interpretations of the same information; and pressures to make critical decisions invariably followed by irreparable results.[62] Law firms, therefore, would benefit from adopting some of the practices that enable HROs to anticipate problems and function safely, efficiently, and continuously. These practices, discussed below, include (1) preoccupation with failure; (2) attention to near-misses and faint signals; (3) reluctance to simplify; (4) deference to expertise; (5) flat communication; and (6) a duty to question.

- *Preoccupation with failure.* HROs continuously consider what could go wrong; what type of problems are likely to be overlooked; how impending problems can be detected in their earliest manifestation; how errors can be reduced, mitigated, or corrected; and how a repetition of similar errors can be

---

[60] See LaPorte, Todd R., & Consolini, Paula M. (1991). Working in practice but not in theory: Theoretical challenges of "High-Reliability Organizations." *Journal of Public Administration Research and Theory, 1*(1), 19. Weick, Karl E., & Sutcliffe, Kathleen. (2001). *Managing the unexpected* (p. 71). San Francisco: Jossey-Bass.

[61] LaPorte & Consolini, *supra* note 60.

[62] Kiser, Randall. (2010). *Beyond right and wrong: The power of effective decision making for attorneys and clients* (pp. 377–383). Berlin, New York: Springer.

avoided. In that sense, they are preoccupied with failure.[63] This preoccupation is not a negative experience. On the contrary, it is an energetic, purposeful, and mindful state of awareness that coalesces everyone in the organization to anticipate, detect, and avert errors. A critical element of this preoccupation with failure is a collective responsibility for preventing failures. As organizational psychologist Karl Weick observes, "There is a strong tendency in companies that aren't high-reliability organizations to isolate failure, to blame the culprit, and to not learn from mistakes. And that's idiotic, because few failures can be traced to a single individual."[64]

- *Attention to near-misses and faint signals.* HROs regard near-misses and minor mistakes as harbingers of serious problems. Instead of ignoring minor errors or feeling relieved after a near-miss, HROs recognize that they experienced a fatal accident whose consequences have been temporarily and fortuitously postponed.[65] HROs avoid the common habit of overlooking seemingly small problems and concentrating efforts on large problems. As Ed Catmull, president of Pixar Animation and Disney Animation, explains, "When we put setbacks into two buckets—the 'business as usual' bucket and the 'holy cow' bucket—and use a different mindset for each, we are signing up for trouble. We become so caught up in our big problems that we ignore the little ones, failing to realize that some of our small problems will have long-term consequences—and are, therefore, big problems in the making."[66]

---

[63]   See Schulz, Kathryn. (2011). *Being wrong: Adventures in the margin of error* (p. 302). New York: HarperCollins. ("When they are at their best, such domains have a productive obsession with error. They try to imagine every possible reason a mistake could occur, they prevent as many of them as possible, and they conduct exhaustive postmortems on the ones that slip through. By embracing error as inevitable, these industries are better able to anticipate mistakes, prevent them, and respond appropriately when those prevention efforts fail.")

[64]   Coutu, Diane L. (2003, April). Sense and reliability. *Harvard Business Review.*

[65]   Gerstein, Marc S., & Ellsberg, Michael. (2008). *Flirting with disaster* (pp. 258–259). New York: Union Square Press. ("It is a safety *sine qua non* that near misses and other forms of weak signals be treated as if they were genuine accidents. They are considered 'free tuition'—valuable lessons without much cost.")

[66]   Catmull, *supra* note 46 at 169.

- *Reluctance to simplify.* Many people handle reality by compressing it into a simpler form and dealing with the aspects that are familiar and relatively easy to handle. This approach reduces cognitive load but precipitates problem-solving errors. HROs recognize the human tendency to simplify, and they counter it by encouraging people to acknowledge, understand, and address the full range of operations, responsibilities, and consequences in complex environments. Leaders must "complicate themselves in order to keep their organizations in touch with the realities of the business world," asserts Weick. "My worry when executives say, 'Keep it simple, stupid,' is that they're underestimating the complexity of their own organizations and environments."[67] Simplifying is inherently attractive and invariably deleterious; it appeals to both leaders and followers and often prevents them from perceiving and responding to threats because they do not appear in simplified versions of complex environments.
- *Deference to expertise.* HROs attempt to counter the dangers of hierarchies by deferring to expertise. This means that the people most knowledgeable about a particular problem and most skilled at solving those types of problems are empowered to determine the solutions. The fact that the person with expertise ranks low in the organizational hierarchy is irrelevant in HROs. As management professor Michael Roberto explains, "They do not let formal hierarchy, status, or power dictate decision-making during times of stress. Instead, they try to ensure that people at lower levels can apply their expertise to solve thorny and urgent problems without fear of retribution from their superiors."[68] Deferring to expertise avoids the problems that frequently occur when people high in organizational structures base decisions on limited or inaccurate information and are not aware of the filters that prevent them from receiving or attending to essential information.

---

[67] Coutu, Diane L. (2003, April). Sense and reliability. *Harvard Business Review.*
[68] Roberto, Michael A. (2008). Why catastrophic organizational failures happen. *Management Department Journal Articles*, Paper 25.

- *Flat communication.* Hierarchies are dangerous decision-making structures.[69] They consolidate power among the people who generally possess the least amount of problem-specific information, and they force organizations to rely on high-status people whose decision making is often cursory, rapid, and final. Hierarchical organizations foster a directive decision-making style that may be effective in crisis situations but tends to be demeaning, demoralizing, and defective in ordinary circumstances.[70] This directive decision-making style discourages innovation, flexibility, and initiative. HROs attempt to reduce the deficiencies in hierarchical organizations by distributing information to and eliciting input from a broad range of people who may be affected by an issue or may have knowledge about it. HROs do not make "the mistake of confusing the communication structure with the organizational structure."[71]

- *Duty to question.* To reduce human error, HROs promote a culture of inquiry and a duty to dissent when inquiry does not result in satisfactory responses or acceptable solutions. This culture promotes initiative, reduces the fear of honesty, and encourages more candid discussions of concerns, reservations, and objections. "If people are trained to listen to their internal alarm bells, search for the causes, and then take corrective action," states James Winnefeld, the former vice-chairman of the U.S. Joint Chiefs of Staff, "the chances

---

[69] See Pentland, Alex. (2010). *Honest signals* (p. 74). Cambridge, MA: MIT Press. ("Since the classic studies of Alexander Bavelas at MIT nearly sixty years ago, we have known that teams with a centrally coordinated structure—the classic "org chart" structure—are good for fixed, well-defined tasks, but not for complex tasks requiring flexibility. Conversely, teams with richer interconnections are good for tasks requiring flexibility.")

[70] Sinek, Simon. (2017). *Leaders eat last* (p. 168). New York: Portfolio. ("Teams led by a directive leader initially outperform those led by an empowering leader. However, despite lower early performance, teams led by an empowering leader experience higher performance improvement over time because of higher levels of team-learning, coordination, empowerment and mental model development.")

[71] Catmull, *supra* note 46 at 64.

that they'll forestall problems rise dramatically."[72] When people adopt a questioning attitude, he adds, they "remain alert for anomalies and are never satisfied with a less-than-thorough answer."[73]

Each of these HRO practices promotes a readiness to detect and respond to unanticipated changes. They incorporate an individual and organizational willingness to adapt to new challenges. The practices also "flatten the authority gradient" by encouraging the dissemination of information and expression of questions and concerns, regardless of a person's position within the organization's hierarchy.[74]

Law firms are hierarchical organizations in structure, function, and leadership. Client matters typically are staffed by senior or junior partners and subordinate senior and junior associates. Law firm operations and strategies are determined by department, practice group, and regional office leaders; an executive committee often comprised of senior partners; and a managing partner or chairperson. These hierarchical arrangements frequently produce decisions based on insufficient and highly filtered information because the attorneys most knowledgeable about specific issues are the least likely to be involved in the decisions, whether related to client matters or firm operations and strategies. Hierarchical organizations like law firms not only consolidate power at the top of their pyramidal structures; they also amass and then neglect the greatest amount of information at the base of those pyramidal structures. Unless law firms adopt HRO practices designed to engage and elicit critical information from people at all levels of their hierarchies, they will continue to make decisions without being aware of the information that could have contributed to better decisions.

---

[72] Winnefeld, James A., Jr., & Kirchhoff, Christopher. Cybersecurity's human factor: Lessons from the Pentagon. (2015, September). *Harvard Business Review*.

[73] Ibid.

[74] See Hallinan, Joseph T. (2009). *Why we make mistakes* (p. 7). New York: Broadway Books. ("In error-speak, this is known as 'flattening the authority gradient,' and it has been shown to be an effective way to reduce errors.")

Civility

Many law firms exhibit an extraordinary tolerance for incivility among attorneys—especially when an uncivil attorney packs a large book of business. In a profession where aggressiveness is considered an asset, many law firms have not distinguished between forceful argument and plain bullying. When law firms tolerate incivility, attorneys disengage from their work, law firm morale declines, clients obtain perfunctory service from their lawyers, and few attorneys are motivated to contribute to a firm's overall success and its long-term goals.[75] The pervasive incivility in many law firms is unlikely to change, as Robert Riordan, an attorney and clinical psychologist explains: "As long as law firms measure success through profitability, partners who are interpersonally challenged yet profitable are not going to be censured for their behavior."[76]

Attorneys become habituated to impulsive, rude, and abusive colleagues. In some firms, routine belittling is considered a rite of passage for new attorneys. An associate attorney, writing in *Texas Lawyer*, thinks that partners who yell at associates may be doing them a favor. "In my opinion," he says, "those are the best partners because when you make a mistake, you will never forget it."[77] As incivility becomes routine and normalized in law firm interactions, it forms a model for future behavior and eventually is integrated into a law firm's folklore and culture.

Very few attorneys see themselves as bullies, but they are unlikely to be accurate judges of their own behavior. Only one in 200 people admits to engaging in workplace bullying, but one in four people has been subjected to bullying at work.[78] Many forms of incivility fall short of bullying but nevertheless inflict serious and unnecessary stress on colleagues: delaying access to information or resources;

---

[75]   See Gillespie, Becky Beaupre. (2012, March 1). No jerks: Some firms argue that collegiality pays. *ABA Journal*.

[76]   McQueen, M. P. (2016, April 13). Your law firm partner is a jerk. Now what? *The American Lawyer*.

[77]   Weiss, Debra Cassens. (2009, August 4). Upset about yelling partners? Too much work? Get over it, an associate says. *ABA Journal*.

[78]   Sutton, Robert. (2017, August 10). How to survive a jerk at work. *The Wall Street Journal*. (In that study, "bullying" was defined as "abusive conduct that is threatening, intimidating, humiliating, work sabotage or verbal abuse.")

belittling others and their efforts; behaving disrespectfully when disagreeing with others; interrupting others; and making demeaning or derogatory remarks.[79] Each of these forms of incivility has a cumulative, negative effect on attorneys' motivation, pride, and self-respect. They convey a strong message that an attorney is not regarded as a professional and does not merit professionalism.

Incivility exacts an enormous toll on individual performance. As business professor Robert Sutton explains, "Leaders who believe that destructive superstars are 'too important' to fire often underestimate the damage they can do."[80] Illustrative studies show that performance deteriorates quickly and significantly after people see or experience incivility:

- A team with a single person who is disrespectful "suffers a performance disadvantage of 30% to 40% compared to teams that have no bad apples."[81]
- Employees interpret incivility as strong disrespect. Incivility and disrespect, in turn, are correlated with lower levels of employee creativity, motivation, productivity, and trust.[82] Incivility creates a toxic work environment where "people feel disrespected, underappreciated, neglected, or abused."[83]
- Simply seeing an employee act rudely toward another employee heightens sensitivity to discourteous behavior and diminishes performance. In one study, employees who witnessed rude behavior in the early morning perceived more acts of incivility throughout the day, and their work performance

[79] Porath, Christine. (2016). *Mastering civility* (pp. 51–52). New York: Hachette Book Group.

[80] Sutton, Robert. (2011, October 24). How a few bad apples ruin everything. *The Wall Street Journal*.

[81] Sutton, Robert I. (2010, September 8). Bad is stronger than good: Evidence-based advice for bosses. *Harvard Business Review*. Felps, Will, Mitchell, Terence R., & Byington, Eliza. (2006). How, when, and why bad apples spoil the barrel: Negative group members and dysfunctional groups. *Research in Organizational Behavior, 27*, 175.

[82] Amabile, Teresa, & Kramer, Steven. (2012, Winter). The progress principle: Optimizing inner work life to create value. *Rotman Magazine*, p. 33.

[83] Ibid.

suffered materially.[84] "Their task performance and goal progress was low, they avoided interactions with their co-workers, and they avoided thinking about work," states management professor Andrew Woolum. "All of a sudden, everyone seemed rude, so they disengaged, which killed their performance."[85]

- When people are subjected to incivility, they quickly reduce their involvement with their work. In a survey of 800 employees and managers, 48 percent reported that they "intentionally decreased their work effort" after encountering incivility.[86] Forty-seven percent said they also decreased the time spent at work, and 38 percent acknowledged that they "intentionally decreased the quality of their work."[87] Nearly 80 percent of the surveyed workers said their commitment to the organization declined.[88]

- Negative interactions at the workplace have five times as much impact on employees as positive interactions.[89] Negative impressions are formed more quickly than positive impressions, and they last longer than positive impressions.[90] People, in short, are more sensitive to negative interactions. As psychologist Roy Baumeister notes, "we found bad to be stronger than good in a disappointingly relentless pattern."[91]

Research also indicates that rudeness is contagious. A single act of rudeness leads to rudeness in subsequent interactions, as the

---

[84] Woolum, Andrew, Foulk, Trevor, Lanaj, Klodiana, & Erez, Amir. (2017, December). Rude color glasses: The contaminating effects of witnessed morning rudeness on perceptions and behaviors throughout the workday. *Journal of Applied Psychology, 102*(12), 1658–1672.

[85] Mitchell, Heidi. (2018, February 19). The big impact of a little rudeness at work. *The Wall Street Journal.*

[86] Porath, Christine, & Pearson, Christine. (2013, January–February). The price of incivility. *Harvard Business Review.*

[87] Ibid.

[88] Ibid.

[89] Miner, A. G., Glomb, T. M., & Hulin, C. (2005). Experience sampling mood and its correlates at work. *Journal of Occupational and Organizational Psychology, 78,* 171–193.

[90] Baumeister, Roy F., Bratslavsky, Ellen, Finkenauer, Catrin, & Vohs, Kathleen D. (2001). Bad is stronger than good. *Review of General Psychology, 5*(4), 323.

[91] Ibid. at 362.

subject of the first rude interaction becomes a "carrier," replicating the rude behavior in his next interaction.[92]

Despite popular depictions of successful attorneys as being self-absorbed, brusque, and overbearing, the empirical evidence demonstrates that jerks and bullies fare poorly in the workplace.[93] People who are perceived as being civil (defined as "treating someone respectfully, with dignity, politeness or pleasantry") are more likely to be regarded as leaders and to be sought out for advice.[94] Employees who believe that their leader is respectful display "92% greater focus and prioritization, 56% better health and well-being, and 55% more engagement."[95] Civility also is correlated with large professional networks, information sharing, team commitment, initiative, creativity, productivity, and performance.[96] One study, moreover, indicates that the most frequent cause of executive failure is an "insensitive, abrasive or bullying style."[97]

If law firms find that, notwithstanding the empirical evidence, their bullies and jerks are thriving, that should be a cause of deep concern, not relief. Those law firms may not be aware of the hidden costs of their most difficult partners, including high staff and attorney attrition rates, unproductive associate attorneys, client defections, and fewer new clients. Law firms harboring fugitives from civility also never know the opportunities they missed for client referrals, firm mergers, or other lucrative ventures. Eric Seeger, a law firm management consultant with Altman Weil, recalls many occasions when "we have approached a firm with a growth

---

[92] Woolum, Andrew., & Foulk, Trevor. (2016, January). Catching rudeness is like catching a cold: The contagion effects of low-intensity negative behaviors. *Journal of Applied Psychology, 101*(1), 50.

[93] See Filisko, G. M. (2013, January) You're out of order! *ABA Journal*, p. 37. (Lawyers blame incivility on "[o]ver-the-top portrayals of lawyers on TV and in films" and the "fuzzy line between aggressive advocacy and rudeness.") (2015, October). Lawyer bullies, incivility: On policing lawyer manners. *Your ABA*.

[94] Porath, Christine. (2016, November 23). Civility at work helps everyone get ahead. *The Wall Street Journal*.

[95] Ibid.

[96] Porath (2016), *supra* note 79 at 26–36.

[97] Ibid. at 36.

opportunity and a key partner has said, 'I would never join Firm A as long as a certain lawyer is in the firm.'"[98]

Diversity

Clients are losing patience with their law firms' failure to diversify their workforce. Law firm leaders assure clients that they are committed to diversity, but they often neglect to implement this commitment in their hiring practices. Rick Palmore, a former general counsel and recipient of the General Counsel Lifetime Achievement Award by New York Stock Exchange Governance Services, says that law firms had "a script of platitudes" when he questioned them about diversity. As he dug deeper and asked them how they tracked diversity data, his inquiries were "met with blank looks."[99] Judges also see through law firms' superficial displays of diversity. U.S. District Judge Terry Hatter, for instance, observes, "On the civil side as well, you get these employment discrimination and various civil rights cases and the firms are smart enough to bring in that one minority associate and put them on the case." Judge Terry adds, "I just sit and laugh about it, but no that doesn't affect me being fair."[100]

About one-half of corporate attorneys state that they do not have confidence in outside counsel creating diversity and inclusion strategies.[101] Since they lack confidence in law firms' diversity programs, corporations are imposing their own requirements on their outside counsel. HP Inc., for example, withholds 10 percent of fees billed by law firms that do not meet its diversity standards.[102] "I think that as customers of legal services, we are entitled to request that the work be performed to our standards and satisfaction," asserts HP Chief Legal Officer Kim Rivera, "and those standards absolutely can include having diverse teams."[103] HP's diversity standards, applicable

---

[98]   McQueen, *supra* note 76.

[99]   Rawles, Lee. (2017, October). How can GCs be a force for change? *ABA Journal.*

[100] Keys, Laurinda. (2015, September 22). Old school. *San Francisco Daily Journal,* p. 2.

[101] Bloomberg Law. (2016). *Diversity and inclusion: Annual report.*

[102] Williams-Alvarez, Jennifer. (2017, February 14). HP's GC says "diversity mandate" embraced by law firms. *San Francisco Daily Journal.*

[103] Ibid.

to law firms with 10 or more attorneys, require them to have "at least one diverse firm relationship partner regularly engaged with HP" or "at least one woman and one racially/ethnically diverse attorney, each performing or managing at least 10 percent of the billable hours worked on HP matters."[104]

Facebook specifically requires that 33 percent of its law firm teams be composed of women and ethnic minorities.[105] In addition, their law firms must show that they "actively identify and create clear and measurable leadership opportunities for women and minorities."[106] Those opportunities, explains Facebook general counsel Colin Stretch, "include serving as relationship managers and representing Facebook in the courtroom."[107] JPMorgan Chase's policy is yet more stringent; it requires that women and diverse lawyers hold at least 50 percent of the leadership positions on litigation teams.[108] Other companies adopting strong diversity policies for outside counsel include Microsoft Corp., CBRE, Inc., MetLife, and Toyota.[109]

For some corporate counsel, law firms' cavalier attitude toward diversity is not only objectionable but borders on being preposterous. Stacey Friedman, general counsel for JPMorgan Chase, recalls a meeting with five white male partners from a large, prominent firm. They were seeking new assignments from JPMorgan Chase, although female attorneys were absent from leadership roles in their firm's litigation teams. When asked about the firm's diversity efforts, "the men had only halfhearted answers to her questions."[110] Shortly after leaving the meeting, Friedman told her colleagues, "We're not hiring them for a year."[111] In an interview conducted in

---

[104] Ibid.

[105] Rosen, Ellen. (2017, April 2). Facebook pushes outside law firms to become more diverse. *The New York Times.*

[106] Ibid.

[107] Ibid.

[108] Rozen, Miriam. (2018, February 2). JPMorgan holds law firms' feet to the fire on diversity. *The American Lawyer.*

[109] Mulvaney, Erin. (2017, October 17). Outside counsel diversity initiatives force companies to confront norms. *The American Lawyer.* Kirby, Lisa, & Stacy, Caren Ulrich. (2017, July 17). Client call for greater diversity at fever pitch. *Law.com.*

[110] Rozen (2018), *supra* note 108.

[111] Ibid.

2012 while she was General Counsel at Reddit, Inc., Rebecca Lynn Eisenberg described similar experiences with some law firms' proposals:

I've had the chance to send out a lot of work on a request-for-proposal basis. One of the things that has always shocked me is when lawyers think that it is OK to send a team that's all white men in 2012. I would say that a lot of us [general counsel] are women. Some of us are minorities. I would urge law firms that we do expect teams to be better diversified, and I don't mean all partners being male and all associates being female. I've expressed that to some of the firms when they've responded to RFPs. I think, "Are you kidding me, you just gave me a 20-staff proposal where they are all male?"

It makes me wonder about the firm: Do they respect women? Are they going to respect me as their client? Do they think I have something to offer? What is that bias? I worry. I just won't hire them. I don't have to. There are so many law firms out there with so many capable lawyers. All things being equal, why would I choose the nondiverse team over the diverse team?[112]

An attorney at another corporation finds that law firms' attitudes toward diversity and inclusion mirror their culture. She sees "a direct correlation between the success of a firm's diversity and inclusion initiatives and the culture of the firm."[113]

As discussed in Chapter 3, law firms presumably do not intend to discriminate against female and ethnic minority attorneys, but the actual effect of their hiring and compensation practices is to reduce opportunities for female and ethnic minority attorneys and to compensate female attorneys, on average, at lower rates than male attorneys. These practices are nonrandom, persistent, and pervasive. They reflect personal and systemic biases that have been

---

[112] Lee, Kevin. (2012, July 9). Moving at byte speed. *San Francisco Daily Journal*, p. 5.

[113] Bloomberg Law, *supra* note 101.

allowed to fester in the legal profession for decades. For perspective on the gravity and duration of prejudice and bias in the legal profession, attorneys need only recall that Harvard Law School did not admit women until 1950, and the American Bar Association explicitly banned Black attorneys from membership until 1954.[114] About 70 years after Harvard Law School first admitted women, the status of women in law firms remains inferior, if not marginal: 22 percent of law firms have no women on their governing committees; 40 percent have only one woman or no women at all on their compensation committee; only 25 percent of firms have a female chair or co-chair of their corporate department; and only 33 percent have a female chair or co-chair of their litigation department.[115]

Law firms claim to be correcting their biases by accelerating their diversity efforts, but clients recognize that firms move faster on issues they perceive to be of greater importance to their profitability. Noting that law firms promptly cut expenses and changed their compensation structures after the Great Recession, yet they have made scant progress in promoting diversity relative to their corporate clients, former Bloomberg BNA Legal President David Perla states:

It does make me wince a little bit when firms have made so much progress around their cost structures and other things in such a relatively short amount of time. Why exactly is this such an intractable problem? If other things that seemed embedded have been changed almost foundationally in less than a decade, is it that there's just no repercussion to not doing this the way there is at larger companies? If the smartest people in America have been working on a problem for 10 years and it really isn't needle-moved, that's a strange thing.[116]

---

[114] Linowitz, Sol M., & Mayer, Martin. (1994). *The betrayed profession: Lawyering at the end of the twentieth century.* New York: Charles Scribner's Sons.

[115] Triedman, Julie. (2015, June). A few good women. *The American Lawyer.*

[116] Schallert, Amanda. (2016, June 1). Women in Law Hackathon aims to find new ways to advance female attorneys. *San Francisco Daily Journal*, p. 4.

The perception that law firms may not be serious about diversity is substantiated by a Bloomberg survey of law firm attorneys. Asked what their law firms do to recognize those people who work on diversity and inclusion strategies, 31 percent of the attorneys responded, "Does not do anything."[117] Only eight percent of the attorneys said that their firms "reward those involved," while 31 percent said their firms "give recognition to those involved."[118]

Attorneys are quite candid in identifying the challenges their law firms face in advancing diversity and inclusion. The most frequently cited obstacle to diversity and inclusion is "implicit/unconscious bias," followed by "lack of diversity on executive committee," "lack of succession planning for institutional client relationships," "not getting asked to go on client pitches," and "lack of diversity on compensation committee."[119] Female and ethnic minority attorneys report that senior partners do not introduce them to their clients, and they are not assigned to lead roles on cases. A "good ol' boys' club mentality," they note, reinforces biases in law firm leadership and creates "a very real ceiling for minority success."[120] One attorney states, "leadership, which is white male dominated, needs to buy into diversity and consider it important, which they do not at the moment. It should not be only window-dressing."[121]

Law firms that intend to move from "window dressing" to actual results in promoting diversity and inclusion should implement, at a minimum, the following 10 practices:[122]

---

[117] Bloomberg Law, *supra* note 101 at 6.

[118] Ibid. See Araya, Kibkabe. (2015, September 3). Corporate counsel retool diversity push. *San Francisco Daily Journal*, p. 1.

[119] Bloomberg Law, *supra* note 101 at 5. For purposes of the Bloomberg Law survey, diversity was defined as "the range of human differences, including but not limited to race, ethnicity, gender, gender identity, sexual orientation, age, social class, physical ability or attributes, religious or ethical values system, national origin, and political beliefs." Inclusion was defined as "involvement and empowerment, where the inherent worth and dignity of all people are recognized. An inclusive organization promotes and sustains a sense of belonging; it values and practices respect for the talents, beliefs, backgrounds, and ways of living of its members."

[120] Ibid.

[121] Ibid.

[122] The 10 measures are derived primarily from Bloomberg Law, *supra* note 101, and the Appendix to ALM Intelligence. (2017). *Where do we go from here?: Big Law's struggle with recruiting and retaining female talent.*

1. Increase diverse representation on firm management and talent development committees by establishing specific representation goals and regularly evaluating whether those goals have been achieved. If the actual representation remains below the goals for two or more years, firms should consider replacing the goals with quotas to overcome their biases. Quotas may be necessary because law firms' diversity goals tend to be more aspirational than effectual. In 2016, for instance, only 24 percent of law firms achieved their annual diversity goals, and in previous years only 9 percent of law firms achieved them.[123]

2. Ensure that female attorneys have 50 percent or more representation on compensation committees. (Firms that have three or more female attorneys on compensation committees achieve "near parity in compensation among men and women equity partners.")[124]

3. Provide transparent monetary incentives for lawyers and practice groups that measurably increase diversity and inclusion.

4. Maintain accurate diversity data regarding all attorneys, including attrition rates, and ensure that governing committees review the data every six months.

5. Conduct a pay audit to determine compliance with "the federal Equal Pay Act, Title VII of the Civil Rights Act, or individual state laws."[125]

6. Provide networking and mentoring opportunities for diverse attorneys, and establish metrics for client pitch meetings to ensure that diverse attorneys are included in those marketing activities and the origination credits that result from those activities.

7. Form a diversity and inclusion committee to monitor the firm's progress in meeting its diversity and inclusion goals and to serve in an advisory capacity.

---

[123] Major, Lindsey, & Africa. (2017). *Law firm recruiting & development survey* (p. 12).

[124] Jackson, Liane. (2017, October). Who's the best? *ABA Journal*. Triedman, *supra* note 115.

[125] ALM Intelligence, *supra* note 122.

8. Redesign attorney interview processes to require structured interviews based on specific competencies and behavioral questions.[126] "Lawyers are particularly susceptible to certain forms of bias," states Paola Cecchi-Dimeglio, a senior research fellow at Harvard Law School's Center on the Legal Profession, "because, ironically, their training leads them to believe they can be fair and impartial, particularly in the hiring process."[127]

9. Ensure that female attorneys constitute a majority of associate attorney hiring and lateral partner hiring committee members.

10. Establish and implement diversity goals for new partner classes.

Chapter Capsule

Effective law firms share five practices: collaboration among attorneys and practice groups; sound decision making in client matters and firm operations; readiness to change perceptions and behavior; civility in relating to colleagues and subordinates; and diversity and inclusion in practice groups, teams, and leadership roles.

Collaboration increases firm revenue, client satisfaction, attorney engagement, and intra-firm referrals. When two practice groups collaborate in serving a client, the revenue from that client does not double; it triples. Collaboration also reduces client defections and attorney errors. Law firms can promote collaboration by learning more about their clients' needs and establishing formal programs in which information about different practice groups and attorneys' specialization areas is exchanged. Informal meetings and activities, where attorneys learn about each other's practice and expertise, also promote collaboration.

Professional decision making can be refined at four levels: preparing to make decisions, making decisions, implementing decisions, and evaluating decisions. Proficient decision makers begin by determining whether they tend to be risk-averse or risk-taking decision makers and then enlisting other people to offset biases

---

[126] See Henderson, William. (2016, February). Solving the legal profession's diversity problem. *PD Quarterly*.

[127] Cecchi-Dimeglio, Paola. (2017). *Nudging law firms to hire and promote more women.* Thomson Reuters Legal Executive Institute.

in their decision-making styles. They also monitor their decision making to assess whether and how their decision-making styles have evolved to reflect their experience, knowledge, and responsibilities. In making decisions, proficient decision makers elicit multiple opinions, practice the art of humble inquiry, generate multiple problem-solving alternatives, and conduct a premortem. When decisions are being implemented, proficient decision makers attempt to test them on a small scale, anticipate how people will respond to decisions at an emotional level, and develop sufficient detachment from their decisions to know when to modify or abandon them. In the evaluation phase, proficient decision makers continually assess the results of their decision and set new and tougher goals for their next decision. They also regard their mistakes as immensely valuable learning opportunities.

Effective law firms exhibit a state of readiness—a commitment to change and an ability to implement changes. Readiness is developed and enhanced by six mindsets: (1) preoccupation with failure, enabling people to detect and solve problems in their earliest stage and prevent similar problems from occurring in the future; (2) attention to near-misses and faint signals, teaching people to regard small errors as harbingers of larger problems; (3) reluctance to simplify, forcing people to acknowledge and apprehend the complexity and potential consequences of problems; (4) deference to expertise, encouraging people to defer to their most knowledgeable, not their most powerful, colleagues; (5) flat communication, facilitating the exchange of information based on functions rather than status in an organization; and (6) a duty to question leaders, legitimizing dissent and promoting initiative, candor, and objectivity.

Effective law firms also are dedicated to civility, diversity, and inclusion. They do not tolerate bullying, and they recognize that abusive behavior in any form saps motivation, decreases productivity, and harms work product quality. Their respect for human dignity and individual rights results in a diverse workforce that meets new, more stringent client requirements. Their clients are convinced that their commitment to diversity is more than window dressing; it is embodied in the firm's culture and reflected every day in its workforce and practices.

8

Systems

Systems are at the intersection of law firms' policies, strategies, priorities, and values. Systems determine whether concepts and ideas become actions and programs. They also serve as tests of the sincerity, depth, and durability of law firms' commitment to changes that are publicly espoused but may be privately deprecated. Until changes are embedded in systems, law firms have not made the tangible investments that demonstrate they are genuinely committed to turn sentiments into operations.

Although systems are often perceived as being dull and uninspired, they actually represent a law firm's view of its attorneys and clients. Systems ultimately reveal the attitudes and beliefs that prevail at a firm, and they strongly affect how attorneys perform their work and how clients are treated at that firm. Systems that strictly curtail individual initiative and autonomy, for example, may reflect a lack of trust, while systems that enshrine independence may indicate that attorney autonomy is more important than uniform client service standards. When no system exists to implement an espoused firm goal, as often occurs with diversity and inclusion efforts, that goal is functionally inconsequential and intended to be overlooked and eventually forgotten. Systems, in short, determine whether an intention evolves into a practice.

This chapter identifies and discusses seven types of systems essential to effective law firms:

1. Quality control, feedback, and evaluation systems
2. Attorney compensation systems
3. Technology and information management systems
4. Lateral attorney integration systems
5. Succession planning
6. Attorney wellness systems
7. Pro bono systems

This list is not exhaustive but instead identifies seven systems necessary to meet minimum standards of effectiveness.

Quality Control, Feedback, and Evaluation Systems

Law firms are usually diligent about conducting formal associate attorney evaluations. But they falter in evaluating their own partners and eliciting feedback from clients. As discussed below, law firms would benefit from changing the method and timing of associate attorney evaluations, reducing palpable biases in evaluating female and ethnic minority attorneys, implementing regular partner evaluations, and obtaining client feedback.

Associate Attorney Performance Evaluations

Employees dread performance evaluations, and their unease is matched by their employers' anxiety in providing them. One in four surveyed employees "said they dread such evaluations more than anything else in their working lives."[1] Most employees, moreover, think performance evaluations are unfair or inaccurate.[2] Their distrust of performance evaluations may be well-founded.

---

[1]   Heen, Sheila, & Stone, Douglas. (2014, January–February). Finding the coaching in criticism. *Harvard Business Review.* Weber, Lauren. (2017, September 1). As workers expect less, job satisfaction rises. *The Wall Street Journal.* (Employees are least satisfied with these five work components: recognition, performance review, educational/job training, bonus plan, and promotion policy.)

[2]   Hancock, Bryan, Hioe, Elizabeth, & Schaninger, Bill. (2018, April) The fairness factor in performance management. *McKinsey Quarterly.* Heen & Stone, *supra* note 1.

In one study, for instance, managers who shared responsibility for directing employees' work rarely agreed on an employee's ratings. "If one said seven, the other said below a four or a five," states R. J. Heckman, president of Leadership and Talent Consulting at Korn Ferry. "There was a shocking disagreement on very basic areas."[3]

Reflecting their own anxiety about presenting evaluations, most managers fail to complete performance reviews thoroughly and on time.[4] They also are unable or unwilling to participate in difficult feedback discussions with employees.[5] Given managers' reluctance to provide timely and meaningful feedback, it is no surprise that 58 percent of executives believe that "their company's current approach to performance management did absolutely nothing to drive engagement or performance."[6]

For many attorneys, the most difficult part of their work is evaluating subordinate attorneys and working with them to correct their performance deficiencies. When asked what keeps her up at night, Barbara Levi Mager, General Counsel and Global Head of Legal at Sandoz, responded,

---

It is not legal issues or cases that keep me up at night, it is people. The emotional part is the hard part; when you have a conversation about gaps in performance or with someone whose self-image is radically different from your own perception. How do you convey your message with clarity and show respect at the same time? How do you find the right balance of challenging and supporting? How do you stay true to your own judgment but keep an open mind for different opinions?[7]

---

[3] Charan, Ram, Barton, Dominic, & Carey, Dennis. (2018). *Talent wins* (p. 115). Boston: Harvard Business Review Press.
[4] Heen & Stone, *supra* note 1.
[5] Ibid. When reviews are conducted, it is critical to limit them to observable behavior; avoid comments about an employee's thoughts or motives; evaluate only behavior than can be independently verified; and focus exclusively on employee actions that are directly linked to client service and firm performance. Cappelli, Peter, & Tavis, Anna. (2016, October). The performance management revolution. *Harvard Business Review.*
[6] Charan, Barton, & Carey, *supra* note 3 at 116.
[7] Major, Lindsey, & Africa. (2018, March 6). Sandoz GC Barbara Levi Mager on following your passion. *The American Lawyer.*

Many attorneys cope with the stress of subordinate attorneys' performance deficiencies by ignoring them. They write off associate attorneys' time and eventually withhold assignments.[8] Since the clients' work still needs to be done, "it is all too often dumped on A players, creating morale problems for the best associates. The C players linger until the firm eventually terminates them for low billable hours or poor performance."[9] The result is a prolonged, inefficient process of extricating poorly performing attorneys—at a cost of $210,000—$280,000 per attorney in lost revenue.[10]

The simplest way to reduce the anxiety of performance reviews and the delays in taking corrective action is to conduct more frequent reviews. Formal annual or semiannual reviews are being replaced by ongoing feedback and informal evaluations. "With a less structured approach," explains Bruce Nolop, the former chief financial officer of E*Trade Financial and Pitney Bowes, "managers have the onus to become more engaged and to anticipate the right junctures to communicate with each individual. It also makes it easier to separate performance reviews from compensation decisions, which facilitates more constructive discussions and fewer surprises."[11]

Companies that have shifted from annual reviews to regular feedback include Adobe, General Electric, Deloitte, Accenture, IBM, and Microsoft.[12] They find that performance problems are identified more rapidly; feedback is more thorough and interactive; employee defensiveness is reduced; and employees' perceptions of fairness and their sense that they "know where they stand" are increased.[13] Ongoing feedback is particularly critical to retaining Millennial

---

[8]   Picht, Jeanne M., & Stacy, Caren Ulrich. (2013, May/June). Solving the multi-million dollar C player problem. *Law Practice Magazine, 39,* 3.

[9]   Ibid.

[10]   Ibid.

[11]   Nolop, Bruce. (2016, September 18). What if performance reviews lasted all year? *The Wall Street Journal.*

[12]   Cappelli & Tavis, *supra* note 5.

[13]   See Buckingham, Marcus, & Goodall, Ashley. (2015, April). Reinventing performance management. *Harvard Business Review.* Feintzeig, Rachel. (2017, May 9). The never-ending performance review. *The Wall Street Journal.* Hoffman, Liz. (2017, April 21). Goldman goes beyond annual review with real-time employee feedback. *The Wall Street Journal.*

generation employees, who expect open and direct communication about their performance and careers. "If you're giving them lots of feedback and being transparent," states Edith Cooper, Goldman Sachs' Global Head of Human Capital Management, "that will create some stickiness."[14]

Law firms are slowly changing their associate attorney evaluation systems. Reed Smith, Blank Rome, and Drinker Biddle, for example, are supplementing their annual evaluations with quarterly performance reviews or considering new methods of obtaining ongoing feedback.[15] Hogan Lovells stopped its annual reviews in 2018 and instituted a new program that encourages associate attorneys to elicit feedback from partners.[16] One feature of the new Hogan Lovells program is "flash feedback," which requires associate attorneys to obtain three feedback items every four months. Steve Immelt, CEO of Hogan Lovells, describes the annual review system as "broken in a number of respects and not really delivering what our people needed and wanted."[17]

Biases in Attorney Evaluations

Recent studies indicate that attorneys' performance evaluations are sometimes tainted by racism and gender bias. In one study, 53 law firm partners evaluated the same memorandum reportedly prepared by an associate attorney (but actually prepared for the study by five senior attorneys). Twenty-nine of the partners participating in the study were told the memorandum was written by "a Caucasian man named Thomas Meyer," and 24 partners were told that the memorandum was written by "an African-American named Thomas Meyer."[18] The partners rated the memorandum, supposedly written by the White attorney, 4.1 on a 1–5 scale.

---

[14] Hoffman, *supra* note 13.

[15] McLellan, Lizzy. (2017, May 12). Young lawyers demand more feedback, firms deliver. *The Legal Intelligencer*.

[16] Lovelace, Ryan. (2018, April 12). Hogan Lovells scraps 'broken' review system for associates. *The American Lawyer*. Eversheds Sutherland also dropped its annual performance reviews in 2018. See Walker, Rose. (2018, May 24). Eversheds Sutherland scraps annual performance reviews. *The American Lawyer*.

[17] Ibid.

[18] Weiss, Debra Cassens. (2014, April 21). Partners in study gave legal memo a lower rating when told author wasn't white. *ABA Journal*.

But the same memorandum, supposedly written by the Black attorney, was rated 3.2.[19] The partners also had difficulties detecting the spelling and grammar errors in the memorandum ostensibly prepared by the White Thomas Meyer; they found only about one-half of the errors in that memorandum. But the same errors in the memorandum by the African American Thomas Meyer were somehow more salient; the partners detected nearly all of those errors. As reported in the *ABA Journal*, "the white Thomas Meyer was praised for his potential and good analytical skills, while the black Thomas Meyer was criticized as average at best and needing a lot of work."[20]

In a study of 253 associate attorneys at a major Wall Street law firm, researchers discovered extensive gender bias that affected female attorneys' partnership opportunities. The partners in that firm prepared numerical ratings and narrative evaluations of the associate attorneys. Only the numerical ratings were considered in partnership decisions. The researchers, using text analysis software and working with independent coders who reviewed the narrative evaluations, concluded:

- The narrative ratings either "favored the women being rated or treated them no less favorably than men."[21] But 14.5 percent of the male attorneys and only 5 percent of the female attorneys received numerical evaluations higher than a 4.5 on a 1–5 scale.[22]
- "Male supervisors judged male attorneys more favorably than female attorneys on numerical ratings that mattered for promotion but offered narrative comments that showed either no sex effects or greater favorability toward women."[23]

---

[19] Ibid.

[20] Ibid.

[21] Weiss, Debra Cassens. (2011, October 26). Study finds disconnect between numbers and narratives in associate job reviews—but only for women. *ABA Journal*.

[22] Ibid.

[23] Biernat, Monica M., Tocci, J., & Williams, Joan C. (2012). The language of performance evaluations. *Social Psychological and Personality Science, 3*(2), 186.

- "Men who were praised for technical competence tended to receive better numerical ratings than women who received the same degree of praise."[24]
- "Women criticized for low interpersonal warmth tended to receive lower numerical ratings than men who were criticized for the same problem."[25]

Joan Williams, one of the study researchers and a professor at UC Hastings College of the Law, states: "This study suggests that one reason law firms can't keep women is that firms' evaluation systems are not correcting for implicit biases that disadvantage women. Law firms need to adopt best practices, including having someone trained to spot gender bias reviewing all evaluations before they become final."[26]

Partner Evaluations

Once an associate attorney becomes a partner, many law firms act as though the evaluation process has served its purpose and can be shut down for the balance of the partner's career. One of the implicit agreements that often attends partnership status is an assurance that a partner's performance shortfalls may be considered in determining compensation but will not be used to coerce substantive behavioral changes. When partners are subjected to evaluations, including 360-degree evaluations from associate attorneys, many partners are dismissive, regarding the evaluations as a trespass onto their prerogatives and a violation of their status. This partner's reaction is illustrative:

And some partners are subjected to 360-degree reviews from their charges. I have a hard time seeing the value of those. The whole process is thankless, time consuming, and generally useless. It is more akin to "security theater" at the airport than an

---

[24] Weiss, *supra* note 21.
[25] Ibid.
[26] Ibid. See also Snyder, Kieran. (2014, August 26). The abrasiveness trap: High-achieving men and women are described differently in reviews. *Fortune.*

> actual system for providing effective feedback and incentives to Biglaw participants. . . . So I am not a big fan of Biglaw reviews today, and consider myself fortunate to have been spared them while I was an associate.[27]

This attitude is consistent with studies demonstrating that, as people ascend the status hierarchy and become more affluent, they pay less attention to others' ideas, opinions, and advice.[28] As management professor Kelly See observed in her study of 200 managers, "They tended to feel they were right, they were more accurate and they felt less need for taking others' advice—even if they were, in fact, wrong."[29]

Partner evaluations are complicated by the fact that partners do not agree on the elements of superior partner performance and how those elements should be measured and weighted. Although associate training, mentoring programs, public service, and law firm leadership are considered valuable contributions, they ultimately receive little attention relative to client origination and gross billings. And although firms frequently emphasize profitability, they may not share common concepts, definitions, or methods of determining profitability. As consultant Jim Hassett, who studied 50 Am Law 200 firms, explains:

> When we asked, "If you compare profitability for two lawyers in your firm, is there a software program or formula used to calculate profitability or is the comparison more intuitive?" a surprising 26% said it was intuitive. For the other 74%, definitions

---

27   Anonymous partner. (2012, October 6). Buying in: Upon further review. *Above the Law.*

28   See, Kelly E., Morrison, Elizabeth Wolfe, Rothman, Naomi B., & Soll, Jack B. (2011, August 2). The detrimental effects of power on confidence, advice taking, and accuracy. *Organizational Behavior and Human Decision Processes,* 116(2), 272-285. Tost, Leigh, Gino, Francesca, & Larrick, Richard. (2012, January). Power competitiveness, and advice taking: Why the powerful don't listen. *Organizational Behavior and Human Decision Processes, 117*(1), 53.

29   Silverman, Rachel Emma. (2011, September 19). Some managers just won't take advice. *The Wall Street Journal.*

and formulas varied widely, including total revenue, profits per equity partner, leverage, several different types of realization, and a variety of approaches to cost accounting.[30]

Hassett points to a managing partner who told him, "I have a $10 million practice. But that could be a disaster for a firm, because it could cost them $11 million to get $10 million. But nobody ever talks about it that way."[31]

Client Evaluations

Law firms do not uniformly seek client feedback, and to the extent they obtain feedback, their attorneys may not respond to it. Although law firms claim they are making great strides in "building closer ties with key clients," less than one-half of law firms conduct systematic client surveys and interviews.[32] When law firms elicit clients' feedback, most of them report that their lawyers are "ambivalent" or "not enthusiastic" about the firm's efforts.[33] One popular way of responding to attorney resistance is to insulate them from client feedback; only one-third of law firms "communicate feedback to lawyers and other staff that actually deal with the client."[34]

Clients report that their law firms rarely elicit feedback. Only 16 percent of clients, according to an Acritas survey, "have been invited to participate in feedback programs in the last 12 months."[35] Tom Trujillo, deputy general counsel at Wells Fargo Bank, recalls only four law firms conducting a client interview with

[30] Hassett, Jim. (2014). *Client value and law firm profitability* (p. 7). Boston: LegalBizDev.
[31] Ibid. at 6.
[32] Cohen, Alan. (2011, December 1). Building a breakout firm. *The American Lawyer*. Olsen, Dana. (2011, June 28). Survey: Half of law firms don't seek client feedback. *Law.com*. Seeger, Eric A., & Clay, Thomas S. (2017). *2017 Law firms in transition* (p. 8). Newtown Square, PA: Altman Weil.
[33] (2011, June 28). LexisNexis: Global survey finds majority of law firms missing benefits of client feedback. [Press release].
[34] Ibid.
[35] Duffy, Elizabeth. (2017, May 18). How client feedback programs benefit law firms and clients. *Law 360*.

him—although he has served as in-house counsel for 18 years.[36] His experience is similar to that of Jennifer Ishiguro, the former chief legal officer of Gateway One Lending & Finance. "It's also the precious few that call from time to time to ask how we are doing, what we are doing well, what we could be doing better and how we could further improve the relationship on both sides," she reflects.[37]

Law firms apparently do not understand that they are the primary beneficiaries of client feedback. Feedback is a gift from clients, not an irritant inflicted on beleaguered attorneys by their unappreciative clients. When clients are irreversibly dissatisfied with their law firms, they simply take their next legal matter to another law firm, and they do not waste additional time on what they see as an unsatisfactory vendor relationship. Client feedback enables attorneys to prevent that defection.

When asked whether his general approach is to "move on from a law firm when you are unhappy with its work product," Daniel McIntosh, general counsel of Content Partners, replies,

---

In the ordinary course, I probably am inclined to move on. . . . There are firms that follow up with you. Usually, it would be someone else from the firm calling to see how the firm is doing and what it could improve. Those are helpful opportunities. I think follow-up from lawyers after a large transaction is helpful. I think that would be a way that rough edges could be smoothed out. I think good law firms may not want to impose on their clients but I think most inside counsel would be happy to help outside counsel improve on their service delivery. I don't really see it as my function to provide input on how they did on a transaction. But I'm happy to respond if someone wants to solicit my view.[38]

---

[36]   Whitaker, Kathryn B. (2018, April 4). Focusing on client retention may mean restructuring the firm. *The American Lawyer*.

[37]   Klam, Jennifer Chung. (2016, July 4). Driving commerce. *San Francisco Daily Journal*.

[38]   Brisbon, Melanie. (2017, February 7). Opening the vault. *San Francisco Daily Journal*, p. 6.

The impetus is on law firms to seek their clients' evaluations. The clients themselves can easily retain other law firms that either provide better client service or at least make an effort to learn how to improve their service.

Compensation Systems

Law firm partners generally are pleased with their compensation. Four out of five partners in the Major, Lindsey, & Africa partner compensation survey state that they are "very" or "somewhat" satisfied with their total compensation.[39] Satisfaction, however, varies significantly with the following individual characteristics: gender, race, partnership status, tenure, client originations, and total compensation. The effects of these factors are summarized below:[40]

- *Gender.* Twenty-seven percent of female partners are "not very satisfied" or "not at all satisfied" with their compensation, compared to 19 percent of male partners.
- *Race.* Thirty-eight percent of Black partners are "not very satisfied" or "not at all satisfied" with their compensation, compared to 28 percent of Hispanic attorneys and 20 percent of White attorneys. Fifty percent of American Indian attorneys report that they are "not very satisfied" or "not at all satisfied" with their compensation.
- *Partnership status.* Sixteen percent of equity partners are "not very satisfied" or "not at all satisfied" with their compensation, while 35 percent of non-equity partners are "not very satisfied" or "not at all satisfied" with their compensation.
- *Tenure.* Eight-four percent of attorneys who have been partners for 21 years or more are very or somewhat satisfied with their compensation, compared with 72 percent of attorneys who have been partners for one to five years. Partner satisfaction with compensation rises uniformly with partnership tenure.

---

[39] Lowe, Jeffrey A. (2016). *2016 Partner Compensation Survey* (p. 24). Major, Lindsey, & Africa.

[40] All data in the bulleted points is derived from Lowe, *supra* note 39 at 24–34.

- *Client originations.* Eighty-nine percent of partners with total originations exceeding $5 million are very or somewhat satisfied with their compensation, compared with 71 percent of partners with originations below $1 million.
- *Total compensation.* More money does seem to make more partners happy. Ninety-four percent of partners with annual compensation exceeding $1.5 million are very or somewhat satisfied with their compensation, compared with only 75 percent of partners making less than $300,000. Partner satisfaction rises uniformly with compensation increases at all levels.

Two systemic factors also affect partner satisfaction with compensation: open versus closed systems and lockstep versus non-lockstep systems. Eighty-two percent of partners in firms with an open compensation system (partners can learn what other partners are earning) are very or somewhat satisfied, compared with 69 percent of partners in closed compensation systems (compensation is known only to compensation committee members).[41] Open compensation systems also are correlated with higher originations. Average partner originations in open systems are $2.76 million, compared with $1.51 million in closed systems.[42] Even when they are fairly implemented, closed compensation systems generally provoke suspicion and incite surmise in the absence of disclosure. As one partner notes, "closed compensation systems allow the decision makers to unfairly compensate people—both high and low."[43]

Surprisingly, partners appear to be more satisfied with lockstep systems, despite the oft-repeated criticism that they penalize individual effort and achievement because partners at the same tenure

---

[41] Lowe, *supra* note 39 at 28. See Burkus, David. (2016, May 30). Why being transparent about pay is good for business. *The Wall Street Journal.* ("One study . . . found that participants who were shown their earnings and how they compared with others generally worked harder and increased their performance. Another study . . . found that pay secrecy was associated with decreased performance. What's more, evidence suggests that transparent pay conditions tend to reduce the gender wage gap and other forms of pay discrimination.")

[42] Lowe, *supra* note 39 at 19. See Zenger, Todd. (2017, August 13). The downside of full transparency. *The Wall Street Journal.*

[43] Nye, Ronald J. (2014). *Changes law firm partners would like to see in their compensation systems* (p. 4). Washington, DC: Major, Lindsey, & Africa.

level earn the same compensation. Ninety-two percent of partners in lockstep systems are very or somewhat satisfied with their compensation, compared with 79 percent of partners in non-lockstep systems.[44] Average partner origination in lockstep systems is $3.64 million, compared with $2.37 million for partners in non-lockstep systems.[45]

The relative dissatisfaction with non-lockstep systems may result more from their execution than from the concept itself. Unfortunately, although non-lock systems can be implemented fairly and with minimal personal discretion, they often reflect the individual biases of the compensation committee members and hence are frequently considered "subjective" or "subjective–objective" systems.[46] "We have an open compensation system, so I know how everyone else is compensated," a partner comments. "What I don't know is why the others are compensated the way they are."[47]

When asked what factors are most important in determining their compensation, partners rank these factors, in descending order, as "very important" or "somewhat important": originations, receipts, realization, billable hours, management responsibility, cross-selling, citizenship, seniority, and nonbillable hours.[48] Most partners also rate originations as being more important than profitability in determining compensation.[49] Ironically, the firms whose partners rate originations as being more important than profitability experience lower annual increases in profits per equity partner than the firms whose partners rate profitability as being more important than originations.[50]

---

[44] Ibid. at 59. See Simmons, Christine. (2018, March 23). Partner exits, compensation shifts keep lockstep firms under pressure. *The American Lawyer*.

[45] Nye, *supra* note 43 at 20.

[46] See Aderant. (2015, October). *Your partner compensation system can be better: Here's how.* ("In firms where the partner compensation process is particularly fraught, it probably stems from an overall sense that the decisions are arbitrary, unfair or lack transparency.")

[47] Nye, *supra* note 43 at 2.

[48] Lowe, *supra* note 39 at 36.

[49] Seeger & Clay, *supra* note 32. See Bostelman, Jack. (2015, June 15). Matter profitability. *Law Practice Today*. Simons, Hugh A. (2017, October 30). Aligning partner compensation to actual contribution. *The American Lawyer*. Simons, Hugh A. (2017, July 28). How firms should be measuring the profitability of matters. *The American Lawyer*.

[50] Seeger & Clay, *supra* note 32 at 31.

Despite their general satisfaction with compensation, partners acknowledge that compensation systems do not give adequate weight to qualitative factors critical to the firm's success. These qualitative factors, according to Major, Lindsey, & Africa's survey, include "firm management, client management, quality of legal services, good behavior and citizenship, mentoring junior partners and associates, community involvement, commitment to diversity, speaking engagements that raise the profile of the firm, and pro bono representations."[51] Although billable hours fuel firm revenue, the qualitative factors ultimately determine whether new clients initially consider the firm and whether existing clients remain satisfied with its services.

Partners' comments regarding their firm's compensation systems are revealing:[52]

"There are a lot of people at our firm who bill a lot of hours and are paid very well but do little or no work that benefits the firm in other ways. . . ."

"[M]anagement makes little or no effort to explain the connection between specific personal accomplishments or shortcomings, and pay. To the contrary, management is enraged by any systematic attempt to understand a relationship between available information and compensation."

"I would like to see a more nuanced system of origination credit that allows multiple contributors to be credited on some sort of weighted basis."

"[G]reater attention needs to be paid to the relative profitability of originations in valuing partner contributions. Too many partners are rewarded for work that is unprofitable. . . ."

"The entire private practice profession is becoming stratified into two classes: highly paid rainmakers and a class of underpaid working partners who service the clients and where the real lawyering skills flourish."

---

[51] Nye, *supra* note 43 at 2.
[52] Ibid. at 2–4.

These comments illuminate many of the deficiencies in compensation systems: an undue emphasis on origination over profitability; little or no incentive to devote time to firm management, collaboration, mentoring, associate attorney training, public service, and pro bono activities; opaque criteria for determining compensation; insufficient communication regarding compensation decisions; and scant attention given to efficiency, innovation, and client satisfaction.[53] Conventional compensation systems, unfortunately, "focus on top line revenue growth, as opposed to profitability to the law firm arising from reducing costs and providing effective services."[54] If all partners actually responded to typical compensation system incentives, the firms would find that revenue increased in the short term and fewer partners were interested in the factors that contribute to the firms' long-term stability—profitability, efficiency, quality, client satisfaction, reputation, collegiality, leadership, professional development, and community service. The risk in contemporary law firm compensation systems is that they may be dangerously effective in promoting short-term financial benefits while disregarding long-term organizational imperatives.

Technology, Cybersecurity, and Information Resources Systems

Law firms are not at the forefront of technological innovations, and many of them remain skeptical about the benefits of technology. Zev Eigen, the former global director of data analytics for Littler Mendelson, finds that "law firms are starting to try to do stuff, but firms were not set up to do anything that's innovative. It's like a horse-and-buggy company: How can a horse-and-buggy company design cars when their whole business model and all its

---

[53] See Zeughauser, Peter. (2017, October 16). New post-recession metrics for Big Law partner success. *Law 360*. Concoran, Timothy B. (2018, March 7). Outdated partner comp plans are an obstacle to growth. *The American Lawyer*.

[54] Carr, Jeffrey, Lamb, Patrick, McKenna, Patrick J., & Reeser, Edwin B. (2009, November 3). If you pay for hours, you get hours. *San Francisco Daily Journal*, p. 5.

individuals are incentivized by how many horses they can make run faster?"[55]

Still tied to hourly billing models, law firms are struggling to devise a new model for developing, implementing, and pricing technology that simultaneously reduces attorney time, improves work product quality and reliability, shortens product delivery cycles, largely eliminates human error—and maintains or increases law firm profitability. Not surprisingly, many attorneys perceive technology more as a threat than an advantage because it reduces inefficiencies and hence billed time. One managing partner, for example, attempted to introduce a new IT system to provide more efficient client service and was nearly "impeached" by his board: "They asked why we would want to spend all that money to get less fees from clients."[56]

Eighty-six percent of law firm leaders believe that "using technology to replace human resources will be a permanent trend going forward."[57] But only 51 percent of those law firm leaders report that their law firms are actually using technology tools to replace human resources and "increase efficiency of legal service delivery."[58] Among the law firms that have implemented technology tools, only 40 percent believe that their efforts have "resulted in a significant improvement in firm performance."[59] Consistent with the lackluster results that firms reportedly derive from technology, law firm leaders rank "invest in technology" as their second least important strategic priority.[60] ("Standardized process/procedure" is the least

---

[55] Lopez, Ian. (2018, March 26). "Half-assed innovation:" Do law firms need to change incentives to innovate? *The American Lawyer.*

[56] Johnson, Chris. (2010, September 17). Letter from London: Europe's GCs warn of more pressure on fees. *The American Lawyer.*

[57] Seeger, Eric A., & Clay, Thomas S. (2018). *2018 Law firms in transition* (p. 61). Willow Grove, PA: Altman Weil.

[58] Ibid. at 53. See Intapp. (2018, September 25). The lawyer survey: Majority of law firms aren't investing in technology fast enough to meet client demand. [Press release]. ("Although 86 percent of law firms agree that automation is important to deliver insights and analytics to clients, only 18 percent have, to date, made the investment necessary to embed this capability into their service delivery models.")

[59] Ibid. at 54.

[60] The Remsen Group, & Jaffe. (2016). Re-envisioning the law firm: How to lead, change and thrive in the future.

important.) Reviewing law firms' progress in adopting technology, Stephen Poor, former chair of Seyfarth Shaw LLP, states, "the reality is that Big Law—both law firms and legal departments—are laggards in the development and implementation of technology designed to enhance the delivery of legal services."[61]

Law firms' tendency to neglect or underutilize technology is more than a business failure; it may constitute an ethical failure as well. ABA Model Rule 1.1, as modified in 2012 and adopted by more than one-half of the states, requires lawyers to "keep abreast of changes in the law and its practice, including the benefits and risks associated with relevant technology."[62] Steven Puiszis, a partner at Hinshaw & Culbertson LLP, identifies six specific aspects of legal representation that are implicated by Rule 1.1:[63]

1. *Data security*—safeguarding the information that clients provide to their attorneys
2. *Electronic discovery*—preserving, reviewing, and producing electronic information for use in litigation
3. *Law practice management*—using technology to operate law practices, including "communicating with clients and third parties, transmitting information, electronic research and software applications for document generation, electronic calendaring, and docketing." This technology also may include cloud computing and cloud storage.
4. *Client technology*—safeguarding the technology clients use to "design and manufacture the products they sell"
5. *Courtroom technology*—using and protecting technology to present evidence and arguments in litigation matters
6. *Social media*—complying with confidentiality duties, advertising and solicitation rules, and other ethical requirements

In each of these six aspects, attorneys must comply with the duty of competence by understanding and, if appropriate, applying the

---

[61] Poor, Stephen. (2016, November 8). Investing in tech is just one piece of "Big Law" puzzle. *Bloomberg Law*.

[62] MODEL RULES OF PROF'L CONDUCT R. 1.1 cmt. [8]

[63] The six categories and their descriptions appear in Puiszis, Steven M. A lawyer's duty of technological competence.

relevant technology. As Suffolk University Law School Dean Andrew Perlman writes, "Technology is playing an ever more important role, and lawyers who fail to keep abreast of new developments face a heightened risk of discipline or malpractice as well as formidable new challenges in an increasingly crowded and competitive legal marketplace."[64]

Although attorneys are ethically required to understand relevant technology and assess the security of the technology they use in their practices, many attorneys adopt a casual attitude toward technology. Nearly one-half of attorneys surveyed by the American Bar Association stated that "they were not ethically required to stay apprised of legal technology developments, or that they were unclear regarding their ethical duties."[65] This nescience is irresponsible and ethically hazardous. Model Rule 1.1, as modified in 2012, "precludes a lawyer from pleading ignorance when it comes to technology or the risks associated with its use. Lawyers are expected to have at least a basic understanding of the technologies they use and the risks associated with those technologies."[66]

Apart from the ethical issues related to technology, law firms should adopt technological innovations at a faster pace because technology will dominate their practices and strategies during the next 20 years. Technology already has altered or transformed many practice areas, including contract analysis and management, discovery, case outcome prediction, compliance, attorney hiring, fee estimates, and flat fee pricing.[67] McKinsey & Company estimates that about 40 percent of professional services consist of data processing and data collection, and 23–32 percent of lawyers' work could be automated now.[68] A more conservative estimate is

---

[64] Roberts, Tyler. (2018, February 2). What is a lawyer's duty of technology competence? *National Jurist.*

[65] Diaz, Luis J., & Stueben, Christina A. (2017, February 8). Latest technology survey of lawyers reveals troubling trends. *E-discovery law alert.* See Cal. State Bar, Formal Op. 2010-179 (2010).

[66] Puiszis, Steven M. (2016, April 12). Perspective: Technology brings a new definition of competency. *Bloomberg Law.*

[67] See Savarino, Julie. (2016, May 12). A look at the start of the art in business development software and analytics. *Law Practice Today.*

[68] Michael Chui, Manyika, James, & Miremadi, Mehdi. (2016, July). Where machines could replace humans—and where they can't (yet). *McKinsey Quarterly.*

provided by Frank Levy, a labor economist, and Dana Remus, a law professor. They assert that, if attorneys implemented all currently available technologies, billable hours at law firms would be reduced by 13 percent.[69] The front-line casualties of automation are and will continue to be first-year associate attorneys. Thirty-five percent of law firm leaders expect them to be replaced by artificial intelligence in the 2020–2025 period.[70]

Whether 13 percent or 32 percent of attorneys' work could be automated today—or whether first-year associate attorney positions will disappear today or five years from now—is of little significance. The critical fact is that technology will irreversibly change the practice of law and lower the standard of living currently enjoyed by maladaptive attorneys as it wrings out the inefficiencies and excesses in the legal services industry. Law firms can choose to direct this disruptive technology or bemoan its consequences.

Lateral Attorney Integration Systems

In the late 1990s, Harvard Business School Professor Boris Groysberg began studying leading professionals in investment banking, marketing, public relations, and law. He focused on star performers who changed companies or firms and, specifically, how they performed after they left the organization where they had initially achieved a stellar reputation. He found that "top performers in all those groups were more like comets than stars. They were blazing successes for a while but quickly faded out when they left one company for another."[71]

---

[69] Strom, Roy. (2017, August 31). A case for letting associates drive technology advances in law firms. *The American Lawyer.*

[70] Weiss, Debra Cassens. (2015, October 26). Will newbie associates be replaced by Watson? 35% of law firm leaders can envision it. *ABA Journal.* Peter Kalis, the former chairman of K&L Gates, is skeptical of the survey result regarding first-year associates and suspects the survey participants misunderstood artificial intelligence. "One hundred percent of law firm leaders," he jokes, "don't know anything about AI." Triedman, Julie. (2015, October 24). Computer vs. lawyer? *The American Lawyer.*

[71] Groysberg, Boris, Nanda, Ashish, & Nohria, Nitin. (2004, May) The risky business of hiring stars. *Harvard Business Review.*

In a detailed analysis of 1,052 star analysts employed by investment banks, Groysberg tracked salaries, bonuses, industry sectors, annual rankings by institutional money managers, and numerical performance scores. He also conducted 167 hours of interviews with 86 analysts and supervisors. His conclusion: "When a company hires a star, the star's performance plunges, there is a sharp decline in the functioning of the group or team the person works with, and the company's market value falls. Moreover, stars don't stay with organizations for long, despite the astronomical salaries firms pay to lure them away from rivals."[72] The worst performing stars were those hired to build new businesses or strengthen existing teams—the typical purposes for which law firms hire lateral partners.

Only 3 of the 24 investment banks that Groysberg studied in depth successfully integrated the star analysts. Those banks developed and implemented systems to select, assist, monitor, and promote the new star analysts. This process began well before the employment offer was made; the successful companies had already identified the qualities of their internally created stars, and they sought to replicate those qualities in hiring stars outside their company. By the time the new star arrived, the company also had compiled extensive research on the star's prior performance, and it had "started building a presence in the star's area of expertise before the individual arrived." Some of the company's clients, moreover, had already been prepared to receive research reports from the new star analysts. The successful companies took one more action that does not occur in law firms: they offered their "homegrown" and previously hired stars the same range of compensation. As Groysberg remarks, "firms must never forget the stars they already have."[73]

Law firms' success in selecting lateral partners has been no better than the results of a coin toss. As discussed in Chapter 4, "more than half of laterals do not meet expectations in terms of books of business brought in and/or personal productivity."[74] Thirty-eight percent of lateral partners, moreover, depart within five years of

---

[72] Ibid.
[73] Ibid. See also Groysberg, Boris. (2010). *Chasing stars: The myth of talent and the portability of performance*. Princeton, NJ: Princeton University Press.
[74] Clay & Seeger, *supra* note 32 at iii.

joining a new firm.[75] One reason for law firms' mediocre record in selecting and retaining lateral partners is the lack of systems to integrate the partners into their new firms. Only 60 percent of large law firms prepare business plans for lateral partners before they join the firm, and only one in ten firms have formal monthly check-ins after they join the firm.[76] Not surprisingly, given this minimal involvement with the new lateral partner, all firms report that they experienced challenges with lateral partners in "bringing the expected volume of portable business"; and 75 percent have encountered difficulties with lateral partners "expecting more work to be given to them than is reasonable."[77]

Law firms' uneven integration efforts lead many partners to ask, "Why are we spending such an inordinate amount of time, effort and resources finding and hiring laterals and so little time and effort to ensure they stay with our firm?"[78] To avoid disproportionate investments in recruitment and retention, effective law firms carefully plan each phase of the integration process and develop systems to facilitate new partners' performance. These systems include:

- *Peer mentor*.[79] The firm should assign a peer mentor to new lateral partners. That person functions as an informal source of advice and provides connections with other firm partners. An ideal candidate is "someone the new hire connected with during the recruiting process so that they have already established a level of interpersonal trust."[80]
- *Early attention to lateral partners*. Law firms cannot afford to take a "wait and see" attitude toward new partners because they may fail shortly after joining the firm. "Research on the emotional state of new hires has found that an early sense of

75   Simons, Hugh A., & Ellenhorn, Michael A. (2018, January 28). Recent survey shows firms aren't doing right due diligence on laterals. *The American Lawyer*.
76   Ibid.
77   Ibid.
78   Savarino, Julie. (2013, July 9). Successful lateral integration for law firms. *Blomberg Law*.
79   Gardner, Heidi K. (2017). *Smart collaboration* (p. 56). Boston: Harvard Business Review Press.
80   Ibid.

euphoria and excitement is typically followed by a dip when reality strikes," observes Stuart Sadick, a partner in the consulting firm Heidrick & Struggles. "Finding a place in the new team and possibly in a new market, reconnecting with previous clients to explain the change and ramping up new business from a different platform can be a lonely process."[81] For that reason, the entire hiring team needs to work closely with the new partner from the outset.

- *Business plans.* New lateral partners should prepare and discuss detailed business plans before or immediately after they join a new firm. "The plan should have both short- and long-term dimensions," state consultant Patrick McKenna and former Baker & Daniels' Chair Brian Burke. "The first 100 days at the firm are critical and could determine whether the new lawyer will succeed there, so insist that the plan be as specific as possible about what the lawyer intends to do and what the lawyer will need from the firm during that period."[82]

- *Introductions to clients.* Law firms are sometimes hesitant to introduce new partners to their clients, thinking that they should see how the partner "works out" before enabling them to meet with their clients. This hesitancy indicates that the selection process is insufficiently thorough, and the integration process is preventing the new partner from being quickly and successfully incorporated into the firm.[83] It also conveys to the new partner an overall sense of distrust and lack of confidence, decreasing the new partner's ability to meet the firm's performance goals. If the firm is uncertain about introducing a new lateral partner to its clients, that partner should not have been selected in the first place. Even when firms intend to promptly introduce clients to new lateral partners, "very often that doesn't happen, and the firm doesn't follow up to make sure it happens."[84]

---

[81]   Sadick, Stuart. (2015). Hiring rainmakers as client leaders. In Normand-Hochman, Rebecca (Ed.). *Leadership for lawyers* (p. 33). Surrey, UK: Globe Law and Business Ltd.

[82]   McKenna, Patrick J., & Burke, Brian K. (2011). *Serving at the pleasure of my partners* (p. 61). Eagan, MN: Thomson Reuters.

[83]   Ibid. at 60.

[84]   Li, Victor. (2017, April). Value proposition. *ABA Journal*, p. 32.

- *Organized meetings and visits with partners.* Within 30 days after a new lateral joins the firm, a schedule and budget for meeting other partners should be established. The specific partners who will conduct the introductions should be identified, and those partners should report their progress to the practice leader. Some of those meetings should include presentations by the new lateral partner on his or her practice areas, and those meetings should be attended by likely collaborative partners.[85]
- *Culture of inquiry.* New partners have multiple questions that they may hesitate to ask. Fostering a culture of inquiry enables new partners to ask questions that are critical to their integration. They need to feel free to ask questions that the firm has not anticipated, and, equally important, they need to know whom they should ask. Firms also benefit from asking what strikes new partners as being different from their previous experiences and what methods might be imported to improve the firm's work processes. Firms invariably obtain a new perspective on their own processes when they ask the simple question, "What has surprised you the most since you joined the firm?"
- *Conditions on new lateral hiring.* Law firms should impose accountability on practice groups by conditioning their ability to hire future laterals "on how successfully they integrate each newcomer. You might not be able to see immediate financial results, but you should be able to track activity: How many partners have used the newcomer's expertise to develop joint pitches, to create new IP such as white papers or conference presentations, or to visit clients?"[86] Accountability acts as a strong incentive to promote the new lateral partner's practice and forces existing partners to be more mindful of their individual roles in learning about and collaborating with the new lateral partner.

Overall, these systems deliver a clear, convincing message that new lateral partners are not auditioning and are valued resources and active participants in the firm.

---

[85]   Gardner, *supra* note 79.
[86]   Ibid. at 57.

Succession Planning

Contemplating his impending retirement, a name partner and co-founder of a Beverly Hills law firm reflects, "The firm will go over to the younger attorneys, and they'll have to decide what they want to do and if they want to rename it. I have almost no concerns over it, because my selfish view would be to just close the doors."[87] Although his funereal views may not be representative of most retiring partners, they reflect the attitudinal challenges that have thwarted succession planning in many law firms. Faced with the prospect of losing about one-half of their partners due to retirements over the next 10 years, many firms are unjustifiably confident, peculiarly indifferent, and remarkably unprepared.

Law firm partners are taken aback when they learn that some of their corporate clients have no C-suite succession plans. But they show little concern about the absence of succession planning in their own firms. "Many law firms are not formalizing their succession planning process," states ALM Intelligence senior analyst Daniella Isaacson, "in direct contradiction to the very same advice they give clients."[88] One-third of large law firms do not have a succession plan for their firm leadership or client teams.[89] The partners of those firms say that it is "not an immediate concern" and is "too sensitive an issue to discuss with firm leaders."[90] When law firm leaders are asked whether they are "proactively grooming" their successor, only 22 percent respond affirmatively, while 33 percent respond, "somewhat," and 45 percent respond, "No."[91] Consistent with the lack of formal succession plans and informal preparation and training, only 27 percent of law leaders believe that their firms are "doing a good job identifying and grooming its future leaders."[92]

---

[87] Hodkowski, Ryne. (2012, October 30). Small firms increasingly facing leadership quandaries. *San Francisco Daily Journal.*

[88] Jeffreys, Brenda Sapino. (2017, December 28). Change at the top? Many law firms remain unprepared. *The American Lawyer.*

[89] Ibid.

[90] Ibid.

[91] The Remsen Group & Jaffe, *supra* note 60.

[92] Ibid.

One factor contributing to lackadaisical succession planning is law firms' reluctance to specify the duration of managing partners' terms and their reticence in imposing term limits. About one-half of law firms do not define the length of the managing partner's term, and 89 percent of law firms have no term limits.[93] When no one at a law firm knows when the chair or managing partner will depart, it is difficult to summon the motivation to select and prepare candidates for law firm leadership positions. The absence of formal terms also makes it politically hazardous for individual partners to raise the issue of succession planning, thwarting the orderly transition necessary to effectuate succession planning. The neglect of succession planning may be no accident in the one-third of law firms whose governance model is described by their managing partners as a "benevolent dictatorship" or an "established oligopoly."[94]

Another factor that stymies succession planning is the apparent lack of suitable candidates for leadership positions. In their drive to recruit lateral partners, law firms have given short shrift to developing leaders among their senior associate or junior partner ranks, as law firm consultant Brad Hildebrandt explains,

---

Part of that is because so much of the growth in the past three to four years has been through lateral partners. So there were very little associates [that] made equity partners. And I think what you've had is a kind of bulk-up in the middle, but not all those people performing all that well. The long-term issue is where is the new talent coming from? That's the issue.[95]

Since most law firms are planning to increase the number of associate attorneys and decrease the number of equity partners at

---

[93] Ibid.
[94] Ibid.
[95] Strom, Roy. (2017, December 14). In 2018, law firms will face greater challenges than slow growth. *The American Lawyer*.

their firms, the pool of partners available for leadership positions will continue to diminish.[96]

In law firms where partners recognize the importance of succession planning and can expressly address leadership transitions, succession planning begins years before the leadership transitions occur. Christopher Bockman, a leadership development consultant, identifies four stages of the succession process:

- *Developing the next generation of leaders.* Leadership development is "an integral and ongoing part of how a firm is being managed," states Bockman.[97] In the leadership development process, law firms need to show how they define and value leadership—"the more transparent and shared the understanding about what constitutes leadership, the less the chances of misunderstanding during the succession process."[98]
- *Deciding who the next leader should be.* After creating a class of possible successors in the leadership development stage, law firms identify the qualities necessary in a leader and then select a candidate to match that profile. A common error at this stage is basing the leadership profile on the incumbent managing partner instead of recognizing that a different profile is required because the firm has reached a different stage of development.[99]
- *On-boarding the new leader.* In this stage, the firm is "supporting the successor in managing the gap between their personal expectations, their firm's expectations and the realities of adjusting to the new role."[100] Three basic challenges arise at this stage: (1) the successor's skill set has to be broadened to deal with a range of issues outside the leader's previous experience; (2) the successor has to renegotiate her relationships with colleagues and "establish a new basis for influence and

---

[96] Ibid.
[97] Bockman, Christopher. Leadership succession in law firms: Continuity or renewal? In Normand-Hochman, *supra* note 81 at 120.
[98] Ibid. at 121.
[99] Ibid. at 126.
[100] Ibid. at 120.

authority with other partners in leadership roles"; and (3) the successor has to make personal adjustments, shifting from an external source of satisfaction (clients) to an internal source (firm attorneys).[101]

- *Stepping down and out for the incumbent leader.* When the successor leader replaces the incumbent leader, the firm must ensure that the process is dignified, respectful, well organized, and complete. The firm should acknowledge the incumbent leader's accomplishments; and the incumbent leader needs to "create the space for the successor to flourish, apply his own leadership style, make independent decisions and help to contribute to the renewal that the succession is supposed to feed."[102]

In considering succession planning, a pivotal question often arises: Is there an ideal tenure for managing partners? There is no comprehensive statistical evidence on this issue in the law firm context, but a study of chief executive officers of 356 U.S. companies provides some guidance. The researchers in that study examined the strength of firm–employee relationships and firm-customer relationships and the magnitude and volatility of stock returns.[103] They discovered that as CEO tenure lengthens, firm–employee relationships become stronger, but firm–customer relationships become weaker. The researchers explain this phenomenon:

Early on, when new executives are getting up to speed, they seek information in diverse ways, turning to both external and internal company sources. This deepens their relationships with customers and employees alike.

But as CEOs accumulate knowledge and become entrenched, they rely more on their internal networks for information, growing less attuned to market conditions. And, because they have

---

[101] Ibid. at 130.
[102] Ibid. at 131.
[103] Luo, Xueming, Kanuri, Vamsi K., Andrews, Michelle. (2013, March). Long CEO tenure can hurt performance. *Harvard Business Review.*

more invested in the firm, they favor avoiding losses over pursuing gains. Their attachment to the status quo makes them less responsive to vacillating consumer preferences.[104]

In the law firm context, the lesson from this research is that, as partners and law firm employees become more satisfied with the managing partner, the firm may be losing its clients and market share.

So, what is the optimal tenure length? The researchers concluded that it is 4.8 years. By that measure, about one-half of managing partners have already served longer than their optimal tenure.[105]

Attorney Wellness Programs

Law firms are taking an increasingly proactive approach to their attorneys' health and well-being. Eighty-three percent of large firms now provide wellness programs, and 42 percent of those firms encourage employee participation through financial incentives.[106] The efforts to promote wellness include educational programs; tobacco cessation programs; fitness classes; disease management programs; weight loss challenges; nutrition classes; hotlines to access confidential counseling and health coaching with a behavioral health professional; gym membership reimbursements; and mindfulness programs.[107] Some firms also provide onsite physical

---

[104] Ibid.

[105] The Remsen Group & Jaffe, *supra* note 60. See also Wesemann, Ed. (2014, November 1). Managing partners: full or part time? EdWesemann.com. Retrieved from http://edwesemann.com/articles/governance/2014/11/01/managing-partners-full-or-part-time/. ("Although the average tenure of managing partners has grown from an average of seven years to almost ten years, there is still a likelihood that most law firm leaders will not retire directly from a management position.")

[106] Jackson, Erin. (2017, July 16). How to set up an effective workplace wellness program.

[107] Ibid. Pressly, D. Finn, & Wethall, Judith. (2017, November 13). Wellness programs on the run. *Best Lawyers.* Good, Crystal. (2006). Wellness matters. *Absolute Advantage.* (Some wellness programs may be subject to the Health Insurance Portability and Accountability Act [HIPAA], Americans with

therapists, counselors, massage therapists, flu shots, and preventive health screenings.

Law firms adopt wellness programs for practical and altruistic reasons. Some law firms report reductions in employee absenteeism and health care insurance premiums, and some programs, like Akin Gump's Be Well program, have been so successful in promoting workplace health that they earned the American Heart Association's Silver Workplace Health Achievement award.[108] "I think all law firms are interested in caring for their professionals and this [is] coming out of a sincere interest in taking care of your folks," states Casey Ryan, Reed Smith's Global Head of Legal Personnel.[109] "The legal [profession], it is individual and person dependent," she explains. "And so if you have your lawyers operating at their best, at their highest potential, then it's better for them, it's better for the client [and] it's better for the firm."[110] Reed Smith's wellness program is centered on four practices (stress reduction, mindfulness, work-life balance, and health and wellness); and it organizes quarterly events with health experts, provides educational resources on its internal network, and sponsors other events like a 5K race to support its wellness initiatives.

Attorneys have an acute need for wellness programs. Gallup's study of attorney engagement shows that attorneys score lower on measures of physical well-being than other advanced degree holders. In assessing attorneys' physical well-being, Gallup found that only 35 percent of attorneys are "thriving," while 56 percent are "struggling" and 9 percent are "suffering."[111] Attorneys also compare

---

Disabilities Act [ADA], Employee Retirement Income Security Act [ERISA], Genetic Information Nondiscrimination Act [GINA], and other federal and state laws and regulations. See Jones Day. (2013, August). Employer wellness programs: What financial incentives are permitted under the law? *Jones Day Commentary.*)

[108] Akin Gump. (2017, September 12). Akin Gump's wellness program recognized by American Heart Association. [Press release].

[109] Tribe, Meghan. (2018, January 25). Reed Smith launches workplace wellness initiative. *The American Lawyer.*

[110] Ibid.

[111] Gallup, & AccessLex Institute. (2018). *Examining value, measuring engagement* (p. 18). Washington, DC: Gallup.

unfavorably with executives on exercise and fitness scores. The Center for Creative Leadership collected health data from law firm attorneys over a two-year period and then compared the attorneys' results with data collected from executives attending its Leadership at the Peak program (LAP) over a 10-year period. The results suggest that wellness programs are a necessity for law firms:

- "60 percent of the attorneys in the survey were very dissatisfied with their fitness level, compared to 23 percent of LAP executives.
- 42 percent averaged less than an hour a week of aerobic exercise, compared to 35 percent of LAP executives.
- 52 percent averaged less than an hour of resistance training each week, compared to 40 percent of LAP executives.
- 35 percent reported they received no support or encouragement from their firm for fitness, compared to 12 percent for other executives."[112]

About one-half of the attorneys also acknowledged that their diets were unhealthy. Most importantly, for purposes of justifying attorney wellness programs, 64 percent of the lawyers said that "they wished their firm would do more to support their fitness levels and wellness."[113]

The National Task Force on Lawyer Well-Being also reports that attorneys' level of well-being is disturbingly low and can be improved with law firm wellness programs. The task force reviewed research regarding attorneys' mental health and substance use disorders, noting that "too many lawyers and law students experience chronic stress and high rates of depression and substance use. These findings are incompatible with a sustainable legal profession, and they raise troubling implications for many lawyers' basic competence."[114]

---

[112] McDowell-Larsen, Sharon. *Improving performance by promoting attorney health.* Greensboro, NC: Center for Creative Leadership.

[113] Ibid.

[114] National Task Force on Lawyer Well-Being. (2017, August 14). *The path to lawyer well-being: Practical recommendations for positive change.*

The task force concluded that "the current state of lawyers' health cannot support a profession dedicated to client service and dependent on the public trust."[115] The specific recommendations for law firm wellness programs, as advanced by the task force, include: (1) form a lawyer well-being committee to identify workplace policies and procedures that create mental distress, ascertain methods of promoting well-being, and track the progress of well-being strategies; (2) use anonymous surveys to continually assess attorney well-being and firm attitudes toward mental health and substance use problems and treatment; (3) establish procedures for lawyers to confidentially express concerns about colleagues' mental health or substance use; (4) monitor lawyers for signs of work addiction and poor self-care; (5) provide education and training on well-being; (6) offer well-being programs like meditation, yoga sessions, and resilience workshops; and (7) ensure that attorneys know about resources, including lawyer assistance programs, to assist with mental health and substance abuse disorders.[116]

Surveying the studies regarding attorneys' substance abuse and mental health problems, former American Bar Association president Hilarie Bass states: "Sadly, our profession is falling short when it comes to well-being. Law firms need to emphasize that mental health is an indispensable part of a lawyer's competence and work to educate lawyers on mental health and addiction issues."[117] She notes that the number of lawyers struggling with mental health issues is "shocking," and she urges law firms to consider education, mentoring, and preventive programs to enable lawyers to handle stress and "to try to stop struggling attorneys from feelings of isolation."[118]

---

[115] Ibid.

[116] Ibid. at 31–34. See Lovelace, Ryan. (2018, May 15). Akin Gump adds on-site counseling as firms fret over mental health. *The American Lawyer.* ("Beginning last month, an on-site behavioral assistance counselor from the workplace wellness consulting and counseling company Lytle EAP Partners is spending one day a week at the firm. Akin Gump chief operating officer Sally King said the counselor is already booked solid through the end of June.")

[117] Bass, Hilarie. (2018, March 30). ABA president sees call to action in Quinn Emanuel partner's story of depression. *The American Lawyer.*

[118] Ibid.

In responding to Bass' urgent call for action, law firms should recognize that wellness programs are necessary to promote attorney well-being and to protect both attorneys and clients from the serious risks posed by untreated mental and substance abuse disorders. Constructively supporting impaired attorneys, though, is a difficult challenge for law firms. Their leaders acknowledge that depression, anxiety, and drug and alcohol addiction are prevalent among their attorneys, but they also report that the legal profession stigmatizes these disorders.[119] Eighty-one percent of Am Law 200 law firm leaders, for example, believe that a stigma is associated with "suffering from depression"; and 44 percent believe that the legal profession stigmatizes "seeing a mental health professional."[120] Behavioral health consultant Patrick Krill finds that these stigmas have a devastating effect: "Lawyers don't seek help for their problems because they fear that someone will find out. Assuming you were an attorney at a large firm, where stigma around behavioral health issues clearly exists, it is perfectly understandable why you would fear others finding out that you had a problem and needed help."[121]

Pro Bono Systems

Being financially successful and being committed to pro bono services are often seen as contradictory objectives for law firms. The time spent on pro bono work is frequently regarded as time taken away from billable work. In reality, many of the most financially successful law firms also operate the most extensive pro bono programs. Three of the five firms with the highest gross revenue in 2016, for instance, were selected for American Lawyer's "A-List," which weights pro bono service in addition to revenue per lawyer.[122]

---

[119] Krill, Patrick. (2018, September 24). Big Law leaders say stigma comes with addiction and mental health problems. *The American Lawyer*.

[120] Ibid.

[121] Ibid.

[122] Zeughauser Group. (2017). *The ZGuide to the 2017 Am Law 200 and 2016 Global 100*. Only 20 firms are selected for the A-List. The selection is determined by a firm's rankings in pro bono, revenue per lawyer, associate satisfaction, diversity, and the percentage of female equity partners. A firm's rankings in revenue per

Those firms are Kirkland & Ellis, Latham & Watkins, and Skadden, Arps, Slate, Meagher & Flom. The attorneys in those firms spent an average of 84 hours per attorney on pro bono services in 2016, and 81 percent of their attorneys spent a minimum of 10 hours on pro bono services.[123]

Many attorneys assume that providing pro bono services is easier for large firms, due to their high staffing levels and financial stability. As the Thomson Reuters Foundation notes, "At Large Firms it is likely that finances and manpower would be available to support the development of a structured pro bono practice within the firm, and the number of lawyers would mean that there would be capacity amongst the lawyers within the firm to get involved in more pro bono initiatives."[124] In fact, attorneys in small firms devote the greatest number of hours to pro bono services. Attorneys in small firms spend an average of 42 hours per year on pro bono services, while attorneys in large firms (200+ attorneys) and medium-sized firms (50–199 attorneys) spend an average of 35 and 28 hours per year on pro bono work, respectively.[125]

Attorneys in small firms also display higher participation rates in pro bono services. More than half of all attorneys in small firms spend more than 10 hours per year on pro bono services. In large and midsize firms, however, only about 25 percent of their attorneys spend more than 10 hours per year on pro bono work.[126] This data suggests that small firms bear a disproportionate responsibility for pro bono services and that medium-sized and large firms could devote considerably more resources to them. Since 58 percent of firms use pro bono activities for attorney training and skills development, increased pro bono services would accelerate attorneys' professional development while providing legal services to historically underserved populations.[127]

---

lawyer and pro bono are given twice the weight of the other factors in calculating a firm's overall score.

[123] Thomson Reuters Foundation. (2017). *TrustLaw index of pro bono 2016* (p. L3).
[124] Ibid. at B2.
[125] Ibid. at B1.
[126] Ibid. at B2.
[127] Ibid. at C2.

The existence of formal systems strongly influences the extent of attorneys' participation in pro bono activities. "Across all firms," the Thomson Reuters Foundation reports, "the findings suggested that the average pro bono hours and the average proportion of lawyers performing 10 or more hours of pro bono increased when the firm had at least one of a pro bono coordinator, a pro bono committee or a pro bono policy in place."[128] The specific effects of coordinators, committees, and polices are notable and summarized below:[129]

- *Pro bono coordinator.* A pro bono coordinator oversees the administration, coordination, and assignment of pro bono matters. Law firms with a pro bono coordinator record an average of 38.7 pro bono hours per attorney, as compared with 17.4 average hours in firms without a pro bono coordinator.
- *Pro bono committee.* A pro bono committee typically is responsible for policy, strategy, approval of pro bono matters and clients, and the general administration of the pro bono program. Surprisingly, the Thomson Reuters Foundation finds that "lawyers at firms with pro bono committees performed less pro bono on average than those at firms without a committee—34.3 hours compared to 36.4 hours. This difference became more pronounced amongst Medium-sized Firms where lawyers at firms with committees performed 19.2 hours on average compared to 40.2 hours at firms without a committee."
- *Pro bono policy.* A pro bono policy usually specifies the firm's intent, eligibility criteria for pro bono clients, and the roles of the pro bono coordinator and committee. In firms with a formal pro bono policy, attorneys work an average of 44.8 hours per year on pro bono matters; in firms lacking a formal pro bono policy, the average annual pro bono hours drop to 14.7.

Law firms that lack any element of pro bono infrastructure (coordinator, committee, or policy) exhibit significant decreases in pro

---

[128] Ibid. at D3.
[129] The data in the bulleted paragraphs is derived from Thomson Reuters Foundation, *supra* note 123 at D3, D4, and D6.

bono activities relative to firms that have at least one element. In medium-sized firms operating without a coordinator, committee, or pro bono policy, "average hours dropped to just 3.7 from 33.2, and the percentage of lawyers performing 10 or more hours of pro bono fell to 8.7 percent from 30.9 percent. At Large Firms average hours fell to 1.5 from 35.7 and the proportion of lawyers performing 10 or more hours of pro bono decreased to 2.6 percent from 26.7 percent when there were no elements of pro bono infrastructure."[130]

Formal incentives, integrated into firm systems, also have a measurable impact on attorney participation in pro bono services.[131] Attorneys in firms that factor pro bono work into compensation perform an average of 39.3 pro bono hours, compared with an average of 28.5 hours in firms that do not consider pro bono work in compensation decisions. When pro bono services are part of attorneys' performance evaluations, attorneys perform an average of 40.2 pro bono hours; but in firms that exclude pro bono work from evaluations, the average pro bono hours drop to 20.7. Mandatory targets for pro bono work also are correlated with significantly more pro bono hours. Firms with mandatory targets report an average of 65.5 pro bono hours per attorney, compared with 31.7 hours in firms with aspirational targets.

The data cited above demonstrates that effective pro bono services require effective law firm systems. These systems include formal incentives and a pro bono infrastructure consisting, at a minimum, of a pro bono coordinator and a pro bono policy. The coordinator does not have to work exclusively on pro bono matters. In small firms, 42 percent of pro bono coordinators continue to have fee-earning responsibilities, and in medium-size firms 24 percent of the pro bono coordinators have ongoing fee-earning responsibilities.[132]

Pro bono services are an integral part of legal professionalism and a duty deeply embedded in the American legal system. John Tucker, the widely respected trial attorney, observed a decline in

---

[130] Thomson Reuters Foundation, *supra* note 123 at D3.
[131] All data in this paragraph is derived from Thomson Reuters Foundation, *supra* note 123 at A9.
[132] Thomson Reuters Foundation, *supra* note 123 at D5.

pro bono services near the end of his career and reminded attorneys that pro bono cases are often "the most interesting and personally gratifying experiences" of an attorney's career.[133] In his book, *Trial and Error*, he writes,

---

Gratifying or not, providing a reasonable amount of pro bono legal work is an obligation every lawyer undertakes when he or she accepts the monopoly conferred by the license to practice law. Every student emerging from law school who considers joining a law firm should have a clear understanding of that firm's policy and practice (not just its rhetoric) regarding pro bono work, and should decline to join any firm that refuses such work or penalizes lawyers who undertake it. Those who proclaim that American lawyers have no obligation to serve the public are not worthy of the title "lawyer."[134]

Chapter Capsule

Systems reflect a law firm's values, beliefs, and priorities. Systems indicate whether an idea has been accepted and integrated into a firm's operations. If a firm espouses client service but has no method of evaluating its client service and informing attorneys of the evaluation results, for example, one can conclude that client service is a mere idea.

Effective law firms, at a minimum, establish seven outstanding systems: (1) quality control, feedback, and evaluation systems; (2) attorney compensation systems; (3) technology and information management systems; (4) lateral attorney integration systems; (5) succession planning systems; (6) attorney wellness systems; and (7) pro bono systems. Each of these systems fulfills a primary purpose in a law firm, enabling the firm to meet client expectations,

---

[133] Tucker, John C. (2003). *Trial and error* (p. 342). New York: Carroll & Graf Publishers.
[134] Ibid.

motivate its attorneys, improve legal services delivery methods, retain and direct lateral attorneys, develop new law firm leaders, protect attorneys' physical and psychological health, and satisfy attorneys' need for meaning and a broader social purpose.

Although systems receive scant attention in popular perceptions and people are more likely to be intrigued by leaders than systems, the strongest determinant of an organization's success might be its systems. As noted author Malcolm Gladwell observes in his study of Enron's collapse and the consulting company McKinsey's role in that collapse:

> The broader failing of McKinsey and its acolytes at Enron is their assumption that an organization's intelligence is simply a function of the intelligence of its employees. They believe in stars, because they don't believe in systems. In a way, that's understandable, because our lives are so obviously enriched by individual brilliance. Groups don't write great novels, and a committee didn't come up with the theory of relativity. But companies work by different rules. They don't just create; they execute and compete and coordinate the efforts of many different people, and the organizations that are most successful at that task are the ones where the system *is* the star.[135]

---

[135] Gladwell, Malcolm. (2002, July 22). The talent myth. *The New Yorker.*

9
Leaders

Leaders embody and advance an organization's principles, standards, and aspirations. They motivate people to honor, animate, and improve an organization's distinct features—its vision, values, practices, and advantages. In the broadest sense, as Microsoft CEO Satya Nadella explains, leaders are the curators of an organization's culture.[1] They are responsible for its care, enhancement, and perpetuation.

Law firm leaders generally are not prepared to be the curators of their firm's culture. They usually are selected for their seniority or success in building a practice, not for their leadership skills.[2] Many are selected because they are self-confident, tall, powerful, talkative, or dominant.[3] The convention of selecting successful lawyers

---

[1] Nadella, Satya. (2017). *Hit refresh* (p. 100). New York: Harper Business.
[2] Hayse, Roger. The role of leadership in law firm success or failure. The Remsen Group. Reynolds, Kylie. (2013, December 20). Law firms give office leader roles to the next generation. *San Francisco Daily Journal*, p. 3. See Innocenti, Natasha. (2012, September). The next generation of law firm leaders. *Law Practice Today*. ("Your best leaders may not be the biggest rainmakers or most senior people. Have the courage and business sense to put your most capable leaders in the most important leadership roles, including practice leadership.")
[3] See Tarakci, Murat, Greer, Lindred L., & Groenen, Patrick J. F. (2015, November). When does power disparity help or hurt group performance? *Journal of Applied Psychology, 101*(3), 415. Bottger, P. C. (1984). Expertise and air time as bases of actual and perceived influence in problem-solving groups. *Journal of Applied Psychology, 69*(2), 214–221. Botelho, Elena Lytkina, Powell, Kim Rosenkoetter, Kincaid, Stephen, & Want, Dina. (2017, May-June). What sets successful CEOs apart. *Harvard Business Review*. ("For example, high confidence more

without demonstrated leadership skills has resulted in a "disconnect between qualities that enable lawyers to achieve a leadership position and qualities that are necessary once they get there."[4]

Law firm leaders often lack the experience, education, training, foresight, vision, resilience, and communication skills necessary to direct law firms and optimize the immense talents of their attorneys. Although the average large law firm generates gross revenue exceeding $600 million and accommodates more than 800 attorneys, the development of law firm leaders is generally haphazard.[5] Since partners must meet billable hour requirements, manage associate attorneys, and generate new clients, law firms present "little or no incentives or encouragement for them to build their leadership skills or volunteer for early leadership experiences. The leadership learning mode is therefore high risk and almost entirely sink-or-swim."[6] Under these circumstances, it is difficult for law firm leaders to know how to protect, let alone enhance, a law firm's culture.

Apart from their lack of preparation for law firm leadership positions, many managing partners are reluctant to separate themselves from their client relationships and assume full-time leadership positions. Even when law firms afford leaders the opportunity to devote all of their time to leadership responsibilities, many leaders are concerned about losing the financial power and security attendant to controlling a large book of business or are simply disinterested in full-time leadership.[7] As Morton Pierce, the managing

---

than doubles a candidate's chances of being chosen as CEO but provides no advantage in performance on the job. In other words, what makes candidates look good to boards has little connection to what makes them succeed in the role.")

4   Rhode, Deborah. (2011). What lawyers lack: Leadership. *University of St. Thomas Law Journal, 9*(2), 476.

5   See Harris, Joanne. (2016, June 23). Revealed: Global 200 deliver £81 bn revenue in 2015. *The Lawyer.* (2016, April 25). Firms ranked by revenue per lawyer. *The American Lawyer.*

6   Westfahl, Scott. (2015). Learning to lead: Perspective on bridging the lawyer leadership gap. In Normand-Hochman, Rebecca (Ed.). *Leadership for lawyers* (p. 80). Surrey, UK: Globe Law and Business Ltd. See Press, Aric. (2011, November 22). The talent. *The Am Law Daily.*

7   See Giuliani, Peter A. (2008, December). Best practices for setting managing partner pay. *Law Practice, 34*(8), 38. See Walker, Carol. (2002, April). Saving your rookie managers from themselves. *Harvard Business Review*, p. 97.

partner of Dewey Ballantine who billed 3,200 hours while leading the firm in his "spare time," commented, "Management is not my passion."[8]

Legal education does not provide the leadership training missing from law firms' professional development programs and minimized in their operations and incentives. Law schools, asserts Scott Westfahl, director of Harvard Law School Executive Education, do not show law students how to collaborate with colleagues, work on teams, manage projects, and function as leaders.[9] Nor do they teach students the technical legal skills required to practice law. In the early stages of their careers, therefore, lawyers "need to focus most of their attention on building technical legal skills because they did not learn them in law school. The attention this requires crowds out the equally important building of professional skills such as leadership."[10]

Considering the lack of leadership training and incentives, it is not surprising to discover that the quality of law firm leadership is highly variable. Herb Rubenstein, the author of *Leadership for Lawyers*, bluntly assesses leadership quality:

Lawyers think they are leaders, and good leaders, just because they are lawyers. However, since law students receive no training in leadership development and only a few, but growing number, of continuing legal education courses teach leadership development, there is a truth that our profession would hate to acknowledge. That truth is that many lawyers are terrible leaders, or worse yet, not leaders at all. In fact, most lawyers know so little about leadership theory or good leadership practices, they don't have a clue how bad a leader they are.[11]

---

[8] Koppel, Nathan. Big law firms try new idea: The true CEO. (2007, January 22). *The Wall Street Journal.*

[9] Westfahl, *supra* note 6.

[10] Ibid.

[11] Rubenstein, Herb. Why leadership development is such a hard sell in the legal profession. See Rubenstein, Herb. (2008). *Leadership for lawyers* (2nd ed.). Chicago: American Bar Association.

Rubenstein's assessment of law firm leaders is corroborated by surveys showing that only 14 percent of law firm leaders regard "strong firm leadership" as one of their firm's principal competitive advantages, and only two percent of those leaders rely on their firm leadership to develop the firm's strategic plan.[12]

To orient attorneys to their leadership duties and to improve their leadership skills, this chapter highlights six responsibilities: awareness; vision and strategy; innovation and change management; crisis management; talent development; and execution. These six leadership duties are by no means exhaustive, but they serve to inform and remind law firm leaders of their critical roles and minimum responsibilities.

Awareness

The threshold requirement for leadership is awareness. Although vision, self-confidence, and assertiveness may be the qualities that first come to mind when people think of leaders, the fundamental requirement is awareness. Leaders must be alert to and knowledgeable about the social, political, economic, and organizational context in which they intend to act; and they must be aware of their own emotions, biases, reactions, and competencies. When leaders fail, the factor most frequently overlooked is their misplaced confidence in their understanding of the dispositive facts. Many leaders, unfortunately, are making decisions and taking actions based on highly filtered or inaccurate information and an ignorance of their own biases, feelings, and ambitions. Even highly intelligent, experienced, and respected leaders fail when they lack a deep understanding of external factors and the self-awareness necessary to see how their personality and emotions affect their perception of those factors. For that reason, the following sections discuss the importance of external awareness and self-awareness.

---

[12] ALM Legal Intelligence. (2012, October). *Thinking like your client: Strategic planning in law firms*, pp. 20, 28. LexisNexis.

External Awareness

Leaders are particularly vulnerable to incomplete, inaccurate, and unduly optimistic information. Because they have the power to obtain information and people compete for their attention, they assume that they are receiving a broad range of information and opinions necessary to make decisions and lead organizations. In fact, as leaders advance within an organization, they become increasingly isolated and ignorant. Walt Bettinger, the CEO of Charles Schwab, finds that leaders have to make a deliberate effort to elicit information that challenges their assumptions or portends new problems because no one is motivated to convey that information. He sees the problem as taking two forms: "people telling you what they think you want to hear, and people being fearful to tell you things they believe you don't want to hear."[13]

Leaders' isolation and the resultant illusion of knowledge are pervasive. Leaders continually fall victim to what is called "the fallacy of centrality." This is the belief that, because leaders are in a central position, they would know if something serious had happened.[14] If they don't know about a phenomenon, leaders reason, "it isn't happening."[15] The fallacy of centrality has an insidious effect on people working with leaders. They assume that leaders know what they know, and they fail to convey critical information out of a fear they are wasting leaders' time. They also become less observant and vigilant, as crisis management experts Dawn Gilpin and Priscilla Murphy explain: "When everyone believes that information flows freely and efficiently, people are less likely to pay close attention to their surroundings, assuming that anything important has already been discovered."[16]

Leaders intent on overcoming their isolation and obtaining accurate information adopt two simple but effective methods: they ask good questions, and they surround themselves with diverse teams.

---

[13]   Gregersen, Hal. (2017, March–April). Bursting the CEO bubble. *Harvard Business Review*, p. 78.

[14]   Weick, Karl E., & Sutcliffe, Kathleen M. (2007). *Managing the unexpected* (p. 158). San Francisco: Jossey-Bass.

[15]   Ibid.

[16]   Gilpin, Dawn R., & Murphy, Priscilla J. (2008). *Crisis management in a complex world* (p. 133). New York: Oxford University Press.

"The important and difficult job is never to find the right answer," declared Peter Drucker, "it is to find the right question."[17] For that reason, exceptional leaders consider what they might be overlooking and persistently question their colleagues to discover facts they might be reluctant to discuss and to detect incipient problems before they become crises. Strong leaders probe and make it clear that they expect honesty and can adroitly handle negative information. Karen Silverman, the former managing partner of Latham & Watkins' San Francisco office, describes her approach to eliciting information: "Watch, listen and learn. Repeat. A lot. I read some and ask questions, also a lot. The questions get smarter before I do."[18]

Successful leaders also make sure that their teams are cognitively diverse. Although the term "diversity" is most frequently associated with *identity* diversity (e.g., ethnicity and gender), the most important type of diversity for leadership and decision making is *cognitive* diversity (differences in beliefs, preferences, and perspectives).[19] Identity diversity frequently, but not necessarily, results in cognitive diversity.

The critical value of cognitive diversity is that it upgrades organizational leadership and decision-making quality in four dimensions: diverse ways of seeing and representing situations and problems; diverse ways of interpreting and classifying events, situations, and outcomes; diverse ways of inferring cause and effect; and diverse ways of generating solutions to problems.[20] Diversity in these dimensions results in a broader range of information being considered by leaders, fewer assumptions, better group analysis and deliberations, more creative problem solving, and fewer decision-making errors. As Professor Scott Page discovered, "diverse groups of problem solvers—groups of people with diverse tools—consistently outperformed groups of the best and the brightest. If I formed two groups, one random (and therefore diverse) and

---

Drucker, Peter. (1954). *The practice of management*, p. 305. Oxford, UK: Butterworth-Heinemann.

[18] Innocenti, Natasha. (2012, September). The next generation of law firm leaders. *Law Practice Today*.

[19] See Reynolds, Alison, & Lewis, David. (2017, March 30). Teams solve problems faster when they're more cognitively diverse. *Harvard Business Review*.

[20] Page, Scott. (2007). *The difference*. Princeton, NJ: Princeton University Press.

one consisting of the best individual performers, the first group almost always did better. In my model, diversity trumped ability."[21]

In data-driven organizations, leaders are tempted to rely on financial performance data and neglect the seemingly inefficient practices of asking questions and working closely with diverse team members. Unfortunately, financial performance data can foster an illusion that all critical information is being collected, analyzed, and integrated into decision making when only the most salient and easily captured information is being reported. Conventional data gathering also tends to provide information that was pertinent to yesterday's problems and threats and may have little utility in anticipating tomorrow's dangers and risks. It can measure the extent of an organization's current success but has little value in discerning the outline of its future competitors. Unless leaders are probing for new information and encouraging robust discussions in a cognitively diverse team, their attention may be focused on data that accurately depicts but cannot forcefully direct their organizations. Drucker called this "finding the right answer rather than the right question."[22]

Self-Awareness

Although leadership seems to be focused exclusively on understanding, motivating, and directing other people, it turns out that the foundation of effective leadership is self-awareness—the ability to understand, motivate, evaluate, improve, and direct yourself. Anthony Tjan, managing partner of the venture capital firm Cue Ball and author of *Heart, Smarts, Guts and Luck*, finds that self-awareness is the most important leadership skill: "there is one quality that trumps all, evident in virtually every great entrepreneur,

---

[21]   Ibid. at xxv–xxvi. See Hong, Lu, & Page, Scott. (2004, November 16). Groups of diverse problem solvers can outperform groups of high-ability problem solvers. *PNAS, 101*(46), 16389.

[22]   Drucker, Peter. (2007). *The practice of management*, p. 304, Abingdon-on-Thames, UK: Routledge. See Day, George S., & Schoemaker, Paul J.H. (2006). *Peripheral vision* (p. 169). Boston: Harvard Business School Press. (Leaders tend to "console themselves by gathering more information, but unless they focus this gathering on expanding the field of vision, no matter how carefully they look, they won't see opportunities and threats unless their scope is broad enough.")

manager, and leader. That quality is self-awareness. The best thing leaders can [do] to improve their effectiveness is to become more aware of what motivates them and their decision making."[23]

The significance and dimensions of self-awareness are illustrated by these insights from respected leaders and a leadership scholar:[24]

- "Of all a leader's competencies, emotional and otherwise, self-awareness is the most important. Without it, you can't identify the impact you have on others. Self-awareness is very important for me as CEO. At my level, few people are willing to tell me the things that are hardest to hear."—Andrea Jung, former Chair and CEO of Avon Products.

- "Self-awareness is the key emotional intelligence skill behind good leadership. It's often thought of as the ability to know how you're feeling and why, and the impact your feelings have on your behavior. But it also involves a capacity to monitor and control those strong but subliminal biases that all of us harbor and that can skew our decision making."—Howard Book, Associate Professor, Department of Psychiatry, University of Toronto.

- "Authentic leadership begins with self-awareness, or knowing yourself deeply. Self-awareness is not a trait you are born with but a capacity you develop throughout your lifetime. It's your understanding of your strengths and weaknesses, your purpose in life, your values and motivations, and how and why you respond to situations in a particular way. It requires a great deal of introspection and the ability to internalize feedback from others."—William George, former Chairman and CEO of Medtronic.

In a study of 72 senior executives conducted by Cornell University's School of Industrial and Labor Relations, the researchers examined leadership traits to determine their effect

---

[23] Tjan, Anthony K. (2012, July 19). How leaders become self-aware. *Harvard Business Review.*

[24] The comments appear in Leading by feel. (2004, January). *Harvard Business Review.*

on multiple performance measurements such as financial results, talent development, and strategic intellect. Their conclusion: "A high self-awareness score was the strongest predictor of overall success."[25] The self-aware leaders may not have possessed every quality necessary for exceptional organizational performance, but their self-awareness enabled them to accurately assess their own skills and collaborate effectively with colleagues who excelled in skills that the leaders lacked.[26] Self-awareness prevented leaders from overestimating their own capabilities, and, equally important, it enabled them to be "especially good at working with individuals and in teams."[27]

Vision and Strategy

Vision and strategy are closely aligned in healthy organizations. In the simplest sense, vision is the concept, and strategy is the implementation of that concept. When organizations flounder, they usually have disconnected vision from strategy and subordinated strategy to pedestrian planning and budgeting tools. They lose sight of their organization's overarching values, principles, and ambitions and define success as any incremental increase over the prior year's financial performance. Because vision and strategy should have a close, symbiotic relationship, they are discussed together in this section.

Vision

Vision has become an overused, ambiguous term in leadership. Its meaning can range from the articulation of a minor organizational goal to the unveiling of a preposterous financial target; its scope can range from the next quarter's earnings to the next century's business model. Stripped of contemporary jargon, vision is an optimistic perception of an organization and its members that crystallizes their highest purpose and their greatest value. Vision reflects the most

---

[25] American Management Association. (2010, November 4). New study shows nice guys finish first.

[26] Ibid.

[27] Ibid.

imaginative extension of an organization's present capabilities, the most expansive deployment of its members' skills, and the most meaningful impact it can have on its members and customers.

Barrie Conchie, the co-author of *Strengths Based Leadership,* finds that vision is an essential part of leadership. He describes how vision distinguishes exceptional leaders from ordinary leaders:

> Successful executive leaders are able to look out, across, and beyond the organization. They have a talent for seeing and creating the future. They use highly visual language that paints pictures of the future for those they lead. As a result, they seem to attain bigger goals because they create a collective mindset that propels people to help them make their vision a reality.
>
> These leaders also recognize that through visioning, they showcase their values and core beliefs. By highlighting what is important about work, great leaders make clear what is important to them in life. They clarify how their own values—particularly a concern for people—relate to their work. They also communicate a sense of personal integrity and a commitment to act based on their values.[28]

Conchie seeks answers to three questions when he determines whether an organization is encouraging its leaders to develop and express a vision: Who contributes to, controls, or communicates the "big picture"? Are leaders encouraged to "paint pictures" of the future? What opportunities do leaders have to talk about and shape the future?[29]

For law firm leaders, vision is, arguably, their most important responsibility. To develop vision, "the chairman must have a keen understanding of the competitive landscape, the markets in which the firm chooses to operate (those would include geographic, client, industry, and practice area markets), and the distinctive value the firm can offer, based on their chairman's insights into the firm's

---

[28] Conchie, Barry. (2004, May 13). The demands of executive leadership. Gallup.
[29] Ibid.

talent, experience, and client base."[30] If law firms are selecting leaders for the right reasons, the chair should be uniquely qualified to develop and articulate the firm's vision. Many attorneys usually can match a chair's operational and organizational skills, but no one should be more qualified than the chair to imagine, define, and articulate its vision.

Strategy

Strategy, unfortunately, has become intertwined with planning and has lost its identity in "strategic planning" and "strategic plans."[31] Despite contemporary perceptions, a strategy should not be the same thing as a plan, and developing a strategy should be considerably more complex than preparing a plan. Roger Martin, the former dean at the University of Toronto's Rotman School of Management, finds that "mistaking planning for strategy is a common trap."[32] It occurs, he contends, because leaders find it "safer to supervise planning than to encourage strategic choice," and "Wall Street is more interested in the short-term goals described in plans than in the long-term goals that are the focus of strategy."[33] Martin describes how planning differs from strategy: "Planning typically isn't explicit about what the organization chooses not to do and why. It does not question assumptions. And its dominant logic is affordability; the plan consists of whichever initiatives fit the company's resources."[34]

Planning in most organizations is focused on leveraging existing resources (human, financial, technical).[35] In a planning exercise, the analysis of marketplace competitors also centers on competitors' existing resources.[36] This approach is dangerous because

---

[30] Zeughauser, Peter. (2006, December). Leading by serving. *The American Lawyer*.

[31] Martin, Roger L. (2014, January-February). The big lie of strategic planning. *Harvard Business Review*.

[32] Ibid.

[33] Ibid.

[34] Ibid.

[35] Dobbs, Richard, Ramaswamy, Sree, Stephenson, Elizabeth, & Viguerie, S. Patrick. (2014, September). Management intuition for the next 50 years. *McKinsey Quarterly*. Hamel, Gary, & Prahalad, C. K. (2005, July–August). Strategic intent. *Harvard Business Review*.

[36] Hamel & Prahalad, *supra* note 35.

tomorrow's competitors do not look like today's competitors; and competitors that eventually dominated their markets "invariably began with ambitions that were out of all proportion to their resources and capabilities."[37] When organizations substitute planning for strategy, they lose the peripheral vision necessary to detect trends and competitors before they are overtaken by them.[38]

Devising strategy is harder work than making plans. Strategy demands a higher level of analysis and risk taking because it necessitates larger, bolder assumptions about the future. Planning, in contrast, usually evades strategic thinking as it centers on incremental revenue increases and presumes the continuation of existing products and services. Expanding an existing law firm practice area by hiring more lateral partners, for instance, is generally depicted as a strategy, but it more closely resembles a plan. Since plans usually contain variations of actions already taken, they are more easily understood, accepted, and implemented than strategies. Plans also foster the illusion that organizations have strategies when, in fact, they have practiced "consensual neglect" in avoiding major strategic decisions.[39]

Michael Watkins, a business school professor and author of *The First 90 Days,* posits a definition of strategy that distinguishes it from planning: "A business strategy is a set of guiding principles that, when communicated and adopted in the organization, generates a desired pattern of decision making. A strategy is therefore about how people throughout the organization should make decisions and allocate resources in order [to] accomplish key objectives."[40] A strategy is necessarily broader in purpose, scope, and effect than a plan. A strategy also is more focused on the future than a plan; a strategy aims to alter future behavior, while plans generally seek to enhance prior behavior. For that reason, a strategy must contain "a set of guiding principles or rules that defines the actions people in

---

[37] Ibid.

[38] See Day & Schoemaker, *supra* note 22.

[39] See Vermeulen, Freek, & Sivanathan, Niro. (2017, November–December). Stop doubling down on your failing strategy. *Harvard Business Review.*

[40] Watkins, Michael D. (2007, September 10). Demystifying strategy: The what, who, how, and why. *Harvard Business Review.*

the business should take (and not take) and the things they should prioritize (and not prioritize) to achieve desired goals."[41]

Law firms' strategies and plans frequently suffer from a lack of imagination and peripheral vision. They typically reflect a firm's responses to three questions: Where are we now? Where do we want to be? How will we get there? To answer these questions, law firms are encouraged to assess their current market position, determine their current practice strengths, set "realistic" goals, and prepare an implementation plan. These questions may be suitable for a short road trip, but they do not address the types of issues that already have disrupted and financially damaged law firms. These questions also give law firms an illusion of control, indicating that they can direct their future in an otherwise static world. They encourage law firms to build yesterday's law firms with today's ambitions. Answering these types of questions would not have prepared law firms for many of the external challenges they have confronted during the last 10 years. Nor would answers to those questions force law firms to determine how the practice of law will change during the next 10 years.

Most law firms' strategic plans, unfortunately, emphasize their internal processes and preferences instead of their external challenges. In a survey of law firm leaders, only 20 percent said that their strategic plans are focused primarily on external factors such as clients and emerging practice areas.[42] The remaining law firm leaders said that their strategic plans are focused on internal factors like website design and pricing, billing, and collection policies.[43] Ironically, the law firm leaders who reported the highest level of satisfaction with their strategic planning process "also had the most internally focused plans and implemented the least."[44]

To develop viable strategies, law firms need to recognize that they are already behind other industries and professions in anticipating changes and adapting to market demands. Law firms must rapidly ascertain (1) what services clients will expect in the future; (2) how

---

[41] Ibid.
[42] Parnell, David. (2017, June 9). Law firm strategic planning and deployment: A report on the state of the art. *Forbes.*
[43] Ibid.
[44] Ibid.

those services will be performed, delivered, evaluated, and compensated when clients, not law firms, determine their necessity and value; (3) which presently neglected markets can be serviced with new, profitable business models; (4) what technological capabilities they must develop to serve their clients; (5) how they will attract, compensate, and retain lawyers and nonlawyers as the definitions of competence and proficiency evolve throughout their careers; and (6) what incentives, training, and oversight will be necessary to promote professional ethics when technology and other innovations present ethical dilemmas not squarely circumscribed by existing rules. Law firms also need to decide how they will respond to Millennial generation attorneys who are more persistent than Baby Boomer generation attorneys in expecting meaningful work, regular feedback, a healthy work/life balance, and flexibility in work hours and office presence.[45]

If law firms continue to build their plans and strategies by extrapolating from current competitive advantages and market conditions, they will remain in a reactive role. They will be continually surprised by external changes as they lose market share to corporate legal departments, alternative legal service providers, software vendors, and new waves of tech-savvy, entrepreneurial competitors. By comparing themselves to other law firms and assuming that strong practice groups will only get stronger, law firms ignore their actual competitors and overlook exogenous threats to their business models. The conventional practice of measuring law firm performance relative to other law firms may provide no guidance or advantage when changing conditions and new competitors have redefined the practice of law and established new performance metrics. Like the Nokia engineers who thought their phones were superior to Apple iPhones because their phones survived intact a rigorous five-foot "drop test," law firms may misunderstand their markets and competitors.[46]

---

[45]   See McQueen, M. P. (2016, February 29). Here come the Big Law millennials. *The American Lawyer*. Tribe, Meghan. (2017, August 28). How Big Law firms are adapting to meet millennials' needs and why that's good for clients. *The American Lawyer*.

[46]   See Troianovski, Anton, & Grundberg, Sven. (2012, July 18). Nokia's bad call on smartphones. *The Wall Street Journal*.

Innovation and Change Management

Patrick McKenna, a law firm consultant, posed this question to more than 500 members of LinkedIn's Legal Innovation Group: "Is there a law firm anywhere, with a culture that consistently encourages innovation?" The responses were tellingly quiescent. "As I fully expected, thus far there has not been one single response," states McKenna.[47] "It is sadly reminiscent," he notes, "of an article that appeared a few years ago wherein forty-five Chief Legal Officers, meeting in Europe, were asked: 'What is the single most innovative practice proposed or used by your outside counsel in the last 12 months?' The unanimous answer . . . Nothing."[48] Consistent with McKenna's experience and personality assessments showing that lawyers generally are reluctant to innovate, only 11 percent of surveyed law firm leaders select "innovation" as one of their competitive advantages.[49] And these leaders may be exaggerating their innovation bona fides because only four percent of corporate counsel report that they have seen any significant innovation from law firms within the last three years.[50]

McKenna's frustration with law firms' lack of innovation is not unique. Stephen Poor, the Chair Emeritus of Seyfarth Shaw, encountered similar problems in his efforts to change legal service delivery. His conclusion: "Never underestimate the resistance to change from lawyers. Even more likely, never underestimate the ability of lawyers to describe virtual status quo efforts as revolutionary change." Poor discovered that law firm attorneys were not the only obstacles to innovation; corporate counsel also adamantly resisted innovation. "What we did not anticipate," Poor relates, "was the resistance from other crucial stakeholders—especially clients."

---

47 McKenna, Patrick. (2009, April 21). Post #391—Is innovation In BigLaw an oxymoron? Retrieved from http://www.patrickmckenna.com/patrickjmcken nabrainmatterrantsraves9.aspx?ID=46&PageID=39

48 Ibid.

49 Lazere, Cathy. (2012). *Thinking like your client: Law firm strategic planning* (p. 21). New York: ALM Intelligence.

50 Thompson Hine. (2018). Closing the innovation gap. (In response to the question, "Over the past three years, how much innovation have you seen from law firms?" 15 percent stated, "None"; 38 percent stated, "Hardly any"; 43 percent stated, "A little"; and 4 percent stated, "A lot.")

This resistance stemmed from the fact that "our clients are lawyers, too, and many of them are the products of the culture of their own business."[51] Poor is correct in noting that corporate counsel, like their law firm counterparts, generally prefer the status quo and view change with skepticism, if not criticism. In-house counsel taking the Caliper personality assessment, for instance, score low on flexibility, accommodation, resilience, and creativity.[52]

Attorneys find innovation to be objectionable because it challenges methods of practicing law that they adopted early in their careers and have not seriously questioned for decades. Innovation forces them to consider the possibility that their methods could have been improved earlier and signals that new habits and behaviors are now required.[53] Law firm consultant Mike Lowe finds that, although other organizations have embraced innovation, law firms and their attorneys are unique in resisting innovations that necessitate changes in individual behavior:

> When I speak to my clients [law firms] about how to make their projects successful, I am told how difficult it is to get attorneys to change their behaviors. They want to install a system to capture and share matter information, for example, but don't want to impose upon matter teams to actually enter information into

---

[51] Poor, J. Stephen. (2012, May 7). Re-engineering the business of law. *The New York Times.*

[52] Hartmann, Markus, Mordan, Bill, Schoenfelder, Thomas E., & Sweeney, Patrick. (2011, July/August). The perfect legal personality. *ACC Docket,* pp. 29–42.

[53] See Dysart, Joe. (2012, July). Mind meld: How to understand legal minds to defeat tech fears. *ABA Journal.* ("'Lawyers seem far more resistant to technology than people in the general business community' says Bruce A. Olson, a long-time litigator and president of Onlaw Trial Technologies, based in Appleton, Wis. 'In some cases, they see no incentive to achieving the increased productivity that properly deployed technology can offer.'") Levin, Leslie. (2009). Bad apples, bad lawyers or bad decisionmaking: Lessons from psychology and from *Lawyers in the Dock. Georgetown Journal of Legal Ethics 22*(4), 1552, fn. 30. Ho, Catherine. (2014, December 21). New leaders at law firm Pillsbury Winthrop experiment with changes to business model. *The Washington Post.* ("Lawyers are not receptive to change," states Sheila Harvey, the leader of Pillsbury's Futures committee. "We're mired in the past, that's how we're trained, to look at what's been said in the past by courts.")

the system. Somehow firms want to transform how they do business without asking attorneys to change how they work. The experience of management consulting for the past decade has been that change is now the norm, and will continue to be the norm. The organizations that are most adept at adapting are best positioned for success.[54]

Lowe's experience with law firms suggests that lawyers may accept innovation if it does not require any change in their behavior. This is like endorsing exercise as long as it does not require exertion.

To mitigate attorneys' resistance to change and successfully implement innovations, law firm leaders may benefit from these five basic strategies:

- *Linkage to firm culture and clients.* Attorneys' resistance to innovation decreases when they can see that a change reflects concepts, values, and principles derived from the firm's culture, history, and client service standards. In explaining why Seyfarth Shaw attorneys more readily accepted some innovations, former managing partner Poor states, "We consciously developed methodologies that linked to the history and culture of our firm or used client voices to support and build the business case for change. As we were able to demonstrate success on smaller scales, we were able to build agents for change that effectively permeated the firm."[55]
- *Clear goals and support from firm leaders.* Innovations fail when leaders are unclear about their goals and ambivalent about achieving them. To effectuate durable innovations, leaders must persuasively communicate the reasons for and benefits of the innovation; express their unequivocal

---

[54] Lowe, Mike. (2012, June 21). Transforming law firms—lessons learned from management consulting (Part II). Hildebrandt Institute. Retrieved from https://hildebrandtblog.wordpress.com/2012/06/21/transforming-law-firms-lessons-learned-from-management-consulting-part-ii-2/

[55] Poor, *supra* note 51. See Venus, Merlijn, Stam, Daan, & van Knippenberg, Daan. (2018, August 15). Research: To get people to embrace change, emphasize what will stay the same. *Harvard Business Review.*

commitment to it; demonstrate that the innovation is important to them; allocate sufficient resources to implement it; and identify the specific goals and deadlines that will indicate the innovation has been successful.[56]

- *Early communication with resisters.* Leaders often ignore or avoid people who object to their ideas. To be an effective innovator, however, law firm leaders must identify likely resisters and attempt to obtain their support at the earliest opportunity. Instead of following the instinct to marginalize people who object to innovative ideas, adroit leaders are solicitous and respectful of resisters. This "puts you in a better position for people to be sympathetic to your idea, to listen to you, to move toward you emotionally as opposed to away."[57]

- *Monitoring and recognition of incremental achievements.* Innovation initiatives are fragile; they usually fail.[58] Because their success is imperiled, innovation initiatives must be monitored regularly, and small achievements must be recognized, publicized, and celebrated. Complex, long-term innovation projects should be reviewed every two weeks, and relatively straightforward innovation projects should be evaluated every six weeks.[59] Although leaders tend to assume that long-term projects are at greater risk of failure, research indicates that "a long project reviewed frequently stands a better chance of succeeding than a short project reviewed infrequently. Problems can be identified at the first sign of trouble, allowing prompt corrective action."[60] When milestones are achieved and innovations start to yield minor improvements, those events merit attention and accolades. That recognition, in turn, enhances attorneys' commitment to the innovation and motivates them to be

---

[56]   See Schaffer, Robert H. (2010, September). Mistakes leaders keep making. *Harvard Business Review*. Miles, Robert H. (2010, January–February). Accelerating corporate transformations (don't lose your nerve). *Harvard Business Review*. Sirkin, Harold L., Keenan, Perry, & Jackson, Alan. (2005, October). The hard side of change management. *Harvard Business Review*.

[57]   Kehoe, Jeff. (2010, October). How to save your good ideas. *Harvard Business Review*.

[58]   Sirkin, Keenan, & Jackson, *supra* note 56.

[59]   Ibid.

[60]   Ibid.

more creative and productive; it forms a progress loop of goal attainment, positive emotions, and long-term commitment.[61]

- *Eliciting new ideas from future leaders.* The partners currently serving on firms' executive committees are unlikely to generate the major innovations that will determine their firm's success within the next 10–20 years. Those innovations are more likely to emerge from attorneys who are senior associates or junior partners. For that reason, law firm leaders should form innovation committees composed of attorneys who will serve in the next generation of firm leaders. Those attorneys have the largest investment in the firm's future and tend to be most knowledgeable about technology. To ensure that the innovation committee incorporates the most recent developments in technology and other fields, its members should be replaced regularly with more junior attorneys.[62]

In addition to these five basic strategies, law firm leaders should anticipate likely objections to innovation and then prepare responses that effectively address them. The most common objections to innovation include: "we tried this before and it didn't work"; "the timing is wrong"; "we can't afford this"; "this seems risky"; "we're fine the way we are"; "this sounds like [something horrible that previously occurred]"; "it won't work here because we're different"; "it puts us on a slippery slope"; "let's go back to the basics"; and "no one else does this."[63]

These reactions are rooted in a visceral belief that changes in the status quo invariably threaten one's status, security, and sense of competence. Unless leaders are prepared to respond to these reactions, they will find that innovation is stymied, if not extinguished. Although confident leaders may think that they can handle these

---

[61] Amabile, Teresa M., & Kramer, Steven J. (2011, May). The power of small wins. *Harvard Business Review.*

[62] See Anand, N., & Barsoux, Jean-Louis. (2017, November–December). What everyone gets wrong about change management. *Harvard Business Review.* Strom, Roy. (2017, August 31). A case for letting associates drive technology advances in law firms. *The American Lawyer.*

[63] Reich, Robert, (2000, September 30). Your job is change. *Fast Company.* Kehoe, *supra* note 57.

objections as they are raised, this confidence is frequently misplaced. "Don't wing it," states John Kotter, co-author of *Buy-In: Saving Your Good Idea from Getting Shot Down*.[64] He urges leaders to imagine likely attacks on their ideas and advises, "a few hours of brainstorming with supporters on potential attacks and responses is more than worth the time."[65]

In their efforts to reduce lawyers' resistance to innovation and implement new initiatives, law firm leaders themselves must be innovative. Change leaders at Reed Smith, for example, established an "Innovation Hours" program in which attorneys are given up to 50 hours of billable hour credits for time spent on innovations in technology and operations.[66] Attorney proposals are reviewed and approved by Reed Smith's chief knowledge officer Lucy Dillon and Innovation Hub manager Alex Smith. Approved proposals have culminated in projects ranging from contract and document automation to Breach RespondeRS, an application that simplifies state laws governing data protection. Projects that directly affect clients are placed on a fast-track program and given the highest level of support. "We had a lot of people wanting to engage in new technologies, process improvement, and new ways of working," states Dillon. "Being able to give people billing credit was the breakthrough way to say to people, 'We really value your ideas and we want you to have the time and to be rewarded for the time to think things through.'"[67]

Crisis Management

Leaders are responsible for managing crises in their organizations. Although crisis management is an essential leadership skill, it is assiduously neglected in most organizations. Like crises themselves, crisis management skills are neither anticipated nor apprehended until an emergency has overwhelmed ordinary capabilities. By that

---

[64] Kehoe, *supra* note 57.
[65] Ibid.
[66] Packel, Dan. (2018, May 15). Reed Smith "Innovation Hours" program gives credit for non-client work. *The American Lawyer*.
[67] Ibid.

time, leaders and their organizations are functionally inoperative, having forfeited the ability to characterize the problem, the confidence to show how it will be solved, and the credibility to demonstrate that it will not occur again.

In law firms, crises occur with remarkable regularity. Since each crisis manifests in a different form, law firm leaders tend to regard them as one-off events. For that reason, law firm leaders do not develop comprehensive methods and procedures for dealing with crises in general. Typical law firm crises are major client defections, legal malpractice claims and verdicts, data breaches, large sanctions awards, key partner and practice group defections, and deaths of high-visibility partners.[68] Less common but equally salient are sexual harassment and discrimination complaints, awards, and verdicts; firm disqualification rulings; arrests of attorneys accused of assault, murder, or sexual relations with minor children; on-site shootings of attorneys and employees; the outing of attorneys supporting offensive social or political causes; destruction of firm offices by fire, earthquakes, hurricanes, or tornadoes; and attorney intoxication resulting in fatal automobile accidents or news coverage of uninhibited language and gestures. Each of these incidents presents serious threats to a firm's reputation, financial condition, and stability and requires a crisis management plan conceived and tested months in advance.

In preparing to respond to crises, firm leaders need to consider four basic requirements:

- *Organization.* Before any crisis has overwhelmed its response capabilities, law firms should designate a Chief Crisis Officer and form a crisis management team.[69] The managing partner could be the Chief Crisis Officer, but usually someone else capable of responding immediately, making quick decisions, and devoting full attention to a crisis is better for this position. Attorneys in general are not ideal candidates for this position because they are accustomed to ascribing blame

---

[68] See McLellan, Lizzy. (2018, January 28). Racing against the clock: Firms must move fast to rebuild after defections. *The American Lawyer.*

[69] Haggerty, James F. (2017). *Chief crisis officer.* Chicago: American Bar Association.

and controlling people and events.[70] They will be far outside their expertise and comfort zone because crises, by their very nature, are unpredictable, ambiguous, dynamic, and intractable. The crisis management team should include a social media expert, representatives from the marketing and public relations departments, the Chief Operating Officer, and a partner on the executive committee. This team should meet monthly "to assess the crisis communications plan and various scenarios that may be on the horizon. They should also coordinate training for the entire organization once or twice a year."[71]

- *Preparation.* Law firm leaders, working with their crisis management teams, should prepare comprehensive response plans and conduct simulations of likely crises. The response plans should include a crisis communications plan.[72] Draft statements and talking points in the communications plan may be modified later to reflect the nuances of actual events. By preparing the statements in advance, organizations are able to quickly address subjective needs and expectations that will be overlooked if the response is prepared in the intense, rushed environment immediately following a crisis. The first press releases following an airplane crash, for instance, are prewritten by the airline companies.[73]

- *Speed.* Crises are defined within minutes after they occur. As Derede McAlpin, Chief Communications Officer of the Association of Corporate Counsel, observes, "In this media environment you have about 15 minutes or less to determine the appropriate response."[74] Law firms cannot afford to lose the opportunity to label, describe, and characterize an event shortly after it occurs. If law firms decline this opportunity and respond with the typical statement, "We are evaluating the situation and have no comment at this time," another person

---

[70] See Johnson, Tim. (2018). *Crisis leadership.* London: Bloomsbury Academic.
[71] Haggerty, *supra* note 69 at 46.
[72] Ibid. at 49.
[73] Ibid. at 190.
[74] Ibid. at 200.

or entity will control the narrative and hence the impact of the event. Public relations manager Katie Pemberton sternly warns against "no comment" responses: "If this is something you can envision yourself saying to a reporter asking about a crisis, you must fight the urge to duck and run because that's exactly what a 'no comment' response is: the verbal equivalent of running and hiding under a rock, hoping your bad situation will just go away on its own."[75]

- *Information.* Law firms under stress tend to withhold information. Eric Rose, a partner of the communications firm Englander, Knabe & Allen, calls this a "toxic strategy." Following a crisis, he explains, the public expects answers to four questions: What happened? How did it happen? What are you doing about it? What will you do to prevent it from happening again? Rose urges organizations to "provide as much information as quickly as possible to consumers, customers, employees, shareholders and the media; help the public understand what is occurring; structure contact with the media to eliminate potential dissemination of misinformation; and put out as much factual/positive information as possible and counter-act any negative responses."[76]

Leaders are primarily responsible for crisis management. The crises that irreparably damage organizations are marked by four leadership failures: lack of preparation; slow initial responses; inadequate information; and insensitive communications. Each of these errors is avoidable with foresight, care, and simulated practice. James Haggerty, an attorney and author of *Chief Crisis Officer*, finds that "in nearly every case, it is not the severity of the event itself, but rather a fumbled initial response that is the defining characteristic of any corporate crisis with staying power." After reviewing recent crises ranging from the BP oil spill to the Volkswagen diesel emission scandal, Haggerty concludes, "In every case where the event did negative reputational damage, the first few days—sometimes

---

[75] Pemberton, Katie. (2012, November 7). The no "no comment" rule. From the rock.

[76] Haggerty, *supra* note 69 at 191.

weeks—were characterized by curt, tone-deaf responses, lack of empathy or a fallback to legalistic, usually unfeeling, technicalities." The tools for managing crises are relatively simple, and, with a modicum of organization, preparation, and empathy, most crises can be effectively contained. With proper preparation, some crises can even be managed to reflect favorably on leaders and their organizations.

Talent Development

Law firm leaders faithfully repeat the professional services mantra, "Our assets go down in the elevator every night."[77] But they don't necessarily internalize the implications of leading an organization whose assets are neither stationary nor fungible. One implication of leading a mobile professional workforce is that lawyers will leave firms that are not committed to their professional development and achievement. Another implication is that rainmaker partners in particular must move to other firms if the quality of their current attorney team is inadequate to service their clients. Both of these implications reflect the importance of talent development and demonstrate that talent development is a major challenge and obligation for law firms. Law firm leaders may perceive themselves as being responsible for a firm's financial success, but they can achieve that success only by dedicating themselves to talent development.

Since law firms are selling professional services rather than manufactured products, they are entirely dependent on their attorneys' skills and commitment. If firms do not match those skills and commitment with professional development opportunities, high performance standards, and state-of-the-art resources, their best attorneys will find a more suitable context to support their success. Law firm leaders, therefore, must be committed to talent development, as the best-selling business author Tom Peters declares:

---

[77] Vault Law Editors. (2008, September 29). Our assets go down in the elevator every night. *Vault.*

If you're a leader, your whole reason for living is to help human beings develop—to really develop people and make work a place that's energetic and exciting and a growth opportunity, whether you're running a Housekeeping Department or Google. I mean, this is not rocket science.

It's not even a shadow of rocket science. You're in the people-development business. If you take a leadership job, you do people. Period. It's what you do. It's what you're paid to do. People, period. Should you have a great strategy? Yes, you should. How do you get a great strategy? By finding the world's greatest strategist, not by being the world's greatest strategist. You do people. Not my fault. You chose it. And if you don't get off on it, do the world a favor and get the hell out before dawn, preferably without a gilded parachute.[78]

Although Peters may be speaking with an evangelist's fervor, his core message remains accurate: whether leading a business or a professional services organization, all leaders must be committed to talent development.

Talent recruitment, selection, development, and retention always have been law firms' competitive advantage. "The most precious and essential element of professional practice," states Edwin Reeser, the former managing partner of Sonnenschein Nath & Rosenthal's Los Angeles office, "is identifying, recruiting, hiring, training, mentoring, promoting and retaining those professionals and the properly skilled staff to support them. Systems, procedures and technologies are all important, but they mean little without having the best professionals (unless you aspire to a practice where the quality of the professionals is not important)."[79] Despite the importance of talent development, law firms traditionally devote a tiny fraction of their revenue to formal talent development programs. Their mentorship efforts, moreover, are highly variable. Although

[78] Heywood, Suzanne, De Smet, Aaron, & Webb, Allen. (2014, September). Tom Peters on leading the 21st-century organization. *McKinsey Quarterly*.

[79] Reeser, Edwin B. (2013, September 5). Law firms in the Great Recession: Looking for change in all the wrong places. *ABA Journal*.

law firm leaders claim to be operating their firms more like businesses, they "fail to adopt many of the basic talent management
principles upon which excellent institutions are built."[80]

Law firms' emphasis on leverage and short-term profitability
jeopardizes talent development. In arguing that most large law
firms are destined to fail, law professor Larry Ribstein specifically
points to the high associate-to-partner ratios that limit the amount
of time any single partner can devote to associate attorney training and, he asserts, make "high quality training, mentoring, and
monitoring infeasible."[81] This inability to provide regular oversight
and systematic training results from the contemporary fixation
on short-term profitability, and it eventually erodes a firm's standards and reputation. It also prevents new partners from functioning as leaders and rainmakers. A survey of 5,600 new partners,
for instance, indicated that "only 45 percent were satisfied with
the formal training they received."[82] Most surveyed partners said
their firms did not provide any formal training in business development or leadership skills, and most had never been evaluated
in a 360-degree review."[83] At the associate attorney level, formal
training is similarly sparse. When asked to evaluate his firm's
training programs in a survey of 14,000 associate attorneys, one
attorney, for example, responded, "Training? What is this training
you speak of?"[84]

If law firms were deeply committed to talent development, that
commitment would be evident in at least four critical dimensions:
increases in talent development budgets, improvements in associate attorneys' understanding of partnership admission criteria,
expansion of leadership development programs, and higher levels

---

[80] Rikleen, Lauren Stiller. (2012, July 10). Law firms need to take care of their talent. *Harvard Business Review.*

[81] Henderson, William D. From Big Law to lean law (2013). *International Review
of Law and Economics*, Vol. 3, 2013; Indiana Legal Studies Research Paper No.
271. Available at SSRN: https://ssrn.com/abstract=2356330

[82] Press, *supra* note 6.

[83] Ibid.

[84] Hopkins, Kandy. (2013, October 2). BigLaw "Cold War," atmosphere of
fear cited by survey respondents. The Hildebrant Institute. Retrieved from
https://hildebrandtblog.wordpress.com/2013/10/02/biglaw-cold-war-
atmosphere-of-fear-cited-by-survey-respondents/

of attorney efficiency and client satisfaction. But material progress in each of these dimensions cannot be discerned. Law firms have reduced their talent development budgets; associate attorneys continue to be confused about partnership admission criteria; most firms do not provide formal leadership development programs; and clients perceive little or no improvements in attorneys' efficiency and overall performance.[85] As Terri Mottershead, the former Director of Professional Development at DLA Piper, notes, "law firms have not connected the dots between [how] they manage their talent and their ability to achieve their business performance goals. Firms have properly focused on their pipeline of client work but not as much on building the pipeline of talent to deliver that work."[86] Until law firms connect those dots, they will continue to lose clients and generate dissatisfaction among the clients they keep. In neglecting talent development, law firms exhibit a low regard for their clients' legitimate expectations and perpetuate the illusion that an attorney's skills and competence are static personality characteristics rather than transient qualities that must be continually evaluated and enhanced.[87]

Execution

The success of strategies is dependent on their execution. As Larry Bossidy writes in *Execution: The Discipline of Getting Things Done*, "No company can deliver on its commitments or adapt well to change unless all leaders practice the discipline of execution at all levels. Execution has to be part of a company's strategy and its goals.

---

[85] See Altman Weil (2014). *2014 Chief Legal Officer survey*. Newtown Square, PA: Altman Weil. Exterro. (2017). *2017 law firm benchmarking report*. McLellan, Lizzy. (2017, September 1). Salary hikes keep associates happy. *The American Lawyer*. Shannon, Marcia Pennington. (2010, November/December). Strategic talent management: Top issues and to-dos for firms. *Law Practice, 36*(6), 50. The Remsen Group, & Jaffe. (2016). *Re-envisioning the law firm: How to lead change and thrive in the future*.

[86] Shannon, *supra* note 85.

[87] See Colvin, Geoff. (2008). *Talent is overrated*. New York: The Penguin Group. Dweck, Carol. (2006). *Mindset*. New York: Ballantine Books. Tough, Paul. (2012). *How children succeed*. New York: Houghton Mifflin Harcourt.

It is the missing link between aspirations and results."[88] Despite its importance, execution is rarely successful. Most employees rate their organization as being weak on execution, and about 70 percent of strategic plans do not achieve their goals.[89] The most commonly cited causes of poor execution are lack of clear and decisive leadership; poor communication of the strategy; lack of accountability or follow-through; excessive focus on tactics rather than strategy; poor coordination across groups or units; overemphasis on short-term results; failure to make strategy meaningful to front liners; inability to measure impact; lack of time and resources; and conflicting priorities.[90]

Execution is sometimes considered the crucible of leadership.[91] If execution is indeed the crucible, many law firm leaders might prefer a more charitable test of their performance. When law firm leaders are asked, "How much of your last strategic plan has been implemented?" only 3.2 percent of them respond, "almost all of the plan."[92] When asked to evaluate how well their firms have implemented their strategic plans, only 10 percent of law firm leaders respond, "Excellent."[93] The difficulties in implementing strategic plans cannot be blamed on the dynamic nature of law firms' strategic plans; two-thirds of firms report that their firm's strategies have not changed at all "in light of disruptive changes going on within the legal profession."[94] Most firms, moreover, do not regularly review and revise their strategic plans.[95]

---

[88] Bossidy, Larry, & Charan, Ram. (2002). *Execution: The discipline of getting things done* (p. 19). New York: Crown Business.

[89] Ewenstein, Boris, Smith, Wesley, & Sologar, Ashvin. Changing change management. (2015, July). *McKinsey Quarterly.* Neilson, Gary L., Martin, Karla L., & Powers, Elizabeth. (2008, June). The secrets to successful strategy execution. *Harvard Business Review.*

[90] (2010, July–August). How hierarchy can hurt strategic execution. *Harvard Business Review,* p. 75.

[91] See Manyika, James. (2009, September). Google's view of the future of business: An interview with CEO Eric Schmidt. *McKinsey Quarterly.* ("In a corporation the role of a leader is often not to force the outcome, but to force execution.")

[92] Parnell, *supra* note 42.

[93] The Remsen Group & Jaffe, *supra* note 85.

[94] Ibid.

[95] Parnell, *supra* note 42.

The major obstacle to law firms' execution of their strategic plans is the absence of a link between objectives and actions. The results of ALM Legal Intelligence's survey of law firm leaders are illustrative:[96]

- "Growing the firm's revenue" is the highest priority for law firms. But only 56 percent of firms have a "plan in place to build, track and measure client loyalty and satisfaction." Only 21 percent of leaders would like to "provide higher service levels," and only 9 percent would like to "institute client satisfaction surveys/interviews." Increasing revenue without tracking and improving client service strikes most people in business as incongruous, if not impossible.

- "Talent acquisition and retention" is the second highest priority for law firms. Nearly every firm (96 percent) intends to emphasize lateral partner acquisitions. Seventy-six percent of law firms report that they are "aggressively pursuing" lateral partners. But only 28 percent of firms state that their lateral strategy has been "very effective" during the last five years. As Rutger van der Wall, Vice President of Global Products at LexisNexis Risk Solutions, asks, "How sustainable are growth models tied to an on-going 'musical chairs' game of lateral talent shifting from firm to firm? Is anyone focused on a plan for organic growth?"[97]

- "Improving firm profitability" is the third highest priority for law firms. But only 5 percent of firms regard "improving realization rates" as a high priority, and only 15 percent have taken steps recently to de-equitize partners.[98] When asked, "How do alternative fee arrangements affect firm profitability?" 65 percent of firms respond, "too soon to tell" or "don't know/ can't say." If firms do not know whether their alternative fee arrangements are profitable, their efforts to improve firm profitability may be futile.

---

[96] All results reported in the bulleted paragraphs appear in ALM Legal Intelligence, *supra* note 12 at 9, 13, 14, 19, 21, 22, 27, 29, 30, 31, 33.

[97] Ibid. at 5.

[98] Only 20 percent of law firms measure attorney productivity by any metric other than billable hours. Exterro, Inc. (2017). *2017 Law firm benchmarking report*, p. 25.

When objectives are isolated from actions, as occurs in law firms, it is virtually impossible to effectuate strategies and enforce priorities. Execution is dependent on a clear and persuasive statement of objectives, action items tied to timetables, and rigorous systems for monitoring and enforcing timely completion of the action items.[99] Attorneys resist these incursions into their autonomy, even when they recognize that they are designed to achieve firm-wide objectives. A relatively simple requirement like preparing a personal client development plan often provokes pushback, followed by complaints and procrastination. Consistent with this recalcitrant attitude, attorneys in law firms of all sizes state that their greatest source of dissatisfaction with strategic plans is "implementation with designated responsibility and time lines."[100] Many law firms, consequently, avoid attorneys' resistance by not presenting specific action plans in the first place. If specific action plans are presented, pushback is often averted by not requiring compliance.

Apart from their failure to execute strategies by linking objectives with actions, law firms are neglectful in eliciting attorneys' participation in developing the strategies, reviewing and revising the strategies on a regular basis, and communicating the strategies throughout the firm. These oversights have serious consequences. Firms that involve a majority of their partners in preparing the strategic plan are more successful in implementing the plan; and when plans are reviewed throughout the year, more elements of the plan are actually implemented.[101] Communicating the strategic plan also is essential to its execution. As Burkey Belser discovered in his study of successful law firms, "92 percent of successful firms communicated the strategic plan all the way down the chain of command to associates and staff, while only 43 percent of failed firms did so."[102]

Absent a willingness to execute strategies, consultant David Maister states, "many law firms will not function well as firms but will remain what they are today: bands of warlords, each with his

---

[99] See Mankins, Michael C., & Steele, Richard. (2005, July–August). Turning great strategy into great performance. *Harvard Business Review.*

[100] Parnell, *supra* note 42.

[101] Ibid.

[102] Belser, Burkey. (2012, June 28). Why firms fail: A diagnosis of the death of Dewey LeBoeuf.

or her followers, ruling over a group of cowed citizens and acting in temporary alliance—until a better opportunity comes along."[103] In deferring to attorneys' demands for autonomy, law firms often forfeit their strategies and, ultimately, their viability, for recalcitrant, opportunistic attorneys who may not stay with their current firm anyway. In their efforts to mollify their attorneys, firms may end up relinquishing their most important objectives for many of their least committed attorneys.

Chapter Capsule

Law firm leadership skills are scarce. Neither law schools nor law firms devote sufficient attention to leadership development, resulting in "sink-or-swim" learning and suboptimal performance. Many law firm leaders are convinced they have been selected for their leadership skills, but most are selected for their seniority, popularity, rainmaking abilities, or legal skills. Other leaders are selected because they are "consensus" candidates—unlikely to alienate powerful partners and unlikely to lead the firm in any direction that could provoke dissent.

Law firm leaders must fulfill six fundamental responsibilities: awareness; vision and strategy; innovation and change management; crisis management; talent development; and execution. If they evade any of these responsibilities, their tenure usually is marked by poor decisions, unsuitable strategies, stalled innovation efforts, underperforming attorneys, partner defections, declining revenue, and a palpable listlessness that tells clients the firm may be competent, but it will never be dynamic.

Law firm leadership requires a distinct skill set that respects attorney autonomy but convinces attorneys that yielding some of their autonomy will increase their financial security, afford a broader range of professional opportunities, and enhance their reputation and status. Because attorneys are sensitive to intrusions upon their autonomy, they are more comfortable with leaders who do not appear to be seeking power and have few ego needs of their own. Attorneys' insistence on autonomy and their aversion to ambitious,

---

[103] Maister, David. (2006, April). Are law firms manageable? *The American Lawyer.*

powerful leaders sometimes result in "stealth" leaders who spend most of their time trying to build consensus, mollify their partners, and underplay their own ideas and aspirations. Management professor Laura Empson describes these leaders as being capable of "interacting politically while appearing apolitical."[104] Very few firm leaders meet these job requirements, and even fewer would want the position under these conditions. As Empson observes, "I have found that in law firms, which are filled with highly educated, independent thinkers, who do not like being told what to do, it is not easy to find lawyers who are happy to identify themselves as followers. Furthermore, finding lawyers who are happy to put themselves forward as leaders is even harder."[105]

---

[104] Empson, Laura. (2015). Leadership, power and politics in law firms (p. 98). In Normand-Hochman, *supra* note 6.
[105] Ibid. at 89.

10
Conclusion

If peripatetic lawyers journeyed into the Brazilian rainforest and explored the distant Maici River, they would encounter a tribe known as the Pirahã. The tribe has about 700 members living among four villages. The Pirahã visit each other frequently, traveling by canoes. Despite their isolation, they enjoy a sense of superiority and show a disdain for other cultures, believing that they have "the best possible way of life."[1]

Catholic missionaries first attempted to convert the Pirahã to Christianity in the 1700s. After a few years they gave up, convinced that the Pirahã were "the most recalcitrant group they had ever encountered."[2] Although other missionaries have attempted to convert the Pirahã after the first Catholic mission failed, not a single Pirahã has ever converted. When Daniel Everett, an evangelical Christian missionary, related stories from the Bible to the Pirahã in the late 1970s, they asked him, "What color is Jesus? How tall is he? When did he tell you these things?"[3] Everett answered, "Well, you know, I've never seen him, I don't know what color he was, I don't know how tall he was."[4] The Pirahã responded abruptly, "Well, if you have never seen him, why are you telling us this?"—effectively

---

1 Everett, Daniel L. (2013). Recursion and human thought: Why the Pirahã don't have numbers. In Brockman, John. *Thinking* (p. 276). New York: HarperCollins.
2 Ibid. at 280.
3 Ibid. at 277.
4 Ibid.

thwarting Everett's efforts because the Pirahã believe only what has been personally seen and experienced.

The Pirahã are unique in many respects. Their language is unrelated to any other language. It strikes non-natives as indecipherable and confounding, and it lacks conversational lubricants like "thank you" and "sorry."[5] It has no words for numbers or counting and, as a consequence, the Pirahã lack the linguistic tools necessary for scientific measurement and analysis.[6] The Pirahãs' language, moreover, is what linguists call "non-recursive"; it cannot build upon a concept, and hence it remains linear, protracted, and, arguably, inefficient.[7] The Pirahã, for instance, do not say, "John's brother's house," but instead say in separate sentences, "John has a brother. This brother has a house."[8] In their trades with Brazilians, the Pirahã do not store or accumulate any goods but instead consume any acquired items immediately.[9] If they trade sex for two pounds of sugar, for instance, they quickly pour the sugar in a bowl and eat all of it.[10] They do not build permanent shelters, maintain tools, or otherwise allocate resources for future use.[11]

The Pirahã also are adamant about how they define their responsibilities and what they are willing to learn. Although they are dependent on canoes for trading, fishing, hunting, gathering plants, and socializing, they refuse to build canoes—even after a Brazilian canoe master spent days teaching them how to select the wood and use tools to dig out a canoe. When Everett gave them the tools and suggested they make canoes, they said, "Pirahã don't make canoes."

---

[5]   Barkham, Patrick. (2008, November 9). The power of speech. *The Guardian*. Colapinto, John. (2007, April 6). The interpreter. *The New Yorker*.

[6]   Everett, *supra* note 1 at 275, 284. Barkham, *supra* note 5.

[7]   Everett, Daniel L. (2007, June 11). Recursion and human thought: Why the Pirahã don't have numbers. Available at: https://www.edge.org/conversation/daniel_l_everett-recursion-and-human-thought. Substantial controversy exists about recursion and the Pirahã language. See Nevins, Andrew, Pesetsky, David, & Rodrigues, Cilene. (2009). Pirahã exceptionality: A reassessment. *Language, 85*(2), 355–404. Everett, Daniel L. (2009, June). Pirahã culture and grammar: A response to some criticisms. *Language, 85*(2), 405–442.

[8]   Everett, *supra* note 1 at 271–272.

[9]   Colapinto, *supra* note 5.

[10]   Everett, *supra* note 1 at 285.

[11]   Leith, William. (2012, April 10). Daniel Everett: Lost in translation. *The Telegraph*. Barkham, *supra* note 5.

As Everett explains, "that was the end of it. They never made a canoe like the Brazilians, even though I know that some of them have the skills to do that."[12] After living with the Pirahã for more than 20 years, Everett concludes that there is "just a strong conservative core to the culture; they don't change, and they don't change the environment around them much either."[13] Everett abandoned his efforts to convert the Pirahã in the 1990s.

Although it's unlikely that North American attorneys have traveled into the Brazilian rainforest to coordinate strategies with the Pirahã, they share many practices that appear to be imprudent or nonsensical when displayed by the Pirahã and cautious or conventional when implemented by attorneys. Attorneys tend to be insular and do not incorporate practices from other disciplines and professions; their language is exclusionary, complicated, and confusing to clients and the general public; their mannerisms often are seen as brusque, insensitive, and arrogant; they lack a mathematical or scientific tradition; the profits from their practices are distributed rapidly without reserves for research and development; and they unilaterally define what they will and will not learn. Like the Pirahã, attorneys rely primarily on their own experiences and are convinced their way is the best, despite objective evidence that their way of life has become untenable.[14]

The first chapter of this book discussed the untenable condition of many law firms and introduced Jim Collins' concept of getting the right people on the bus, getting the wrong people off the bus, getting the right people in the right seats, and steering the bus in the right direction. In this concluding chapter, it also may be helpful to consider Collins' five stages of organizational decline and corrective steps, as identified in his book, *How the Mighty Fall*.[15] These five stages serve as warning signs and a helpful checklist for law firm

---

[12]   Everett, *supra* note 1 at 277.
[13]   Everett, *supra* note 1 at 280.
[14]   See Dysart, Joe. (2012, July). Mind meld: How to understand legal minds to defeat tech fears. *ABA Journal*. (Quoting Daniel Siegel: "It's the nature of the profession. We all think we're smart and our way is right. So it's hard to change.")
[15]   Collins, Jim. (2009). *How the mighty fall* (pp. 20–23). New York: HarperCollins.

leaders determined to avoid obsolescence and overcome conventional thinking:[16]

- *Stage 1—Hubris born of success.* This initial stage of decline "kicks in when people become arrogant, regarding success virtually as an entitlement, and they lose sight of the true underlying factors that created success in the first place." They begin to think that their success results from who they are rather than what they do, and they stop evaluating the ongoing effectiveness of their methods and actions.
- *Stage 2—Undisciplined pursuit of more.* In this overextending stage, organizations embrace "the doctrine of more"—more people, more income, more locations, and more recognition. They "stray from the disciplined creativity that led them to greatness in the first place, making undisciplined leaps into areas where they cannot be great or growing faster than they can achieve with excellence, or both."
- *Stage 3—Denial of risk and peril.* Hubris in Stage 1 and the pursuit of "more" in Stage 2 begin to produce internal warning signs in Stage 3. But leaders "explain away" or dismiss these warning signs. In Stage 3, Collins explains, "leaders discount negative data, amplify positive data, and put a positive spin on ambiguous data. Those in power start to blame external factors for setbacks rather than accept responsibility."
- *Stage 4—Grasping for salvation.* In Stage 4, the evidence of decline can no longer be ignored or rationalized. In response, the leaders look for a quick salvation in "a charismatic visionary leader, a bold but untested strategy, a radical transformation, a dramatic cultural revolution, a hoped-for blockbuster product, a 'game changing' acquisition, or any number of other silver-bullet solutions."
- *Stage 5—Capitulation to irrelevance or death.* If an organization stays in Stage 4 without effective remedial action, it invariably declines into Stage 5. By Stage 5, the organization's

---

[16] The stages are described in Collins, Jim. (2009, May). How the mighty fall: A primer on the warning signs. *Businessweek.* All quotes in the bulleted paragraphs appear in that article.

financial strength has been compromised, and "leaders abandon all hope of building a great future. In some cases, their leaders just sell out; in other cases, the institution atrophies into utter insignificance, and in the most extreme cases, the enterprise simply dies outright."

The data and analyses in this book indicate that many law firms have entered Stage 3, but they perceive themselves as possibly entering Stage 1. Their perceptions might have been accurate if they were describing their condition and prospects a decade ago. "A majority of firms still behave as if the past 10 years really haven't happened," observes James Jones, a senior fellow at Georgetown Law's Center for the Study of the Legal Profession. "Sure, they've adopted things like some technological changes—but they really have not reoriented the way they go about or think about their practices."[17] Since Stage 3 results from the initial overconfidence in Stage 1 and the heedless expansion in Stage 2, the transition to Stage 3 is imperceptible to many law firms. Their capacity to assess and recalibrate is not simply impaired; it has been disengaged.

Fortunately, the problems that currently threaten law firms are largely self-inflicted. They occurred as a result of attorneys' affluence, complacency, insularity, and hubris. In that sense, attorneys and their law firms have become victims of their own success. Attorneys certainly have the intelligence and analytical abilities—if not the motivation—to overcome these errors and oversights. The major risk now is that the attorneys who wield the most financial and political power in law firms will be the least inclined to effectuate reforms due to their impending retirements and short-term perspectives. Controlled by senior factions that have the lowest levels of interest and risk in the future, many law firms suffer from a lack of vision, investment, and innovation. Some senior partners' determination to preserve the status quo is, in fact, making it highly unlikely that prospective partners will

---

[17] Strom, Roy. (2018, January 30). As law firms stall, who will overtake them in the innovation race? *The American Lawyer.*

realize the benefits and advantages presently enjoyed by those senior partners.[18]

"There is no law of nature that the most powerful will inevitably remain at the top," asserts Collins. "Anyone can fail, and most eventually do."[19] But with equal conviction, Collins asserts that every organization can reverse declines and recover its vibrancy, adaptability, and value at any time before it reaches Stage 5. This book has identified and described the elements of that recovery in a law firm's culture, character, practices, systems, and leaders. It has attempted to demonstrate that law firms' success and resilience are based on specific elements capable of coalescing the energy, dedication, intelligence, creativity, and judgment of each attorney in a law firm. The firm's collective skill and vibrancy, in turn, produce exceptional client service, strategies, innovation, financial performance, and career satisfaction.

For those attorneys realistic about the challenges confronting law firms, this book provides reasons, methods, and directions for meeting those challenges. That endeavor is buttressed by the realization that law firms are engaged in an enterprise considerably larger than profit generation. They promote the rule of law, provide independent judgment in advising clients, facilitate conflict resolution, foster predictability in commercial transactions, protect contractual and constitutional rights, and render pro bono legal services to historically underserved populations. In their most critical role, explains Ben Heineman, former general counsel for General Electric, law firms exist to restate, for each generation of attorneys, "the historic concept of what it means to be a legal professional."[20] A central tenet of that concept, Heineman asserts, is that "private lawyers have public responsibilities beyond their immediate self-interest and beyond the needs of

---

[18] See Strom, Roy. (2017, June 17). Barnes & Thornburg's efficiency push: A change management story. *The American Lawyer*. ("On that change management front, the traditional law firm hierarchy often stands in the way of new ideas. Partners who wield the most power within their firm are often the least likely to see any reason to change the system that has benefited them.")

[19] Collins, *supra* note 15 at 8.

[20] Heineman, Ben W., Jr., & Lee, William F. (2010, May 20). Truth, justice and the Big Law way. *The American Lawyer*.

their immediate clients."[21] Historically fulfilling both private and public imperatives, attorneys and their law firms have a singular responsibility to assert leadership, set ambitious standards, and advance innovation in every dimension of client service and legal professionalism.

---

[21] Ibid.

Index